Gilles Pudlowski
Photography by Maurice Rougemont

Great Women Chefs
of Europe

Flammarion

CONTENTS

Preface
Trailblazing Women

During the past century, women in professional cuisine, as in many other fields, have been wresting power from their male counterparts and blazing new trails for themselves. Recognition for their contributions to the field is overdue: the time has come to redress the balance. Although the contributions made by women to the fields of politics, sport, art, and culture are well documented, their inroads into the traditionally masculine preserve of haute cuisine have remained relatively unpublicized. Now, however, they are beginning to earn their due. Women are finally being given equal status with their male (and often highly chauvinistic) competitors.

Until very recently women were still confined to the restricted world of the domestic kitchen, where they often labored tirelessly over the family stove. The common image in the past was that of the nurturing mother (as opposed to the autonomous woman), who respected tradition more than creativity. But today women are setting new goals for themselves. In Italy, for example, women are now beating the men at their own game. Although there may be fewer than twenty women in all boasting stars in the demanding French *Michelin* guide, its no less demanding Italian counterpart lists four three-star chefs, three of which are women. Nadia Santini, Luisa Valazza, and Annie Feolde are women who do not merely "cook"—they take their customers on a trip around the world, imposing their own distinctive style and inspiring a host of imitators.

None of our women chefs fits a single mold. Some are maternal, some sensitive, some sensual. Some are rotund, some slender, some wreathed in smiles, some shrewd and calculating, some benignly devilish, seductive, charming, and clever. But all are practical, as is necessary for anyone working with in this kind of environment. The great Italian women chefs we have used as our models in the following pages are all of this and more. As a matter of fact, their French counterparts still lag behind in the kitchen and the dining room, and French women chefs have a way to go before they succeed in imposing their authority in competition with their male counterparts.

However, all of the women described here—a total of thirty-three chefs, plus an exceptional pastry chef—have many points in common. Their excellence in their chosen field reflects passionate conviction and total commitment rather than commercial considerations. They give their time unstintingly and never count the hours worked. Some, like Christine Farber, frequently rise at three in the morning to be the first to check new produce as it comes into their kitchen. They're imaginative and inventive, and have also given new life to old recipes.

Above all, they are militants in the cause of fine cuisine, and we've chosen each chef for her enthusiasm and dedication. Some have already earned coveted stars, some are famous only in their own country or region, some are promising unknowns just beginning to make a mark. These are today's new culinary "*mères*," as Hélène Darroze puts it when

PRECEDING PAGE, FROM LEFT TO RIGHT: THE MENU AT OLYMPE'S; JOCELYNE LOTZ-CHOQUART'S BURGUNDY SNAILS WITH SPINACH; FLORA MIKULA COOKING CALAMARI; A FEW LEAVES OF "ERYTHRONIUM" IN THE HANDS OF ISABELLE AUGUY; COPPER CAULDRONS OF CHRISTINE FERBER'S FAMOUS JAMS; JUDITH BAUMANN'S FRESH WILD HERBS; THE LIQUEUR CORNER AT LÉA LINSTER'S; JUDITH BAUMANN'S HIBISCUS FLOWER INFUSION ACCOMPANIED BY A JUICY CUBE OF WATERMELON. FACING PAGE: THE ELEGANT HANDS OF JOHANNA MAIER HOLD A PLATE READY FOR SERVICE.

she describes her club for youthful women chefs (including Ariane Daguin in New York and Barbara Lynch in Boston, plus some of the women listed in these pages), which meets annually to prepare a meal for charity. These women amaze, dazzle, beguile, and enchant us. We have chosen them on the basis of their talent and enterprise, their instinctive appeal.

More often than not they're surrounded by men who support them—in every sense of the word—assist them, back them up, encourage them, and inspire them to even greater heights. In Luxembourg, Austria, Spain, Belgium, and Switzerland, these women fearlessly challenge old assumptions, but are innately modest and rarely put themselves forward. But their restaurants, products, and the menus that often read like poems—outstanding examples being Judith Baumann at La Pinte des Mossettes and the unassuming Chantal Chagny at Fleurie in the Beaujolais region—are attractions in their own right.

Most of these women are self-taught, and learned their early lessons from a father, brother, mother, or husband, before striking out on their own and making an independent name for themselves (like Johanna Maier at Fitzmoos). Their stories are adventurous, often legendary. A prime example is the modest Annie Feolde of Nice, who in Florence is considered the honorary duchess of Tuscany; or the discreet Jocelyne Lotz-Choquart, whose life is like something out of a Hector Malor novel. Today, they all tend to shun the limelight, emulating Olympe, who—after several flamboyant years in Paris—abandoned Montparnasse and the radio and television shows for a quiet street in the "New Athens" of the ninth arrondissement.

They sometimes dominate the gourmet landscape of their own countries, from an isolated corner of the Po Valley (in the case of the ebullient Nadia Santini at Canneto Sull'Oglio) to the banks of Lake Orta (the gentle Luisa Valazza at Sorriso al Soriso) and constantly outdo their male counterparts (like Léa Linster of Luxembourg, the first and only woman to have won a world-class international culinary competition, the 1989 Lyon Bocuse d'Or). But self-effacing modesty and discretion remain their hallmarks.

We love them all—each in their own special way, of course. Each one of these chefs has her own unique statement to make. Whether based in Paris or in a less-traveled locale, all are Europeans at heart, while at the same time being rooted in their respective regions—from Gruyère or Catalonia, Piedmont or Maremma, Flanders or the Basque Country, Alsace or Latium. They are introducing us to a new kind of cuisine, one that's clever, sensual, warm, and sometimes unusually daring.

They have their own way of doing things, their own special sauces and succulent pan gravies, their unyielding respect for their local suppliers from the Bay of the Somme (for Marie-Christine Klopp) to Beaujolais (for Chantal Chagny), their own "tricks of the trade" (for example, Gisèle Lovishi's shredded garlic on Corsican vegetables, her dash of olive in country soup), their flashes of genius (Carmen Ruscalleda's windowpane scampi ravioli), their magnificent desserts (Lydia Egloff's Irish coffee).

Each chef has her own distinctive style. From Alsatian Suzel's clever originality to Judith Baumann's poetic playfulness, they all demonstrate that cuisine by women chefs has finally come of age. This book is both proof of that fact and a tribute to these chefs' achievements. Their time has come!

ELENA ARZAK

SAN SEBASTIAN, SPAIN

In the tourist capital of the Spanish Basque country you'll find
a father-daughter duo working at the pinnacle of fine Iberian cuisine.
Their names are Juan-Mari and Elena Arzak, a warmhearted
and lively pair of native Basques who consistently delight their customers.

In San Sebastian (known as "Donostia" in Basque) stands a building with a gleaming façade
containing a cozy dining room and snug, friendly bar. The house is like a wise magus stand-
ing guard over Basque taste. As Juan-Mari Arzak notes, "My travels take me all over the
world, and I'm constantly on the lookout for new products and unfamiliar spices that will
work well with our own style."

At just over sixty years of service, the oldest three-star restaurant still operating in Spain
(the stars were awarded in 1989) still maintains a policy of constant innovation. Juan-Mari
Arzak—who trained under Paul Bocuse, the Troisgros brothers, Alain Senderens, and Gérard
Boyer—has turned his venerable restaurant, located on the busy traffic artery, Alto de
Miracruz, into a table d'hôte open to all and a congenial "laboratory" of innovation. He was
preceded by his grandfather, José-Maria, and his father, Juan-Ramon—who unfortunately
died before his time. His mother also produced a rustic brand of "pure Basque" cuisine. Juan-
Mari himself is primarily interested in contrasts, in combining the crisp with the soft, the
sweet with the sour, and in emphasizing the delicacy of gelatin, curds, and tender farmhouse cheese.

His thirst for learning about, understanding, and exploring new combinations betrays a
traditional spirit teamed with the mind of a chemist. Today, he's been replaced by his daughter, the raven-haired Elena, who is ever-present and makes a continuous effort to improve
and enliven her offerings. She trained at the hotel school in Lucerne, Switzerland, and then
worked as an apprentice with some of the greatest contemporary chefs: in Paris, with Alain
Dutournier at Le Carré des Feuillants and with Claude Peyrot at Vivarois; and in Catalonia
with Ferran Adria at his restaurant El Bulli, and—lastly—with Pierre Gagnaire, the magician of rue Balzac in Paris. It is thus not surprising that she has infused her father with a fresh
determination to forge ahead.

Father and daughter are a sight to be seen, working very closely together, discussing and com-
paring flavors, tastes, textures, and consistencies in their small, unremarkable, secret laboratory

ELENA ARZAK AND HER FATHER JUAN-MARI
(SHOWN BELOW, IN THEIR KITCHEN) KEEP BASQUE CUISINE
ALIVE. THEIR CREATIONS, SUCH AS SEARED BONITO WITH
ONIONS (BELOW RIGHT) AND SHRIMPS WITH GREEN SALAD
(PAGE 11) DEMONSTRATE THEIR CONSTANT INNOVATION.
EACH DISH IS THE RESULT OF A LONG BUT LOVING
PROCESS. LEFT: THE WAITING ROOM DOUBLES AS
A BAR WHERE YOU CAN ENJOY AN APERITIF.

next to the restaurant, where they decide together what the following day's menu will feature. They're a dynamic couple, the two of them, never tired of exploring the new, always fascinated by everything they hear about and taste, determined to find that rare blend, perfect touch of acidity, ideal flavor, sweet or tangy nuance. "Our goal is to expand our own tastes," they explain. These aims are grounded in the distinctive Basque style that Juan-Mari forged during his years of training. A style that is both conservative and innovative, and totally beguiling. Today Elena has become the guardian of the flame.

A meal at their restaurant is a kind of lesson in gastronomy. In the attractive, well-lit dining room, women servers dressed in gray aprons wait on tables where men are not required to wear neckties—a sign that eating here is a casual, extended celebration. Offerings are based on fresh market produce adapted to the Arzak "manner," new ideas that change frequently, fish and shellfish from the shores of San Sebastian and lively variations on local products.

Among the many delicious offerings are sea scallops marinated in tomato aspic, figs with bacon in bean vinaigrette, a caramelized triangle of melon, yogurt, and pigeon livers. The cuttlefish in its own ink magically changes color from black to red when covered in a delicious lemongrass broth. Then there's the shrimp with pasta and asparagus, and the stunning *"fleur d'oeuf"* with truffles—all sleights of hand from two gourmet magicians. Their tender fillet of tuna, skewered on its bone, is highly acclaimed. The hake in green sauce with clams and the marinated cuttlefish are tributes to a tradition that has been updated for lightness.

Also noteworthy are the glazed pigeon with peanuts and the unskinned rack of lamb fried in curry—the fruit of trips to foreign climes. Desserts continue the same theme: spicy chocolate with honey and tomato, peppery milk paste, braised fruit. An aromatic counterpoint is provided by Spanish wines such as Txakoli, a fragrant Chivite Chardonnay, an impressive Torre Muga Rioja, a fascinating Contino. The palate is stimulated, titillated, won over. These wines are provocative, overwhelming, sometimes intriguing—and ultimately delightful and enchanting.

This restaurant provides convincing proof that Basque cuisine is a succession of ever-evolving flavors. In other words, the wizardly Arzak, despite increasing competition, and thanks to the continuity today assured by Elena, does not intend to hang up his apron anytime soon.

FACING PAGE, TOP LEFT: ELENA IN HER SPICE STORE (SHE HAS MORE THAN ONE THOUSAND VARIETIES IN CAREFULLY LABELED BOTTLES) AND IN HER EVER-BUSY KITCHEN (BELOW) UNDER THE EYES OF HER EVER-PRESENT FATHER. FACING PAGE, BOTTOM: THE SERVING STAFF ALL WEAR THE HOUSE UNIFORM. FACING PAGE, TOP RIGHT: A STUNNING CREATION WORTHY OF A FIREWORKS DISPLAY: STRAWBERRY BUBBLES.

ELENA ARZAK'S RECIPE:

SHRIMPS WITH GREEN SALAD

PREPARATION TIME: 35 MINUTES
COOKING TIME: 25 MINUTES
TO SERVE: 4

INGREDIENTS

For the shrimps
· 8 jumbo shrimps or
  16 bay shrimps
· 1 tablespoon mixed black
  olives
· Virgin olive oil
· Salt and powdered ginger

For the garnish
· 14 teaspoons (20 g) mixed
  young salad leaves (arugula,
  beet greens, purslane, baby
  spinach)
· 1 large potato
· 3 tablespoons olive oil
· 1 tablespoon rice or sherry
  vinegar
· 1 teaspoon powdered barley
  or dry yeast
· Salt and black pepper

For the coffee-flavored oil
· 2 tablespoons black olives,
  pitted
· 5 tablespoons olive oil
· ¼ teaspoon instant coffee
· Pinch of confectioner's sugar

METHOD

To make the coffee-flavored oil, grind the olives with the olive oil, instant coffee, and the confectioner's sugar in a blender.

To prepare the potato, microwave it for 7 to 8 minutes or cook in salted boiling water for 25 minutes. To make a vinaigrette dressing for the salad, combine the vinegar, olive oil, and barley or yeast. Season with salt and pepper. Add the salad, without mixing it.

Season the shrimps with salt and ginger, then sauté over high heat with 1 tablespoon oil, cooking for 4 or 5 minutes and turning them frequently. Remove from the heat and mix them well with the olive paste. Reserve. Peel the potato and cut it into 4 rectangles.

Arrange a potato rectangle in the center of each plate, and top with the shrimps and seasoned salad. Arrange the leaves so as to give them maximum volume, arranging all the stems in the same direction. Surround with a trickle of coffee-flavored oil.

If the recipe is made with shelled shrimps, they only need to cook for 2 minutes.

ISABELLE AUGUY

LAGUIOLE, FRANCE

THERE ARE TWO GOURMET RESTAURANTS IN LAGUIOLE,
ONE OF THEM RUN BY THE SELF-EFFACING ISABELLE AUGUY.
THIS CHEF MAINTAINS THE HERITAGE OF HER NATIVE AUBRAC
IN A STYLE THAT COMBINES THE TRADITIONAL WITH THE CONTEMPORARY.

Laguiole, located on a windy plateau at an altitude of 1,000 meters (3,281 feet), boasts a population of 1,200 and two gourmet restaurants. One of these is already famous; the other is in the process of forging its reputation. This village used to lie dormant in the winter, when three-star chef Michel Bras closed down his operation on the outskirts of the Aubrac forests, six kilometers (some three miles) from town. Now, however, Isabelle Auguy takes up the torch from the end of November to mid-March, when the snow finally begins to melt in Aubrac. Most people, attracted by the resort's reputation for gastronomy—who travel long distances to sample it—give up their quest during winter, when the village of Laguiole battens down against the cold.

Isabelle Auguy has taken over the inn that was founded by her grandmother in 1926. It stands in the center of the village; just across the way is La Maison Calmels, which markets the traditional cutlery designed long ago by Auguy's ancestor, Pierre-Jean. Calmels has bred imitators, and there are now some twenty cutlery stores selling the "genuine" Laguiole knife with horn handles. Only five of them, however, actually craft the knives, in big and small workshops.

The village also generates income by selling gourmet specialties to tourists. These local products include the salami and ham sold at the Conquet and Bringuier stores, and the cheese also known—like the knife and the village itself—as "Laguiole." This cheese, similar to Salers and Cantal, today boasts the AOC designation and is sold at the Jeune Montagne Cooperative, along with another cheese—a soft variety, similar to Saint–Marcellin, known as Ecir en Aubrac, which is sold at the plateau's cheese store. Other local specialties include Pascal Auriat's cakes and yeast breads, and Claude Rus's tripe and pig's feet from the Drosera Gourmande.

Many people born in the region—such as Marcellin Cazes, who founded the Brasserie Lipp in Paris and has a street near the local church named after him; or the Costes brothers, who acquired numerous restaurants in Paris and whose mother opened a camping ground there—left the area to seek their fortunes in the French capital. But Isabelle Auguy stayed. And when her parents decided to retire, she returned to the family roost.

She was only twenty years old at the time, was armed with a diploma from the Toulouse catering school, and had completed a single three-month apprenticeship at Jean-Claude Dray's Renaissance restaurant at Magny-Cours, in the Nièvre, which then had three stars. Dray taught her not only the classic rib steak with morels and cream, but also more contemporary dishes, such as foie gras with pineapple preserves. When she took over from her mother and grandmother, she continued to practice this style, but in a more modest vein. She started off with traditional fare such as preserved goose with garlic mashed potatoes, and pigs' feet in lentil salad. She gradually began to develop her own style.

Auguy married a fellow student from the hotel school, a man from Angers with a Flemish name, Jean-Marc Muylaert. He took over the dining room and cellar, supervision of table service, and modernization of the premises. On the untimely deaths of Auguy's mother and brother, she assumed complete control of the restaurant. And so, here she is, ensconced in the village even during the depths of winter, a period when tourists are rare. But connoisseurs who take the trouble to visit for an evening to sample Auguy's rustic menus are given a warm welcome at all times of the year.

Her style—like that of her neighbor Michel Bras, who treated his team to dinner at Isabelle's in celebration of his third star—is inspired by the Aubrac countryside, but with a sophisticated twist. Her idea for the "byways of Aubrac" menu might include a medley of rustic country products from the region: tripe, peasant fare, charcuterie.

Starters include homemade charcuterie tapas to "snack on while waiting," flat sausages made from preserved pigs' cheeks and served with creamed lentils and pan juices; blood sausages with apples and cider-vinegar sauce, accompanied by sautéed foie gras; or fillets of trout from the Gagnot pond, served with crisp bacon, Laguiole-cheese sauce and a peasant-style stuffed baby cabbage.

Then, of course, there's the tripe made according to grandmother Eléonore's method, and served in its pan juices; or ham knuckle with braised pigs' feet cooked in a smoked-bacon crust. After the main dish comes a trolley of local cheeses, followed by tempting desserts such as chocolate-caramel mousse with a hazelnut *dacquoise* and purée of orange conserve, or the amusing caramel cigars topping a baked pear served with ginger ice cream and passion-fruit aspic. This is classic cuisine evoking the long local tradition for charcuterie, but Isabelle also loves her sweet desserts, and uses them to add a note of contrast to the rest of her offerings.

At warmer times of the year, diners can sample the "*prémices du temps*" ("early spring") menu, based on a country theme and featuring local morels in a touch of foamy cream sauce; green Italian-style ravioli; or fresh cod served with seasoned raw artichokes, herbs, tomato conserve, and Sicilian olive oil. Not to mention the classic sirloin of free-range Aubrac beef, accompanied by a marrowbone, cannelloni, and braised shallots in a peppery sauce. And, of course, the traditional garlic mashed potatoes, served in its own pot with Tomme cheese.

Travel, a taste for distant Italy, and culinary discoveries made while dining, as a customer, with some of the greatest contemporary chefs—Olivier Roellinger at Cancale, Michel Guérard at Eugénie-les-Bains, Didier Oudill at Grenade-sur-Adour, and Michel del Burgo in Carcassonne, for example—have somewhat lightened and modernized Isabelle's approach. She's raised herself to the topmost ranks of gastronomy, alone, without fuss, in the heart of a village that slumbers through the winter.

ON THE AUBRAC PLATEAU, ISABELLE, PART OF THE THIRD GENERATION AT THE GRAND HÔTEL AUGUY IN THE HEART OF LAGUIOLE, IS LOYAL TO HER COUNTRY. SHE IS NOT AFRAID TO TAKE A BULL BY ITS HORNS (TOP) AND SHE HAS IMMENSE KNOWLEDGE OF THE REGION'S HERBS, FOR EXAMPLE "ERYTHRONIUM" OR "DOG'S-TOOTH VIOLET" (SHOWN IN HER HANDS, FACING PAGE, TOP LEFT). SHE CREATES MENU ITEMS THAT REFLECT THE REGION, FOR EXAMPLE ASPARAGUS AND FROGS' LEGS (PRECEDING PAGE) OR SIMPLY AUBRAC FARM BEEFSTEAK WITH MARCIAC SAUCE (FACING PAGE, TOP RIGHT). SHE EFFORTLESSLY COMBINES THE TRADITIONAL AND THE MODERN, FOR EXAMPLE WITH HER SPICED CIGAR COOKIES ON APPLE PURÉE (FACING PAGE, BOTTOM). FOR HORS D'OEUVRES SHE SERVES COLD MEATS FROM LAGUIOLE (ABOVE) AND, IN HER KITCHEN, SHE ALWAYS PREPARES A TRADITIONAL ALIGOTE (PAGE 16).

ISABELLE AUGUY'S RECIPE:
CARAMELIZED PEAR AND CIGAR-SHAPED COOKIES WITH CINNAMON CREAM

PREPARATION TIME: 50 MINUTES
COOKING TIME: 20 MINUTES
PLUS 4 HOURS REFRIGERATION
TO SERVE: 6

INGREDIENTS
For the caramelized pears
· 6 pears
· 7 ounces (200 g) sugar
For the cigar-shaped cookies
· ½ cup (125 g) butter +
  4 teaspoons (20 g) for the
  cookie sheet
· 1 ¼ cups (175 g) all-purpose
  flour
· ½ cup (125 g) sugar
· 4 egg whites, lightly beaten
For the cinnamon cream
· 2 cups (500 ml) milk
· ½ cup (125 g) sugar
· 4 egg yolks
· 2 teaspoons (10 g) flour
· 2 tablespoons (25 g)
  cornstarch
· 1 sheet unflavored gelatin
· ⅔ cup (150 ml) whipping
  cream
· 2 dashes ground cinnamon

METHOD
To make the cigar cookies,
preheat the oven to 350°F
(180°C). Melt the butter
and combine it with the flour
and sugar. Mix well. Add the
lightly beaten egg whites.
Roll out the dough as thinly as
possible and cut out 12 small
rounds with a cookie cutter.
Butter a cookie sheet and place
the rounds on it, well spaced.
Bake for 7 to 8 minutes or
until golden. Remove from the
oven and quickly roll up each
one to obtain large "cigars."
To prepare the pears, peel and

dice them. Cook the sugar in a
dry skillet until it caramelizes.
Add the pears and cook them
until golden, but still slightly
crunchy. Drain them.
To make the cinnamon cream,
boil the milk with half the
sugar. Remove from the heat
and leave to infuse for
10 minutes.
Combine the egg yolks with
the rest of the sugar, then
add the flour and cornstarch.
Gradually dilute the mixture
by beating in the milk.
Cook this pastry cream, stirring
constantly, until it thickens.
Soften the gelatin in cold
water. Wring it out and add it
to the warm pastry cream.
Stir until the gelatin has
dissolved. Leave to cool.
Pour the whipping cream into
a bowl and beat it into stiff
peaks with electric beaters.
Mix it with the pastry cream
and flavor with the cinnamon.
Refrigerate for at least 4 hours.
Use a small teaspoon or piping
bag to fill the cigar pastries
with the cream. Arange the
pear on the plate and serve
the cigar pastries on the side.

As an accompaniment I serve
a spiced honey ice cream,
made from a custard sweetened
with half sugar, half honey,
and flavored with 1 cinnamon
stick, 1 vanilla pod, 1 teaspoon
green aniseed and powdered
ginger, and the grated zest
of 1 lemon. The sweet and
sharp notes harmonize with
the delicate texture and flavor
of the pears.

JUDITH BAUMANN

CERNIAT, SWITZERLAND

IN THE IDYLLIC MOUNTAIN LANDSCAPE OF FRYEBURG LIES A TREASURE
CONNOISSEURS DISCOVER ALMOST BY CHANCE—A SELF-TAUGHT COOK
WITH A PURE HEART WHOSE DISHES ARE ODES TO MOTHER NATURE.

She closes on Sundays, Mondays, and Tuesdays; and also from the end of October through
the middle of March. She's glaringly absent from the *Michelin Guide*, despite the fact that
for fifteen years past she's been attracting a huge clientele to her Pinte des Mossettes, located
at an altitude of 1,100 meters (3,610 feet) opposite the Gros Bras, Dents Vertes, and
Patrafran mountain ranges. What was once a modest alpine refuge offering refreshment to
passing hikers has now become the most elaborate "simple" restaurant in the world.

"We're only superficially simple," explains the house's majordomo, Jean-Bernard Fasel,
with a laugh. This former teacher, who worked in Italy for many years, has been Judith
Baumann's assistant in the dining room ever since she first started out. He's the man responsible for the little poetic phrases and proverbs, amusing quotations and legends (true and
false) decorating the menus that change daily.

Judith Baumann, the restaurant's presiding spirit, is completely self-taught. Born in
Tavel, Singine, in the German-speaking part of the canton of Fryeburg, she plied many different trades—weaver, furniture restorer, waitress in local cafés—before serving as cook in a
hostel for apprentices. It was then that she discovered the cookbooks of Frédy Girardet, the
wizard of the Lausanne suburb, Crissier, in the canton of Vaud; and also those of Joël
Robuchon, then working at Jamin in Paris. She began by cooking for her friends. In 1988,
when she assumed management of the Pinte des Mossettes, she started out modestly, offering fondues, warm ham on the bone, and "chalet" soup made with wild spinach and nettles.

Baumann gradually developed an interest in cooking with wild plants, composing new
dishes as if they were symphonies, paintings, or poems. She quietly changed the style of the
restaurant, an initiative greeted with enthusiasm by her customers. In 1988 she was named
"chef of the year" by the *Gault-Millau Guide* for Switzerland. She proudly acknowledges her
adherence to the "herb" school of cuisine, along with Marc Veyrat at Michel Bras, Régis
Marcon at Saint-Bonnet-le-Froid, and near neighbor Jean-Paul Jeunet d'Arbois in the
Franche-Comté. But she has her own distinctive style—light, wild, unconstrained, unusual,
and spontaneous.

THE EVER-SMILING JUDITH BAUMANN IS AN EXPERT AT CREATING NATIONAL SPECIALTIES, AND NOW WORKS FROM AN ANCIENT MOUNTAIN CABIN IN FRYEBURG, WHICH HAS RETAINED ALL OF ITS RUSTIC, ALPINE CHARACTER. SHE SELECTS FRESH HERBS EVERY DAY (FACING PAGE, RIGHT), INCLUDING ONE OF HER FAVORITES, COW PARSNIP, WHICH RESEMBLES WILD ASPARAGUS (FACING PAGE, LEFT). IT IS MAGNIFICENT TO VISIT HER RESTAURANT IN SUMMER AND TO EAT LUNCH IN THE SHADE OF THE TREES ON THE TERRACE (BELOW). AT AN ALTITUDE OF MORE THAN 3,000 FEET, ENJOY THE PURE, OPEN AIR. LEFT: AN HORS D'OEUVRE OF CAVIAR AND EGGPLANT SLICES, ATHAMANTHA MOUSSE, AND SUN-DRIED TOMATOES.

Her menus still read like prose poems written by an elf—a diminutive elf with very clear blue eyes and pale blonde hair, playing at mountain cookery. This gentle Swiss enchantress uses little-known herbs and condiments; she obtains them locally, for the most part, although for some she is forced to go farther afield. Judith Baumann has a unique touch, an understated way of expressing herself, and a lyricism that is all her own.

Her menus at the Pinte des Mossettes are themed. For example, "Artemis in the Cauliflower" is composed of fine carpaccio slices of veal with cauliflower mousse and sprigs of artemisia. Then there's her "Rapunzel and the Fricassee," featuring ravioli made with rampion (a rare herb found on mountain pastures) and mushrooms, accompanied by chicken broth with truffles. Or, again, "Tiny Seascape," which is an unskinned cod fillet baked in a crust of bread-crumbs and bacon, and served with spinach, tapenade, smoked-tea aspic, and beet compote.

Diners doubtless have a hard time choosing between the duckling with rhubarb and coriander seed with a sesame wafer; or the rack of lamb with cucumber, borage, and wood sorrel, accompanied by a slice of bread topped with fennel flower ("The Wolf and the Shepherdess"). The menu is wittily explained by Jean-Bernard Fasel, who will also explain the stories behind these intriguing legends. The food is presented by the graceful women of the waitstaff, who are proud of what they serve and—a rarity in contemporary restaurants—able to explain, comment, elaborate, and offer samples for eye and taste.

Many diners are perfectly happy to opt for the divinely appealing vegetarian offerings. Choices include a comfrey fritter with eggplant caviar and wafers flanked with tomato con-serve; or grilled, Swiss-style cottage cheese with fried cow parsnips and preserved orange, broccoli, and cow-parsnip stems; or potato stuffed with a sabayon of pine sprouts and cucumber served with mushroom kebabs in salad. And, for the dessert finale, an almond *financière* pastry in Montbazillac sauce, garnished with elderflowers and elderberries, and melon sorbet.

Desserts represent some of the restaurant's finest efforts. The chocolate fondant *à la Michel Bras* (which, even if it was a little dry on the day I tried it, was delicious nonetheless) is attractively accompanied with dandelion ice cream. The dark Guinness ice cream with old-fashioned unpitted cherries in a purée of their own juice, and the preserved-lemon yogurt and puff-pastry twist make delicious endings to a great meal.

The restaurant's sunny terrace is shaded by a thirty-year-old chestnut tree, and the mountain rises invitingly in the background at this spot where Judith Baumann has put down new roots. The Abbey of Valsainte is nearby; the village of Cerniat is two or three kilometers (about a mile) away—no one knows exactly. We might be at the end of the world.

Although seemingly at home in her own universe at the heart of as-yet unspoiled nature, Baumann's inquisitive spirit is never completely at rest. When she closes the Pinte during the winter, she travels to far-distant India for a medicinal *ayurveda* cure. She also takes the time to renew her energies, ski, and practice tai chi (not in Hong Kong, but at Bulle, in the Swiss canton of Gruyère). These winter breaks give her an opportunity to restore her strength before she returns in the spring—which always promises to be even more creative than the year before. Judith Baumann must be a very happy woman.

IN A RUSTIC DINING ROOM AT PINTE DES MOSETTES, THE TABLE IS CAREFULLY SET (BELOW LEFT). SOME EXAMPLES OF HER CREATIONS: A *financière* CAKE WITH ELDERBERRIES AND MEADOWSWEET ICE CREAM (PAGE 21); GRILLED SERAC, SAUTÉED COW PARSNIP AND CANDIED ORANGE, BROCCOLI WITH COW PARSNIP STEMS (BELOW RIGHT).
FACING PAGE: JUDITH BAUMANN'S PARTNER JEAN-BERNARD FASEL (PICTURED WITH HER IN THE DOORWAY OF THE KITCHEN) ATTENDS TO THE CUSTOMERS AND IS THE POET RESPONSIBLE FOR THE DELIGHTFUL ANECDOTES THAT ENLIVEN THE MENU. FACING PAGE: CHANTERELLE RAVIOLI (CENTER); THE SUN-DAPPLED RESTAURANT FRONTAGE (RIGHT).

JUDITH BAUMANN'S RECIPE:

CHANTERELLE RAVIOLI WITH GOAT CHEESE

PREPARATION TIME: 1 HOUR
COOKING TIME: 3 MINUTES
TO SERVE: 6

INGREDIENTS

For the ravioli dough
· ⅔ cup (100 g) all-purpose
  flour
· 1 egg
· 1 teaspoon olive oil
· Salt

For the filling
· ⅔ cup (100 g) small
  chanterelle mushrooms
· 1 tablespoon clarified butter
  (melted butter from which
  the white milk solids are
  discarded)
· 1 tablespoon minced shallot
· 1 teaspoon cherry brandy
· 30 rampion spikes
· 2 tablespoons (20 g) fresh
  goat cheese
· 1 egg yolk
· Salt and pepper

For the stock
· 1 ¼ cups (600 ml) chicken
  stock
· 1 teaspoon soy sauce
· Salt and pepper

For the truffle
· ½ ounce (15 g) black truffle
· 2 tablespoons (30 ml) olive oil

To garnish
· 6 campanula flowers
· 6 rampion spikes

UTENSILS

· 1 ravioli-making machine
· 1 serrated cookie cutter,
  2 inches (5 cm) in diameter

METHOD

To make the ravioli dough,
mix the flour in a bowl with
the egg and oil. Add the salt.
Knead until you have a stiff
dough. Cover with plastic
wrap and refrigerate until
required.

To prepare the filling, heat the
clarified butter and sauté the
chanterelles. Add the chopped
shallot. Deglaze the pan, adding
the cherry brandy. Season with
salt and pepper. Blanch the
rampion spikes in salted boiling
water. Rinse them under cold
running water.

To assemble the ravioli, roll
out the dough as thinly as
possible in a long strip, using a
ravioli-making machine.
Divide the strip in half. Mark
out the first part in squares
using the cookie cutter.
Arrange the goat cheese,
chanterelles, and rampion
spikes in the center of each
square. Season to taste. Brush
the edges of the squares with
beaten egg yolk. Cover with
the other strip and cut out the
ravioli, using the cookie cutter.
Refrigerate until required.

To prepare the stock, heat the
stock over high heat and
reduce it to 1 ¼ cups (300 ml).
Add the soy sauce and season
with salt and pepper. Keep
warm until required.

Chop the black truffle finely.
Add the olive oil.

Cook the ravioli in boiling
salted water until they are
al dente, about three minutes.
Place 1 ravioli in the center
of a soup plate. Pour the broth
round it. Sprinkle with the
truffle in oil and garnish
the ravioli with the campanula
flowers and rampion spikes.

25

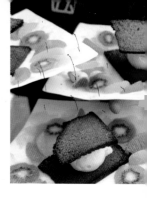

NATHALIE BEAUVAIS

LORIENT, FRANCE

IN BRITTANY THERE IS AN EXPERIENCED YET SELF-EFFACING WOMAN CHEF
WHO CREATES REASONABLY PRICED MARVELS, BASING THE SAVORY CREATIONS
FOR HER JARDIN GOURMAND ON LOCAL PRODUCTS.

Who is the presiding spirit of gourmet cooking in the Morbihan? A diminutive, dynamic woman dressed in a white chef's hat and mariner's sweater who looks like a quiet mouse or a pixie. She won't contradict me when I claim that she's the only outstanding chef in the field of Breton cuisine, although she in no way resembles the "*mères*" who were traditional untrained, pioneers of cuisine; Nathalie Beauvais is something new in the field.

Her husband Arnaud runs the dining room with distinctive flair, extends a warm welcome to their guests, and makes suggestions with a smile, pointing out delicious wines at affordable prices and praising the day's specials with conviction. Alongside him, Nathalie Beauvais has given a serious shot in the arm to a decor that was originally a little drab and old-fashioned. Opting for a contemporary style, she daringly combines modern cuisine with a casual atmosphere. Her Jardin Gourmand concept combines traditional Breton specialties with modern innovations; it is sunny, luminous, and open to the outside world.

The restaurant's stained beech and pear tables are casually set with cloth mats; they encourage informality and conversation. The atmosphere is that of a friendly club where everybody knows everybody else—or soon will. Toasts are frequently made between tables with glasses of a vibrant Sarthois white from the Côteaux de Jasnières, or a red combining Pinot Noir and Cabernet in new casks from the Vendée fiefs of Brem. This background sets just the right tone for showcasing dishes concocted by a woman with magic fingers. Her creations are light, seasonal, and contemporary.

The set menu, which changes daily, is a gift to diners. Nathalie relies on ingredients currently available in the market, and uses them to stunning effect. One day it will feature creamed prawns in a blend of spices known as "*Kari Gosse*," originally invented by a Lorient pharmacist named Gosse whose "curry" soon appeared on all the best local tables. Another day it might feature subtle, mint-flavored zucchini accompanied by shredded smoked salmon and spider crab.

NATHALIE BEAUVAIS REINTERPRETS BRETON CUISINE, WITH AN EMPHASIS ON LIGHTNESS, FRESHNESS, AND MARKET PRODUCE. IN HER SMALL HOUSE WITH ITS GRANITE FAÇADE (TOP LEFT), SHE IS ALWAYS PREPARING TRADITIONAL BUCKWHEAT PANCAKES (TOP RIGHT) AND COOKING GUÉMENÉ SAUSAGE (FACING PAGE, TOP LEFT) IN HER OWN STYLE. SHE ALSO CREATES SMALL DELIGHTS SUCH AS THIS PLATE OF ROQUEFORT WITH DRIED FRUIT (ABOVE) OR TOASTED GINGERBREAD WITH ORANGE SORBET (PRECEDING PAGE). SHE CAN BE SEEN HERE MEETING FISHERMEN IN THE PORT AT LORIENT, SEARCHING FOR THE FRESHEST FISH (FACING PAGE, TOP RIGHT) AND PREPARING SPIDER CRAB WITH HER YOUTHFUL AND DEDICATED TEAM (FACING PAGE, BOTTOM).

A light, amusing, original hors d'œuvre? Perhaps the strips of artichoke with cooked bacon marinated in olive oil and sage—a hint of Provence to set off the local vegetables. The day's fish? Why not an appealing pollack fillet cooked slowly in a buckwheat crust—a nod to the local crêpe, traditionally stuffed and seasoned with a smoky Guémené chitterling sausage. For the pollack, not generally considered a very delicate fish, Beauvais pays tribute to the past by using a traditional cooking method combined with contemporary ingredients.

It's obvious: Nathalie is a discriminating magician with unfailing imagination, a woman who cares about the traditions of her native Brittany and, at the same time—with a wave of her magic wand—transforms ordinary ingredients into a wholly new style that's witty, striking, and versatile. Meanwhile, Arnaud explains the day's suggestions with all the verve of a trial lawyer defending his client's life.

Nathalie learned her craft at the Dinard hotel school and then in Paris with Christiane Massia, who at the time reigned over a battalion of chefs at the Aquitaine on rue de Dantzig. She went on to apprentice with Alain Dutournier at Le Carré des Feuillants, where she served a stint at every single workstation. She's also never forgotten the precious lore she absorbed at her mother's knee.

Her mother was a Breton from Lorient who trained as a schoolteacher and cooked for her extended family on Sundays, preparing different specialties each week for the pleasure of her many guests. She excelled in desserts, as her daughter does today. This explains the evocative delicacies drawn from remembered childhood experiences. These include her astringently refreshing rhubarb au gratin with strawberry sorbet and chunks of fruit, and the warm orange *génoise* fondant with its luscious orange sorbet, accompanied by a salad of strawberries from Madame André in Plouay.

Everything Nathalie Beauvais does seems deceptively simple: easy to make and even easier to enjoy. But her creations are actually based on treasures of lucid invention and a rare finesse. After a tour of the Lorient port, or before a visit to the Port Louis citadel, visitors to the area are delighted to find a Breton wizard of this caliber; one who restores the famished gourmet with offerings that are light as air.

NATHALIE BEAUVAIS'S RECIPE:

ANDOUILLE SAUSAGE FROM GUÉMENÉ/SCORFF WITH OLD-FASHIONED MASHED POTATOES

PREPARATION TIME: 20 MINUTES
COOKING TIME: A FEW SECONDS
TO SERVE: 6

INGREDIENTS
· 3 pounds, 5 ounces (1.5 kg) floury potatoes
· 1 ¾ cups (400 ml) milk
· 1 ¾ cups (400 ml) heavy cream
· 2 pinches grated nutmeg
· 1 ⅓ cups (300 g) softened butter, cut into small pieces
· 1 pound, 5 ounces (600 g) Guémené/Scorff sausage
· Salt and pepper

METHOD
To make the creamed potatoes, first cook them in their skins in salted water. Peel them when they are cooked. Heat the milk and the cream and pour the mixture over the potatoes. Mash them with a potato masher or potato ricer, or with a large fork. Add the grated nutmeg. Add the butter and mix well, lifting the mixture. Season to taste with salt and pepper and keep warm. To prepare the sausage, slice it thinly. Remove the outer black casing and arrange the slices on a cookie sheet. Put the sheet into a preheated 450°F (230°C) oven for a few seconds.
To assemble the dish, arrange the creamed potatoes in a warmed shallow bowl and cover with the slices of sausage.

TIPS
Sausage of this type should be produced by small manufacturers. It is always expensive due to the amount of time spent in making it. This sausage, known as Guémené, consists of pork chitterlings that are seasoned and degreased by hand. The sausage is then cooked in a broth and smoked. This type of sausage is often much more fatty and indigestible when it is manufactured industrially, because the chitterlings have not been fully cleaned of fat. Although this dish is disconcertingly simple, it is very popular with my customers. The success of the recipe will depend solely on the quality of the ingredients, so do not skimp on them. Use the finest butter, the finest cream and milk, and very good potatoes. This will turn the dish into a feast.

SOPHIE BISE

TALLOIRES, FRANCE

On the banks of Lake Annecy, where she supervises restaurants in both Talloires and Doussard, the female heir to the Auberge du Père Bise rules over a marvelous domain. Her luxury restaurant and the contrastingly modest bistro provide her with an opportunity to display the many facets of her talent.

It is a waterside paradise on the banks of the purest lake in Europe, with the peaks of the Lanfon looming above. And then there's the nearby village of Duingt, opposite Talloires, a delightful place for a quiet stay that is frequented by the great and the good—who are of course treated like privileged guests. We're in Doussard, at the end of the lake. The inn is a lively spot, with its shaded terrace, Formica bar, and 1950s-style Art Deco furnishings.

The sign outside is modestly marked Chez Ma Cousine, but the menu is a lesson in spontaneous poetry. "Dig right in," invites a sidebar commentary, going on to state that the appetizers are "an invitation to good eating," that the soups and hot appetizers create a "swirl of traditions offering pure enjoyment." This casual Savoyard tone is applied to a three-cheese fondue with green salad topped by a mini-tart. Cheeses are listed under the banner of "regional taste treats," and include a Saint-Marcellin from Mère Richard, a "shepherd's" selection, and fresh cheese with its own pot of cream and blueberries. Desserts are described as being drawn from the "dawn of the art" and include a vanilla-bean crème brûlée, a *chiboust* with blueberries and lemon sorbet, and a lemongrass-flavored strawberry soup served with Bulgarian ice cream.

Behind these tempting treats stands a benevolent wizard who officiates on the other side of the lake at a gastronomic restaurant, crosses each morning to check that all is going well, and returns at the end of the afternoon, greeting the friends who run the operation with energy and enthusiasm. At her Auberge du Père Bise, in the Talloires mansion made famous by her grandfather Marius and father François, Sophie still serves veal sweetbreads *cassolette*, artic char, and Bresse chicken Miéral.

The *Michelin Guide* played a game of "yo-yo" with Sophie Bise for many years. One star, then two, then three, then two, then one, then two, and then one more. Her restaurant has been fashionable in the past, and it will be fashionable again. The assets of this great old-fashioned mansion, which has retained its timeless charm, include impeccable service, a sumptuous lakeside terrace, cozy dining room, and a snug bar.

AUBERGE DU PÈRE BISE OWES ITS GREAT CHARM
PRIMARILY TO ITS LOCATION IN TALLOIRES, A HAVEN FOR
TOURISTS AND FOOD LOVERS, ON THE SHORES OF LAKE
ANNECY. IN SUMMER, THE TERRACE BENEATH THE TREES IS
DELIGHTFUL. THE FISHERMAN BRINGS ARCTIC CHAR FROM
THE LAKE (ABOVE RIGHT). THE MAGNIFICENT MAHOGANY
BOAT DOCKS ALONGSIDE OTHERS AT THE PORT (FACING
PAGE, BELOW LEFT). IN HER KITCHEN, SOPHIE DISCUSSES
HER NEW DISHES AND MAIN COURSES (FACING PAGE, TOP
RIGHT), FOR EXAMPLE SAUTÉED SLICE OF DUCK FOIE GRAS
AND "DOLCE FORTE" APRICOT MARMALADE (ABOVE LEFT).
SHE ALSO CONTINUES TO PREPARE RESTAURANT CLASSICS,
FOR EXAMPLE STEAMED SOLE (PRECEDING PAGE, TOP)
OR BAKED LOBSTER, BRETON-STYLE, WITH ITS CORAL
(FACING PAGE, TOP LEFT).

Sophie is more "at home" in the laurel-covered family residence, which has won world-wide fame based on a style that can sometimes be a little stiff and formal. Opposite, how-ever, stands the house once run by her cousin (this was called the Sautereau restaurant when her grandfather Marius first courted Marguerite, her future grandmother), and where con-viviality reigns supreme.

One is tempted to say that she's just as comfortable in both places, which gives an idea of the Savoyard serenity characteristic of Ma Cousine. At the Auberge du Père Bise, timeless classicism is the keynote. Diners face some difficult choices. Will they opt for the gratin of crayfish tails "Marguerite Bise," or the warm asparagus with shredded Serrano ham? Will they want the now famous potato upside-down cake with truffles, foie gras, and Périgueux sauce, or the crayfish with sparkling Savoy wine? The arctic char with foamy butter, or the adroitly prepared lake fish (perch meunière, dace *à la grenobloise* with capers), accompanied by a typical Savoyard side dish, forcemeat with prunes?

Here is a versatile chef, firmly rooted in her region, yet capable of producing dishes that are fanciful or chic, depending on the occasion and the place she happens to be working. At the Auberge du Père Bise, the emphasis is on wines from the Rhône Valley and Bordeaux. Doussard, on the other hand, is a little bistro featuring Savoyard wines—for example, a robust white from the Idylle estate in Cruet.

In short, customers have recognized two houses that are different, but each equally appealing in their own way. Wealthy foreigners opt for the Auberge du Père Bise, while—unsurprisingly—locals such as eminent neighbor Veyrat de Veyrier are regulars at Doussard.

SOPHIE BISE'S RECIPE:

ROAST BRETON LOBSTER WITH CORAL AND SAUTÉED PENNE WITH CHANTERELLES AND SCALLIONS

PREPARATION TIME: 45 MINUTES
COOKING TIME: 6 MINUTES
TO SERVE: 4

INGREDIENTS

· 1 cup (250 ml) white wine vinegar
· 1 sprig dried fennel
· 1 tablespoon mignonnette pepper
· 2 lobsters, each weighing around 1 pound, 5 ounces (600 g)
· 2 ¾ cups (700 ml) chicken stock or homemade chicken bouillon
· 2 tablespoons olive oil
· ½ lemon
· 1 tablespoon (15 g) butter
· 1 tablespoon olive oil
· 7 ounces (200 g) chanterelle mushrooms
· 1 shallot
· 2 very ripe medium tomatoes
· 7 ounces (200 g) penne
· 2 garlic cloves
· 2 scallions
· Coarse salt

METHOD

Make a broth for cooking the lobsters by pouring 2 quarts (2 liters) water and the white wine vinegar into a large pot. Add the fennel, the mignonnette pepper, and a handful of coarse salt. Simmer for 15 minutes. Plunge the lobster claws into the stock and cook for 3 minutes. Add the rest of the lobsters and cook for 3 minutes. Drain well and leave to cool.

Shell the lobsters, including the claws and tails. Cut the tails in half. Scoop out the inside of the heads, the coral and creamy parts, and grind in a food processor, then strain. Cook the mixture in a bain-marie to turn them red, stirring constantly. Add 1 scant cup (200 ml) of chicken stock, 2 tablespoons olive oil, and the juice from the lemon.

Check the seasoning and strain through a sieve. Keep warm in a bain-marie, ensuring that this coral sauce does not boil. Melt the butter and 1 tablespoon olive oil in a skillet and sauté the chanterelles and 1 sliced shallot. Cook for around 3 minutes, then remove the skillet from the heat, leaving the contents in it. Skin the tomatoes, cut them into quarters, discard the seeds, and add to the chanterelles.

Cook the penne for 7 minutes in the remaining 2 cups (500 ml) of chicken stock, with 4 halved garlic cloves. Drain and add to the chanterelles. Reduce the cooking liquid of the penne by two-thirds. Finely slice the whites of the scallions, and slice the green parts separately. To assemble the dish, pour the chanterelles, noodles, garlic, tomatoes, and white parts of the scallions into a large saucepan and heat. Add the lobster and sauté for 2 minutes. Add the noodle cooking liquid.

Arrange the mixture in the center of each plate and sprinkle with the green parts of the scallions. Pour a trail of coral sauce around the center and serve immediately.

33

CHANTAL CHAGNY

FLEURIE, FRANCE

In Fleurie, at the heart of the Beaujolais region, there is an auberge
across from the church that showcases
the talents of an exceptional woman, Chantal Chagny.

"We are making a sincere effort to maintain the quality of our service, despite the many problems involved in hiring competent staff. We regret any inconvenience to our customers caused by this situation, and thank them in advance for their understanding." Thus does Chantal Chagny admit, in a small card stapled to the menu, that she faces many difficulties in achieving peerless service. The tone is set: honest, rigorous, disciplined.

We're at the heart of the Beaujolais region—land of wine, laughter, good fellowship, and conviviality—and this is how Chantal Chagny welcomes her customers. Dressed in the dark garb and shawls traditionally worn (like Italian widows) by the women of her native village, she's serious, dedicated, and determined to do things right. Her hallmarks are consistency and honesty, sincerity and rigor. Here's a woman who embodies all of these virtues naturally, without fuss or any attempt to impress. Her tables are filled by a succession of loyal friends and supporters. Among them are Michel Chignard, the outstanding vintner of the Fleurie region, and Georges Duboeuf, the area's leading wine dealer, who is based in Romanèche-Thorins.

When it comes to ordering, customers like these trust Chantal's instincts, barely glance at the menu, and could probably recite all the dishes on it by heart, with their eyes closed. Casual visitors to the restaurant quickly adapt to its unique spirit. The menu's listings, elegantly handwritten in green or purple ink, express Chantal's philosophy and that of the surrounding area. They including such marginal comments as "La Bresse, La Dombes, and the country of Brillat-Savarin" or "From the Burgundy of Val de Saône, a harmonious blend of wine and fine cuisine," with one note set off by an asterisk: "preserving France's regional traditions." Or this one: "Season of growth for wine, buds, flowers, and grapes," or, again, "spring, summer, autumn." And, finally, summing it all up: "Typical of the Beaujolais region."

The aim is obvious: to run a restaurant as if fulfilling a mission. Chantal is everywhere at once, rushing from kitchen to dining room, working at the stove, checking the arrival of premium products for varied sources—the snails known as "*gros gris de Bourgogne*," frogs from Eastern Europe, salads seasoned with oil from the hazelnuts that grow and thrive in the backwoods. And then there's Bresse poultry cooked as for coq au vin and, of course, the poached

CHANTAL CHAGNY, PERFECTIONIST AND LOVER OF GOOD PRODUCE, ALWAYS VISITS HER SUPPLIERS, WHO HAVE OVER TIME BECOME FRIENDS. SHE CAN BE SEEN (TOP LEFT) IN CONVERSATION WITH GENEVIÈVE DUMONT, HER CHEESE SUPPLIER. TRADITIONAL COOKING IS HER PASSION. SHE LOVINGLY PREPARES ESCARGOT, WILD MUSHROOMS (ABOVE) AND FROGS' LEGS (TOP RIGHT). ALL OF HER OFFERINGS REFLECT THE FLAVORS AND FOODS OF THE BEAUJOLAIS REGION, FOR EXAMPLE SAUSAGE IN A LENTIL STEW (PRECEDING PAGE) OR WARM GOAT CHEESE SALAD WITH BACON STRIPS (FACING PAGE, BOTTOM RIGHT). MEMBERS OF HER EXCEPTIONAL STAFF AT THE ENTRANCE TO THE RESTAURANT (FACING PAGE, LEFT).

andouillette created in 1919 by François Chabert, whose son Georges and son-in-law Roger Ducruix keep this tradition of fine charcuterie alive in the village.

Chantal's cuisine is like a philanthropic vocation, extending this tradition and ensuring the perpetuation of its heritage. Flavors strike just the right note, as though integrated into a perfectly tuned musical score. Sauces, featuring onions and shallots with red wine, are subtly focused and tart. The terrine, with its farmhouse-style shallot condiment, evokes memories of childhood. Chantal was raised for six years in a rural area, at her mother's in Finistère. Then her father, who was born in Lancié, packed up the whole family and took everyone back to Beaujolais country. Among the traditional local dishes served at the restaurant are herb soup, fricassee of wild mushrooms, and a matelote of eel braised in wine. Here are dishes that celebrate the passing seasons and the poetry of each day, dishes that have a story to tell.

The village of Fleurie stands quietly at the foot of a bluff dominated by the Chapel of the Madonna, visible from the surrounding vine-covered hills. The inn, located on the square in front of the church, has remained unchanged over the years. It's a rustic spot that is warm and welcoming, preserving the utter simplicity of the past. It once boasted two stars, in the era of Alain Chapel's dedicated pupil Gérard Cortembert—an unassuming colossus of a man who unfortunately died before his time. Today, Chantal sets the style with complete modesty and discreet serenity.

Chantal Chagny is the area's gourmet lodestar. Regulars from nearby have their own napkins reserved for them at the restaurant. Outsiders who happen to drop in while traveling through the lovely wine country between Morgon and Chenas also appreciate this culinary symphony. Chantal composes her dishes with unparalleled brio: roast free-range pigeon, homemade cervelas sausage poached in *ravigote* sauce and served with lentils. To drink with this dish, a full-bodied, aromatic Fleurie from Chignard. And, to round off the meal, a meltingly delicious, creamy-centered Saint-Marcellin cheese. The ideal starter is the *gougère*, a large, puffed, cheese pastry. For dessert, the iced mocha parfait is hard to beat. The "Lancié" blackcurrant special—blackcurrant sorbet served with a tart blackcurrant purée—provides an appealing contrast to its accompanying vanilla ice cream. Afterward come the orange crisps, a delicious cup of coffee, and a glass of marc, the local white brandy made from the seeds and skins of pressed grapes.

This is a symphony like a high mass. Here, across from the Fleurie church, is a woman who respects her customers and her products, and who presents her menus like a sacred liturgy. Nothing is done lightly; everything is elegant. Highlights include perch marinated in lime juice and mixed herbs, freshly caught pike perch sautéed in the skin and served with white-grape verjuice, eggs *meurette* poached in Beaujolais, fillet of Dombes duckling in its pan juices. There is not a false note anywhere. The gourmets of Beaujolais could write an ode to Saint Chantal Chagny.

WARM GOAT CHEESE GRATIN FROM UPPER BEAUJOLAIS WITH ORGANIC BACON

PREPARATION TIME: 30 MINUTES

COOKING TIME: 3–4 MINUTES

TO SERVE: 4

INGREDIENTS

· 4 small semi-dry goat cheeses
· 2 tablespoons olive oil
· 1 tablespoons heavy cream
· 1 egg yolk
· 1 teaspoon minced garlic
· A few flakes of dried thyme
· 5 ½ ounces (150g) lightly smoked pork belly or bacon, thinly sliced
· 8 slices wholewheat bread
· 1 tablespoon goose fat or lard
· 3 cups (300 g) mixed leaf salad
· 2 tablespoons walnut oil
· 2 tablespoons wine vinegar (preferably homemade)
· 2 tablespoons chopped walnuts
· 1 bunch flatleaved parsley, freshly minced
· Sea salt and freshly ground pepper

METHOD

Cut each goat cheese in half crosswise. Sprinkle with a few drops of olive oil. Leave to marinate in a cool place for 2 to 3 hours until they have absorbed the oil.

Combine the cream and egg yolk and brush the cut surface of the cheeses with it. Place them rind downward in a gratin dish.

Sprinkle each halved goat cheese with a dash of sea salt, the minced garlic, sprigs of thyme, and a little olive oil. Place them under the broiler for 3 to 4 minutes to soften the goat cheese and color it slightly. Place the thin slices of smoked pork belly or bacon in a dry skillet and brown on low heat for 2 to 3 minutes.

Cut slices ¼ inch (5 mm) thick from the wholewheat bread. Fry them in the goose fat or lard. Drain them on kitchen paper.

In the center of each plate, put a pile of salad greens seasoned with walnut oil, homemade wine vinegar, sea salt and freshly ground pepper. Add the chopped walnuts.

Around the salad leaves, on each round of fried bread, place a halved goat cheese, as well as twisted slices of bacon. Sprinkle with a little freshly minced parsley.

SALLY CLARKE

LONDON, GREAT BRITAIN

A CORNER BISTRO FEEL WITH VERY DELICIOUS FOOD—THE INSPIRATION BEHIND
SALLY CLARKE'S RESTAURANT IS FRENCH, ENGLISH, AND CALIFORNIAN.

Back on home soil after her stint in California, British-born Sally Clarke is a real Kensington lady, after two decades in London. She heads the restaurant that bears her name and its sister bakery and delicatessen. Organic produce, fresh vegetables, extra-virgin olive oils, clean-tasting and tender meats, succulent fruit: Sally Clarke's is about real cooking from the heart.

Sally was born in Guilford, Surrey, and spent her holidays in France as a child, which was the start of a lifelong love story. She studied in Croydon and followed a Cordon Bleu course, spending one year in Paris training with chefs she had chosen for their love of food. There she discovered Pierre Vedel, who seconded Michel Olivier at the Bistro de Paris. Three months at Le Pactole with Jacques Manière were followed by a longer spell working with Martin Cantegrit, the hot-blooded owner of the Le Récamier.

She learnt about true cooking: the love of fine produce, the value of chance encounters and emotional exchanges. Then out to California, to work with Michael McCarty, owner of Michael's in Santa Monica. Soon she met the chef who was to become her idol: Alice Waters, the great priestess of good and simple food at Chez Panisse in Berkeley. Proper, unadulterated flavors; perfectly selected products at their best; light, clean sauces; Provençal flavors pervaded with herbs; in a word, natural. Now Sally Clarke could really be herself.

By Christmas 1984, she was back in London and had opened Clarke's, followed by the delicatessen & Clarke's, where she brings in all her favourite products, from Italian olive oils to Norman ciders. Soon, her reputation was made. In a city just beginning to rediscover food, Sally Clarke was avant-garde. She published *Sally Clarke's Book* (prefaced by Alice Waters), in homage to the glory of home cooking.

Sally's menus change every day, offering unaffected fare and served by members of her forty-strong staff. Her patrons are as enthusiastic as they are numerous.

What would a typical menu include? It would start perhaps with a spinach soup, with peas, broad beans, thyme, and crème fraîche, served with a thin parmesan baguette; or various smoked fish (swordfish, organic salmon from Ireland) with avocado, beet, and pea

SALLY CLARKE STUDIED CUISINE UNDER PIERRE VEDEL AND JACQUES MANIÈRE IN PARIS IN THE 1980S. HER RESTAURANT AND BOUTIQUE IN LONDON'S FASHIONABLE KENSINGTON (BELOW RIGHT) IS A WORLD OF DELIGHTS, WITH THE EMPHASIS ON QUALITY AND AUTHENTICITY. PRECEDING PAGE: CLARKE SIGNATURE PRODUCTS. HER BAKED SEA BASS WITH PUY LENTILS (FACING PAGE, RIGHT) OR RHUBARB, ORANGE, AND PRUNE TRIFLE (BELOW LEFT) ARE A FEAST.

pods; or a delicious rosemary, leek, and pancetta risotto with mozzarella and Prosecco wine. An ode to simplicity and freshness.

Then herb-roasted sea bass with mustard and lemon mayonnaise, or corn-fed chicken roasted with tarragon cream and lentils; or even her fabulous herby pork sausage balls with a sage jus and apples.

For dessert, exquisite pineapple, mango, and passion-fruit sorbets with delicate tuiles, or sabayon cake with rhubarb, blood orange, and plums.

The wine list favours wines from California (the fantastic Qupé Syrah and Merlot by Havens in the Napa Valley), which remain affordable.

All in all, Sally Clarke's unassuming bistro offers the visitor an enchanting journey. Franco-Anglo-Californian cuisine which is simply "true," as is Sally herself. Impossible not to love it.

SALLY CLARKE'S RECIPE:

BAKED SEA BASS WITH PUY LENTILS, SPRING VEGETABLES, AND HERBED LEMON MAYONNAISE

PREPARATION TIME: 40 MINUTES
COOKING TIME: 25–30 MINUTES
TO SERVE: 6

INGREDIENTS

· 6 sea bass fillets weighing 3 ounces (80 g) each
· Olive oil
· Sea salt and pepper

For the mayonnaise

· 1 whole egg
· 1 egg yolk
· 1 tablespoon of Dijon mustard
· 1 teaspoon French mustard
· 1 cup (250 ml) vegetable oil (or half vegetable, half olive oil)
· Juice of 1 lemon
· Salt and pepper
· 2 tablespoons chopped mixed herbs (tarragon, parsley, and chive, for example)

For the Puy lentils

· 1 ⅓ cups (300 g) Puy lentils
· 2 bay leaves
· 1 teaspoon salt
· 3 cups (750 ml) olive oil
· 1 garlic clove, peeled and crushed
· 1 chili pepper, finely chopped with the seeds
· 1 tablespoon chopped coriander (cilantro)
· 1 tablespoon chopped parsley
· 1 tablespoon chopped chives
· Spring vegetables (see below)

To garnish

· 6 lemon wedges

METHOD

To make the mayonnaise, beat the whole egg and the egg yolk in a bowl with the mustards. Gradually add the oil in a stream, beating constantly to thicken. Add the lemon juice, salt and pepper. Incorporate the herbs just before serving.

To prepare the Puy lentils, pour them into a saucepan, add the bay leaves, season with salt, and cover with cold water. Bring to the boil, reduce the heat, and simmer for 12 to 15 minutes, or until the lentils are soft. Drain and rinse under cold water. Pour the lentils into a sauté pan with the olive oil, the rest of the ingredients, and a little water. Stir and reheat over a gentle heat.

Preheat the oven to 350°F (170°C). Heat a nonstick pan over high heat and add a little olive oil (it should be large enough to hold all the fillets at one time).

Season the sea bass fillets with salt and pepper and place them skin-side downward in the hot oil. Sauté for 30 to 60 seconds, then gently turn them over and slide them onto an oiled cookie sheet. Bake for 3 to 6 minutes, depending on the thickness of the fillets.

Meanwhile, boil a large pot of water. Choose a few spring vegetables that are attractive in color and shape, such as carrots with their tops cut into two or four lengthwise, young trimmed leeks, miniature fennel bulbs, garden peas, and small broccoli florets. Add the vegetables to the boiling water, taking care not to exceed their normal cooking time (carrots first, then the fennel, broccoli, peas, and the leek, i.e. the tenderest, last).

Drain the vegetables in a colander and pour them into a salad bowl. Sprinkle them with olive oil and add a little sea salt, then toss carefully. Divide the vegetables among heated plates, add a sea bass fillet, garnish with the lemon wedges, and serve with the mayonnaise and lentils.

HÉLÈNE DARROZE

PARIS, FRANCE

When Hélène Darroze—who represents the third generation
of a culinary dynasty based in France's Landes region—left her native
Villeneuve-de-Marsan to seek her fortune in Paris, she created a phenomenon
in the French capital that is still going strong. But she has never forgotten her roots.

Ah, she stunned them all, did Hélène—a diminutive woman with the round face typical of people born in the Landes region—when she rose so quickly to the highest echelons in Paris. Although she was an outsider, she never really understood why she was shunned when she first arrived. Perhaps her long-established professional peers from the southwest were afraid that, with her youthful and energetic style, unconventional background, and somewhat trendy premises, she'd upset the apple cart.

And, for that matter, is she really a chef? There are those who have their doubts. Not that she isn't perfectly at home behind the stove, wearing the traditional high pleated chef's hat and carefully supervising each delectable dish as it leaves the kitchen for the dining room. At just a little over thirty years old, this young and ambitious woman is proud of bearing the famous name of Darroze, but her own aim is to give that name a new slant. Her antecedents include grandfather Jean, who earned two stars for the family restaurant at Villeneuve-de-Marsan in Les Landes; and father Francis, who made one of the best French Armagnacs available anywhere, and was followed in this vocation by her brother Marc. There's also her Uncle Claude in Langon and Uncle Henri in Toulouse . . . one can easily become transfixed by the Darroze family tree, and Hélène—the latest branch—has grown out in a different direction, although one still linked to this venerable heritage.

Hélène, who spent her childhood years tagging along behind her father in the kitchen, is doing things her own way. First came serious university study, focused not on cuisine, but on management. Her meeting with Alain Ducasse—who, lest we forget, was also born and bred in the Landes region—was a wake-up call. After discussing her ambitions, Ducasse decided to take her under his wing. His first step was to apprentice her for six months at his restaurant in Monaco, where she "washed lettuce and carved butter curls."

Hélène was next assigned to the office where, from 1990 through 1993, she served as an administrative assistant and learned all the ins and outs of the "Ducasse system." She also spent

CONTEMPORARY RED AND BLACK DECOR COUNTERPOINTS
THE WOODEN FLOORS: THIS IS THE SETTING IN WHICH
HÉLÈNE DARROZE PERFORMS HER WORK (BELOW).
SHE SERVES HER OWN STYLE OF TAPAS ON THE GROUND
FLOOR, AND ENTERTAINS FINE DINERS ON THE FIRST.
SHE IS PASSIONATE ABOUT GOOD FOOD AND PROMOTES
THE ASSOCIATION OF COOKS, THE "NEW *mères*." HER
DISHES, FOR EXAMPLE THE SLICES OF FOIE GRAS GRILLING
OVER A WOOD FIRE (LEFT), AND HER FRUIT GARNISHES
(FACING PAGE, RIGHT) DEMONSTRATE HER CONSTANT
EFFORTS TO DISPLAY THE GASCON PRODUCE OF TODAY.
HER RANGE OF SWEET DISHES INCLUDES THE
SOPHISTICATED BAKED CHOCOLATE CAKE WITH CHICORY
AND VANILLA FLAVORINGS (PRECEDING PAGE, TOP) AND
THE PURE SIMPLICITY OF THESE SMALL POTS OF HOMEMADE
PRESERVES, SERVED WITH MADELEINE COOKIES (FACING
PAGE, LEFT).

long hours with Alain Ducasse himself, learning about his dedication to authenticity, and helping to prepare the menus for the Louis XV restaurant in Monaco. When she felt she was ready, she left to take over her family's hotel, renaming it the Restaurant Hélène Darroze, and swapping the office for the kitchen.

By 1995 she'd become sole proprietor of the Villeneuve-de-Marsan restaurant, although she still hoped to find the location of her dreams somewhere in the area. She never did find it, unfortunately, and, meanwhile, customers were proving hard to attract during the region's long winters. This is when Hélène embarked on her Paris adventure. Representing the third generation of the Darroze family dynasty, she created a sensation in late 1999 when she opened a brand-new upper-floor restaurant on rue d'Assas, with a bistro (À la Table d'Hélène) below.

There she was in Paris, in Saint-Germain-des-Prés, just a step away from Boulevard Raspail and rue de Rennes, metropolitan nerve center where the media can make or break a reputation. But the diminutive Hélène had talent to spare, and her customers were beguiled by her restaurant's trendy decor in shades of red and black, its highly waxed parquet floor, swift and attentive service, unusual wines (many from the south) and original cuisine.

Hélène's talent is amply borne out by such dishes such as creamed beans and corn with fork-tender salt-cod purée (*brandade de morue*) seasoned with Espelette pepper; chilled shellfish bouillon with fennel; sautéed squid in tomato with piquillo chutney; crisp sea bass with violet artichokes, scallops with *ognasses* (onions from Les Landes); cep mushrooms and chestnuts like an autumn symphony; delicately spiced roast Pauillac lamb; foie gras cooked in a terrine and seasoned with spices, or grilled and served hot with seasonal fruit; yellow Landes chicken with mushrooms inserted under the skin; Landes *escaoutoun* (a kind of polenta made with fresh sheep's-milk cheese and shredded truffles); figs in port accompanied by mountain-honey ice cream; chocolate cake with luscious vanilla ice cream; flamed Armagnac baba with vanilla-flavored whipped cream; tart apple crumble with caramel and green-apple sorbet.

Add to all this her father's collection of Armagnacs and rare wines—such as the Sauvignon la Désirante du Poitou, the Saint-Véran des Deux Roches, or the stunning Fronton de Cahuzac—and you'll understand how Hélène Darroze, by following her own instincts, has been able to create an enduring success. The demanding connoisseurs of Paris were taken by surprise: amazed that such a young woman was able to win such high praise . . . and stars.

But she has experience behind her, supported by her native shrewdness, respect for tradition, and commitment to adding luster to the Darroze name. The staircase leading from the ground floor of her restaurant to the floor above is decorated with a series of black-and-white photos evoking the saga of Villeneuve-de-Marsan and the old family restaurant. This is more than just nostalgia: it's a conscious attempt to recognize the predecessors in whom today's success is rooted, the people who passed on their knowledge to the younger generation; and, by anchoring today in yesterday, to pay tribute to the house's roots.

The diminutive Hélène practices her own special brand of cuisine. "We women don't have the same sensibility men do; we don't look at things the same way; we don't feel things the same way, and so our cuisine naturally reflects all this . . . it's more generous." She keeps her vision constantly before her. She also brings her friends together at the Clubs des Dames Cuisinières (Women Chefs' Clubs), an annual event held in a different location each year and designed to forge links among female chefs everywhere. And yet, despite her obvious success, Hélène Darroze has never been totally accepted in Paris. This uprooted woman from Les Landes is a princess in exile.

HÉLÈNE PROUDLY WEARS AN OLD-FASHIONED CHEF'S HAT, EVEN IN THE HEAT OF THE ACTION (BELOW LEFT AND FACING PAGE). EVEN THE SMALLEST DETAIL IS IMPORTANT TO HER DELICATE, LIGHT, AND LOVINGLY PREPARED CUISINE. IN HER RESTAURANT SHE COMBINES PRODUCE FROM THE ATLANTIC COAST WITH INGREDIENTS FROM THE LANDES AND AQUITAINE REGIONS, AND EVEN SOME MORSELS FROM ITALY, AS IN HER SCALLOPS WITH HAZELNUTS, TRUFFLES, AND ARUGULA (FACING PAGE, RIGHT) AND RAVIOLI STUFFED WITH STEWED VENISON (BELOW RIGHT). HÉLÈNE DARROZE CAPTURES THE SPIRIT OF THE AGE WITH APLOMB.

HÉLÈNE DARROZE'S RECIPE:

SCALLOPS WITH HAZELNUTS, WHITE TRUFFLE ICE CREAM, AND ARUGULA SAUCE

PREPARATION TIME: 45 MINUTES
COOKING TIME: 30 MINUTES
TO SERVE: 4

INGREDIENTS
· 6 tablespoons (80 g) hazelnuts in the shell
· 2 teaspoons (10 ml) hazelnut oil
· 2 teaspoons (10 ml) olive oil
· 16 scallops
· 1 small chili pepper
· 2 teaspoons (10 ml) whipped cream
· Salt and pepper

For the arugula sauce
· 2 pounds, 4 ounces (1 kg) wild arugula
· ⅓ cup (100 ml) chicken stock
· 3 tablespoons (50 ml) olive oil
· Salt, pepper, and chili powder

For the ice cream
· 1 ¼ cups (300 ml) milk
· 4 tablespoons (65 g) whipping cream
· 2 ½ teaspoons (12.5 g) dextrose
· 4 tablespoons powdered milk
· 4 tablespoons water
· 1 unflavored gelatin leaf, soaked in water and squeezed
· ⅓ cup (100 ml) white truffle oil
· Pinch of salt

To finish
· 4 tablespoons (60 g) Parmesan cheese
· ½ teaspoon (2 g) white Alba truffle
· 3 tablespoons (40 g) wild arugula

METHOD
Crack the hazelnuts, toast them to loosen the skins and rub off the skins and toast them again in a dry skillet. Combine the nut oils. Chop the scallops and add half the hazelnuts to them.

Season with salt, pepper, and chili powder. Mix well. Whip the cream and add it in. Refrigerate until required.

To prepare the arugula sauce, blanch the leaves in boiling water for 5 minutes, then cool to fix the chlorophyll. Grind the arugula in a food processor then add the chicken stock and olive oil. Season with salt, pepper, and chili powder.

In a chilled bowl, combine the milk, cream, dextrose, and powdered milk. Pour into a saucepan and bring to a temperature of 185°F (85°C), checking the temperature with a candy thermometer. Add the salt. Cool and refrigerate for 6 hours.

Combine the gelatin with the water then pour the truffle oil into the mixture, beating well until smooth. Gradually add the chilled milk mixture, ensuring that it incorporates smoothly. Pour this into an ice-cream maker and make the ice cream. Freeze until required.

Place a 2 ¼-inch (6-cm) diameter cookie-cutter in the center of a plate and fill it with the scallop mixture. Pour a trail of arugula sauce around it, then sprinkle with some of the oil mixture. Dress the arugula with the rest of the oil mixture.

Slice the Parmesan into 8 shavings.

Slice the white truffle with a mandolin slicer.

Place a scoop of truffle ice cream on the scallop mixture, then add a shaving of Parmesan and some slices of white truffles. Sprinkle with arugula leaves and serve immediately.

PATRICIA DESMEDT

WAREGEM, BELGIUM

In Belgium, near the Flemish industrial town of Waregem,
the exceptional self-taught chef Patricia Desmedt
has created a restaurant that is worth the trip. A must.

A famous restaurant? Not at all—or not yet, at any rate. This gem is so far known only to a select group of Flemish connoisseurs, but everyone should make an effort to remember the name of the town in which it's located: Waregem. The restaurant stands near an industrial zone, at an intersection on the main highway not far from Le Coutrai. We're twenty-five miles (forty kilometers) from Lille, and twenty-two miles (thirty-five kilometers) from Ghent. The Flemish Ardennes Mountains begin here, which lends topographical interest to the otherwise flat countryside. Are you feeling a little lost? Just wait.

The inn is called 't Oud Konijntje, a name that every gourmet should learn to pronounce effortlessly. It means, literally, "The Little Old Rabbit's House," and one can easily imagine wild rabbits playing around it. The hamlet of the same name was established long ago by Desmedt's grandparents. Their granddaughter, who began life in the arms of their daughter, Thérèse, eventually grew up and became a respected mother of three children herself.

First is the lively, blonde Anne-Marie, who brings extrovert warmth to her supervision of the dining room, and treats every diner to an enthusiastic welcome. Next in line is Frank, an expert wine steward who explains offerings from all over the world with passionate conviction, although he clearly has a soft spot for wines from France. His cellar contains some of the best Bordeaux, many of them relatively unknown—have you ever heard, for example, of Château Cantelauze? It's a great Pomerol.

Last in this impressive line-up comes Patricia, who produces truly fine cuisine. This chef is an intriguing anomaly on the culinary scene. She doesn't have the conventional profile of a two-star chef, although she's been one for the past twenty years. A self-effacing and gifted intellectual, she never trained with a "great name," but learned everything she knows from her mother, who supported her aspirations and then, after she'd successfully completed a brilliant degree in economics, became her assistant. The cuisine produced by this conscientious self-taught wizard is technically perfect and meticulously executed, reflecting a flawless instinct for products, cooking methods, and flavorings that is stupefying in its precision. What is Patricia's style? A sort of

"The Little Old Rabbit's House" is the name of the house in which Patricia Desmedt and her family live. Its emblem is the rabbit, as seen here carved from wood (top left) and another engraved in a pane of glass in the front door (facing page, top right). These are just a couple of examples, but the rabbit motif is repeated throughout the building, contributing to the light-hearted decor of the stylish mountain restaurant, designed in a New England style and with a dining room that looks out over the gardens (facing page, top left). The work in the kitchen (above right and facing page, top center) resembles that of an artist: here you can see the hors d'oeuvres being prepared. Baked rabbit and chicken breast with morels (above); duo of bream and crawfish, jasmine rice with leek (facing page, bottom left): Patricia's cooking is fresh and full of vitality.

intricate sonata that is confident, classic, and pure. It strikes just the right tone without needless show or untoward deviations. The goal, in short, is to choose the best, freshest products, and to bring out their true essence.

Wearing a long laboratory smock and serious glasses, her brown hair tied back in a chignon, her expression one of mild surprise, Patricia cuts a figure that first-time customers find intriguing. She looks more like a character from *ER*, the popular TV series, than an experienced chef and member of "*Traditions et Qualité*," a sort of Jockey Club for the international culinary fraternity. Despite her deceptive appearance, however, she definitely belongs among the élite of European restaurateurs. She's not someone who puts herself forward or engages in self-promotion. She lets her art speak for itself.

When diners taste her little foie-gras mousse with port, her tender cubes of marinated salmon, her sautéed eel on an eel-and-tomato aspic, served as an appetizer in the old-fashioned drawing room decorated with a collection of faïence rabbits, they understand that something special is going on in this fashionable suburb of Waregem, a little town lost in the heart of Flanders. The New England-style gray pinewood paneling is enchantingly understated, and the garden is a delight in fine weather.

But the best treats are on the plate. Exceptional products cooked at the height of freshness, preparations that are honest in tone and devoid of frills, true flavors that burst with goodness in the mouth. The chipped potatoes *à la moscovite*, with caviar and horseradish, and the pan of Zeebrugge shrimp with baby turbot—which seems to continue sizzling on the plate—served on a mousseline of potatoes with a tarragon and butter sauce, all eloquently reflect the language of authenticity.

The delicate sweetbread ravioli poached in a fragrant chicken broth and served with grated truffles and aged Parmesan cheese are a nod to Italy. Dishes such as these have inspired people to compare the modest Patricia Desmedt with celebrated self-taught Italian woman chefs such as Nadia Santini (see p. 148) and Luisa Valazza (see p. 164), who outclass their male compatriots and monopolize all the three-star awards. The best hare in the world—the juiciest and freshest—in a pepper-sauce duo, one with cream and the other plain, a visually appealing concoction dubbed "Harlequin" and served with cranberry compote and seasonal fruit, confirm this restaurant's reputation as one of the best in Europe.

Desserts—gingerbread mille-feuille with chicory ice cream and coffee ice, ice cream flavored with Mandarine Napoleon Cognac with puréed oranges—are sweet but not too sweet, and strike just the right note. It's time dedicated gourmets knew about 't Oud Konijntje. At only forty minutes from Brussels and two-and-a-half hours from Paris, it's a feasible destination.

PATRICIA DESMEDT'S RECIPE:
DUO OF BREAM AND CRAYFISH WITH JASMINE RICE AND LEEK

PREPARATION TIME: 45 MINUTES
COOKING TIME: 7–8 MINUTES
TO SERVE: 4

INGREDIENTS
· 1 tablespoon mixed diced vegetables (leek, onion, red bell pepper, diced celery, etc.)
· 6 tablespoons olive oil
· 1 garlic clove
· ⅓ cup (100 g) short-grained or Carolina rice
· 4 slices sea bream weighing 4 ounces, descaled
· 4 large raw crayfish tails, shelled
· 1 scant cup (200 ml) crayfish bisque
· 2 tablespoons Cognac
· 2 tablespoons heavy cream
· 2 leeks, white part only of 1, 1 strip of the other
· 1 tablespoon (15 g) butter
· 4 baby leeks
· Pepper, salt, coarse salt
To garnish
· 4 strips flaky pastry sprinkled with sesame seeds

METHOD
Heat 2 tablespoons olive oil in a skillet and cook the mixed vegetables with the crushed garlic. Add the rice, pepper, and salt. Mix well, then add water to barely cover. Bring to the boil, cover with a lid, and simmer gently.

Line a saucepan with nonstick baking paper and add the rice with three times the volume of water. Cook, drain, then leave to cool. When the rice is cold it should solidify. Cut the solidified rice into short strips and brown them in olive oil. Drain on kitchen paper.

To cook the fish, heat the olive oil in a large baking pan. Add the sea bream, skin-side downward, and season with pepper and salt. Bake in a preheated 375°F (180°C) oven for 7 to 8 minutes.

Steam the crawfish tails.

To make the sauce, reduce ⅓ cup (100 ml) crayfish bisque with the Cognac for 15 minutes on medium heat. Add the cream and return to the boil. Reduce by half.

Cut the white part of the leek into diamonds and steam it. Mix with 1 teaspoon (5 g) butter. Season with pepper and salt. Steam the baby leeks.

To assemble the dish, place a tablespoon of leek diamonds on one side of a heated plate and a strip of rice on the other. Arrange the sea bream, skin side upward, on the leeks, and sprinkle with a little coarse salt. Arrange the crayfish tail on the fish and place a baby leek on the rice.

Pour a little cream sauce around the fish and a little reduced crayfish bisque around the sauce.

Garnish with a stick of sesame-coated strip of flaky pastry.

LYDIA EGLOFF

STIRING-WENDEL, FRANCE

LYDIA EGLOFF IS AN EXPERT IN GASTRONOMY WHO INTRODUCES US
TO THE CHEERFUL DISHES NATIVE TO THE GERMAN BORDER REGION OF LORRAINE.
CONNOISSEURS WILL FIND AN EXCEPTIONAL CULINARY TALENT
WAITING FOR THEM JUST BEHIND THE DOORS OF HER EXCELLENT INN.

There are two of them, each one different from the other. One has straw-blonde hair and a cheerful, mocking manner. The other is brunette, athletic, lively, and incisive. They've both been expertly playing to each other's respective strengths for ten decades past at their amazing inn. We're just a step away from Saarbrücken, in France's Moselle region, at Siring Wendel—once an active coal-mining region. Popular French singer Patricia Kaas was born here, as were Lydia and Isabelle Egloff.

The wonderful sleight-of-hand that this duo has been practicing for so many years has been to convince their customers that sunny Provence begins at the borders of the Sarre. This is not a joke. Their aim has always been to combine the seriousness of Lorraine with the relaxed accents of hot, dry Provence. When it comes to wines, Isabelle—the charming wine steward—suggests Val Joanis or Pibarnon, fine Provence reds with hints of spice and ripe fruit.

In the kitchen, the lively Lydia cooks the way birds sing. She graduated from the Strasbourg catering school and apprenticed at the Négresco in Nice under the supervision of Maximin—which is saying a lot. She is never happier than when concocting a hearty bouillabaisse, a dish of smoked ham with olive oil, sole with bergamot, or lobster with cabbage. These are just a few examples of her specialties, which are served on teak tables in the garden, under parasols. Here's a breath of southern sunshine, lightness and freshness based on such fare as lamb charlotte *en backehoffe*; or cold marinated turbot with summer truffles, grilled hazelnut oil, and aged Parmesan cheese—the wildest of her carpaccios and also the crunchiest. This lilting melody continues with chilled vegetable gazpacho, John Dory sautéed with artichokes, delicate snail tart with goat *brandade*, or foie gras sautéed with pears and served with a glazed sauce.

Cooking is an adventure at La Bonne Auberge, and behind the intriguing windowless façade beside the highway lurk truly wonderful surprises. The important thing when dining here is attitude: customers sit down at their tables the way they would fasten their seat belts for a flight to unknown climes. Fish—for example, sea bass with eucalyptus—is often served after the meat, which might be a flavorful pigeon from the Hoches property flavored with angelica, accompanied by green-coffee quinoa and chorizo preserves.

But this chic restaurant is also a repository of traditional recipes from the past. A splendid example of this would be a popular favorite, pike perch *à la krumberkichl* or *grumbeerekiechle,* i.e. cooked in a potato crust. The two women's cooking is contemporary. Their hearty soup is made with foie gras and described as "rich." The "tango" dessert combines sabayon and grenadine in an evocation of carefree summers in Lorraine.

The restaurant is lively and animated. Spirited servers combine discipline with conviviality. Is this typical of Lorraine? In terms of the unflagging and attentive service, yes, it definitely is. The celebrated Saulnois snails in a delicate pastry, served with Provençal-style fennel flavored with Chinese anis, also comes in another version featuring borage, chanterelle mushrooms, and tomatoes. The sweetbreads meunière are accompanied by a purée of caramelized cauliflower, the veal kidney with endive braised in dark beer. These dishes tell a story of love, of old-fashioned dishes updated for contemporary tastes with lightness and freshness.

Added to all of this are exceptional desserts that are the very soul of tenderness and finesse. For example, there are the much appreciated grenadine tango sauce, referred to above, and the cream soufflé with Irish coffee and a gratin of light beer which is, in the words of Marc Haeberlin of the Auberge de l'Ill, "one of the best desserts in the world." There are also the warm little shortbread cookie with fruit, the sabayon brûlée with spiced ice cream, the soufflé au gratin with Mirabelle plums given a hot and cold twist with the addition of Suzette butter—a fine tribute to this golden local fruit. Then again, you might want to try the raspberry aspic served with a crisp tube of choco-sangria, a semi-frozen Jivara with black-olive chips and a foamy coffee-vanilla cream, or a cardamom and macaroon wafer with Gianduja and grilled coffee that could not be more meticulously produced.

Everything here, including the modern decor and convivial atmosphere, contributes to the feeling that this area has made a miraculous transition, from a mining community to an oasis of greenery recalling the hills of Provence. Although actually located at the gateway to the Sarre just off the autoroute to Alsace, this is definitely one of the great restaurants of the "south."

A LUXURIOUS AND CONTEMPORARY DINING ROOM (BELOW LEFT): THIS IS THE SETTING IN WHICH LYDIA EGLOFF PRESENTS HER WORK. VISITING A CIDER BREWER (FACING PAGE, TOP) AND IN A BLUE AND WHITE APRON (PAGE 52). SHE PREPARES BOTH TRADITIONAL AND MODERN DISHES, INCLUDING A BRIOCHE WITH STEWED RABBIT (BELOW RIGHT), A CHAUD-FROID OF MIRABELLE PLUMS (FACING PAGE, BOTTOM RIGHT), AND SNAIL PASCALINES (PRECEDING PAGE), ALL DELICIOUS TRIBUTES TO THE FOOD OF EASTERN FRANCE.

LYDIA EGLOFF'S RECIPE:
CHAUD-FROID OF MIRABELLE PLUMS

PREPARATION TIME: 40 MINUTES
COOKING TIME: A FEW SECONDS
PLUS 12 HOURS REFRIGERATION
TO SERVE: 6

INGREDIENTS
· 9 tablespoons (130 g) sugar
· 1 pound, 12 ounces (800 g)
Mirabelle plums, preferably
home-canned
· 3 whole eggs
· 4 teaspoons (20 g) all-
purpose flour
· 2 tablespoons (30 g) custard
powder
· 1 ¼ cups (300 ml) light
cream
· ⅓ cup (100 ml) lemon juice
· 1 cup (250 ml) Mirabelle
plum juice
· 3 unflavored gelatin leaves
· 5 egg whites
· A few drops of lemon juice
· ⅓ cup (100 ml) good quality
plum brandy (slivovitz)

UTENSILS:
· Tart rings and silicone
release paper

METHOD
Bring 2 tablespoons (30 g)
sugar and ⅓ cup (100 ml)
water to the boil in a skillet.
Add the plums and let them
caramelize. Remove and
reserve on a dish.
Beat the whole eggs in a bowl
with 4 tablespoons (60 g)
sugar. Add the flour and
custard powder. Bring the
cream to the boil with the
lemon juice and plum juice.
Pour the mixture into the
bowl. Beat with a whisk and
leave the mixture to cook on
a low heat until the custard
thickens.
Soften the unflavored gelatin
leaves in cold water and

squeeze to remove excess
moisture. Incorporate them
into the mixture.
Beat the egg whites into stiff
peaks and add them to the
previous mixture.
Place the tart rings on the
silicone release paper and fill
each circle with the plum
custard. Freeze for 12 hours.
Before serving combine the
remaining 3 tablespoons
(40 g) sugar with a tablespoon
of water and cook in a saucepan
until it turns color. Glaze with a
few drops of lemon juice and
the plum brandy.
Brown the custards under the
broiler for a few seconds.
Carefully unmold the custards
and surround each with
caramelized plums. Coat with
the plum sauce.

NICOLE FAGEGALTIER

BELCASTEL, FRANCE

SHE REIGNS WITH SELF-EFFACING MODESTY OVER ONE OF THE LOVELIEST VILLAGES IN FRANCE.
HERE IS A QUICK GOURMET TRIP INTO THE HEARTLAND OF FRANCE.

This is a story of women, and of a family. But first, the context: a village perched on steep rocks—the "*calades*," as the narrow paved lanes of the Aveyron are called, its castle with five round towers once renovated by architect Fernand Pouillon, its angled five-arch bridge over the river, its church and sarcophagi topped with recumbent figures in armor, its caressing breezes, proximity to Rodez, and luxuriant greenery.

This is truly the heartland of France. Nicole and Michèle Fagegaltier, two sisters whose speech still betrays traces of the local accent, have followed in the footsteps of their forebears and taken over the family inn. Michèle studied law and Nicole attended catering school in Toulouse and Rodez. Members of the Fagegaltier family have manned the stove and welcomed diners here for four generations past, and are still doing so today. All the cooking is done by women. The two sisters acquired the house where first their grandmother and then their mother offered "rustic country cuisine," as they put it so appealingly.

"We're virtually self-sufficient," notes Nicole, the woman in charge of the cooking. "Like my grandfather before him, my father ran the twelve-hectare (thirty-acre) farm. He kept a few pigs, calves, and chickens, and raised vegetables for the family and fodder for the animals. The inn, run by my mother and grandmother, was supplied with produce from my father's garden. It was a "farmhouse-inn" long before the concept became fashionable. Diners feasted on gudgeon from the river, fried chicken with onions, roast kid with sorrel, and *pascade* (stuffed cabbage). Then, one fine day, Nicole started cooking, too. She took up the torch, but also began changing things.

When Nicole returned from hotel school in 1983, she took over her parents' business. She was subsequently joined by her elder sister, Michèle, who was then working for an insurance company. Michèle quickly developed a passionate interest in wine, and it wasn't long before the two sisters won their first star and began attracting customers from all over France. They added one small seven-bedroom hotel, and then another, on the far side of the bridge; they enlarged and modernized the kitchen. The sisters' domain is divided in two by the

NICOLE FAGEGALTIER—WITH HER BAKER, ROGER BAYOL, IN RIGNIAC (TOP)—COOKS DIFFERENT DISHES DEPENDING ON HER MOOD AND THE SEASON. WITH HER HUSBAND, BRUNO ROUQUIER (FACING PAGE, BOTTOM LEFT), IN THE RESTAURANT THAT OVERLOOKS THE BRIDGE IN BELCASTEL (FACING PAGE, TOP LEFT). SHE CREATES INTRICATELY PRESENTED DISHES, SUCH AS POTATOES WITH ANCHOVY AND ASPARAGUS (FACING PAGE, TOP RIGHT) OR SIMPLE AVEYRON VEAL (ABOVE). HER FINE AVEYRON CUISINE IS BOTH TRADITIONAL AND MODERN, LIKE HER NOUGATINE MILLE-FEUILLE WITH ICE CREAM (PRECEDING PAGE) OR HER INVENTIVE APPETIZER OF DRIED POTATO SHAVINGS (PAGE 56).

Aveyron River, a symbolically evocative link. Michèle soon met and married Bruno Rouquier, who from 1978 through 1982 had worked with their celebrated neighbor Michel Bras in Laguiole. The three of them formed a perfect team.

Today their style combines the traditional and the modern, with strong emphasis on the land and the importance of quality local products—Aveyron lamb, free-range Aubrac beef, and Segala veal. Thanks to the twice-weekly Rodez market, fish from Brittany and exotic spices are also common sights in the dining room, which seats thirty-five diners comfortably and has been renovated in a light, uncluttered style.

So what is a typical festive meal at Belcastel? It might begin with light pastry canapés and cherry tomatoes in vinegar to stimulate the appetite. This could be followed by warm potatoes with a green anchovy paste, asparagus, and a purée combining sorrel and fresh cottage cheese. Then a pigs'-trotter sausage combined (surprisingly) with grilled crab, accompanied by puréed potatoes and foie gras seasoned with port sauce. And then, of course, there's the emblematic dish of the region: green lentils with lambs' feet in a vinaigrette seasoned with orange and juniper; or sautéed lamb sweetbreads with an onion wafer.

But this is just the beginning. The exquisite sautéed fillet of cod with asparagus, and the creamed salt cod in truffle broth, are haunting reminders of the traditional dish once served by Aveyron grandmothers. Then there's the sea bass sautéed in brown butter, the grilled almond cream, and the potato purée. And, also, the grilled duck foie gras with celeriac conserve, honey caramel, and pineapple marmalade with dried apricots. And, finally, the shredded lamb curry, and roast lamb and sorrel served with tender peas.

We'll spare a moment for the fine cheeses of Rouergue—sheep, cow, and goat—plus flavorful blue varieties. Then comes the festival of desserts: sautéed spiced bananas and coconut mousse in a crusty wafer with orange ice cream and coriander; saffron-flavored rice pudding with chocolate; nougatine mille-feuille with coffee mascarpone; granita flavored with balsamite (a mentholated herb), sprinkled with strawberry juice, and served with a brochette of fruit and a lemon shortbread cookie. Diners should also save some room for the delicate petits fours (caramels with luscious dried fruit; orange pastry horns filled with almond cream, chocolate, or tea) created by a young pastry chef with a magic touch. Serious attention should also be given to the heady, refreshing, and often complex Gaillac wines from Plageoles or Rotier that perfectly complement the treats on this festive board. These female innkeepers on the banks of the Aveyron have developed a cuisine that is exquisite and highly inventive. In short, diners will find their time at table delightful, and should be sure to take a bracing after-dinner stroll to the castle.

Michèle will continue to keep a benevolent eye on the youthful servers. Working with Bruno, Nicole will continue to develop new culinary ideas for future seasons. They plan to open a country hotel—something Rodez lacks—with a bistro on the premises. You'll find a team of wizards at Belcastel in the Aveyron. Wizards who are chefs, attentive hostesses, and accomplished gourmets—in short, purveyors of excitement and pleasure.

NICOLE FAGEGALTIER'S RECIPE:

POTATOES WITH GREEN ANCHOVY SAUCE AND ASPARAGUS WITH SORREL AND CLABBERED MILK

PREPARATION TIME: 40 MINUTES
COOKING TIME: 25–30 MINUTES
TO SERVE: 4

INGREDIENTS

· 4 floury potatoes weighing around ¾ ounce (20 g) each
· 2 cups (200 g) sorrel
· 2 tablespoons (30 g) butter
· 1 tablespoon heavy cream
· 16 asparagus

For the anchovy sauce

· 2 teaspoons (10 g) minced chervil
· 2 teaspoons (10 g) arugula
· 2 teaspoons (10 g) cress
· 2 tablespoons salt anchovies, rinsed
· 2 tablespoons lemon juice
· 1 tablespoon olive oil
· 2 teaspoons (10 g) ground hazelnuts
· Salt and pepper

For the herbed cheese

· ⅓ cup (80 g) pot, farmer or small curd cottage cheese
· 1 sprig parsley
· 1 chive
· 1 sprig chervil

To garnish

· A few lettuce leaves

METHOD

Wash the potatoes and wrap them in aluminum foil. Bake in a preheated 350°F (175°C) oven for 25 to 30 minutes. Pare 2 opposite sides of each potato crosswise, so as to obtain a top and bottom flat service. Keep warm. Sort, trim, and wash the sorrel. In a skillet, melt the butter, and add the sorrel. Season and leave for few moments, then add a spoon of cream. Remove from the heat and keep warm. Peel the asparagus and cook in salted boiling water. When cooked, refresh in cold water. Trim all the asparagus to a length of 5 inches (12 cm) then cut them in half so as to obtain a 2 ½-inch (6-cm) piece of stem and a 2 ½-inch (6-cm) spear.

To make the anchovy mixture, grind the herbs in a food processor and add the anchovies, lemon juice, olive oil, ground hazelnuts, salt and pepper. Mix the pot or farmer cheese with the herb-and-anchovy mixture and check the seasoning. Just before serving, coat each serving dish with the sorrel, place 4 asparagus stems on it. Spread one side of each potato with the anchovy mixture and place it on the plate. Cover with the asparagus spears. Finish with a mound of the cheese-and-herb mixture. Garnish with a few lettuce leaves.

ANNIE FÉOLDE

FLORENCE, ITALY

FEOLDE WAS THE FIRST WOMAN IN ITALY TO WIN THREE STARS FOR HER RESTAURANT.
SHE HAS TRIUMPHED IN BOTH FLORENCE AND TOKYO; BUT IN TUSCANY—WHERE SHE OWNS
THE MOST SUMPTUOUS WINE CELLAR IN THE WORLD—SHE REIGNS SUPREME.

This is the fairy-tale story of a woman from Nice—whose natural habitat was the promenade des Anglais and its environs—who discovered Tuscany and moved her magic realm there. It's also a love story: the tale of Annie Feolde's passion for a man, and a region. Her parents were longtime employees at Nice's palatial Negressco Hotel, where her father supervised the valet parking and her mother ran the switchboard. Annie, meanwhile, became a self-taught chef and the acolyte of a great man, handsome Giorgio Pinchiorri, the urbane wine steward of the Enoteca Nazionale in Florence, which would eventually bear his name.

Feolde started out as a bureaucrat in Paris, went to England to learn the language, and ended up in Italy, where she embarked on a great adventure and encountered the love of her life. "At first," she explains, embarking on the fascinating tale of a cherished dream come true, "we served just a few dishes to accompany Giorgio's great wines. But, after I started working with him, I found I was really enjoying myself." Her enjoyment bore tangible fruit in the form of the first three stars ever awarded in Italy to a woman. Her restaurant was located in a Florentine palace, with marble floors, frescoed ceilings, salons, patio garden, impeccable service, and a huge wine cellar.

Annie Feolde received the supreme recognition of three Michelin stars some ten years ago. Lured by the siren song of Japanese fans entranced with Florence and her restaurant, she opened a copy of the Enoteca Pinchiorri on the eighth floor of a modern building in Tokyo's Ginza business district, and then a wine store. Meanwhile, however, the *Michelin Guide*—apparently believing that she was spreading herself too thin—downgraded her from three stars to two. Undaunted, Annie was still everywhere at once, serving as chef, owner-operator, and instructor to her apprentices. She sponsored young chefs such as Franck Cerutti ("He's like a son to me," she says. "He was with me for seven years, and I consider him a member of the family"), who then transmitted what he had learned about Tuscan cuisine—sweet-and-sour dishes, pasta, ravioli with black olives, gnocchi with pine nuts and raisins—to Alain Ducasse's famed Louis XV in Monaco.

When it became obvious that Annie was working harder and more effectively than ever before, her efforts were rewarded in the 2004 edition of the *Michelin Guide* by the restoration of her third star. She still remains faithful to her signature style, which consists of great cuisine that is both creative and simple, regional and sophisticated—a tribute to all of Italy, and especially to the majesty of Tuscany. A few of her outstanding dishes from the past twenty years immediately spring to mind. Some examples, among many, include tempura-fried cod with *pappa al pomodore*, an updated Tuscan tomato-and-bread soup; scampi in pancetta with a soup of beans and pearl barley; *pici con le briciole*, tiny pasta dipped in a hard-wheat flour-and-water paste, flavored with anchovies and herbs, and served with creamed Lucca white beans and fried pork rind dredged in Tuscan breadcrumbs. Then there's the admirable variation she rings on porchetta (from Umbria, south of Tuscany, where quail replaces pork): the meat is left unskinned, stuffed with the pepper-seasoned livers, and served on a purée of peas with chickpea croquettes with rosemary. Delicious!

Other dishes are the "guitar" spaghetti shaped on a special wire frame and served with creamed peas and marinated mackerel fillets, to which Annie adds a thin slice of grilled ham; the agnolotti stuffed with sheep's-milk ricotta and mint, saffron, and cinnamon; the Roman salad and shredded salami; the cappelletti stuffed with pheasant and creamed lentils. And, of course, a range of seafood that changes according to the season and the tides. One memorable seafood dish is red mullet with fennel and lemon—something it's unlikely any fisherman from Livorno ever tasted. Today Annie serves red mullet with a sliver of foie gras, a purée of Jerusalem artichokes, and shredded fried artichokes. Her repertoire also includes scallops with tomato-accented coral, cooked like tripe and accompanied by crisp fried ravioli stuffed with zucchini and oregano.

Need we say more? This simple, fresh, traditional cuisine, accompanied by choice wines, has genuine star quality. Giorgio, who created the restaurant's *enoteca* (a cellar containing more than 100,000 bottles) plays a brilliant supporting role. With his team of youthful and talented wine stewards, he presents marvels from all over the world—Tocai from Friuli, Chardonnay from Piedmont, sumptuous Tuscan reds from Sangiovese, Cannaiolo, Brunello—and also exceptional French vintages such as Petrus and Château Yquem. To accompany the restaurant's world-class cuisine, customers often sample a range of great wines by the glass.

Annie Feolde works in a large Florentine house on Via Ghibellina. In summer, you can eat in an open-air courtyard (facing page, top left). Annie runs the show and constructs the menu (below) with its two main courses, creates traditional local petits fours (facing page, bottom) and refreshing dishes, for example tomato gelée with basil and walnut and cheese salad (left).
Page 61: her charming petit fours, shaped like doughnuts, to be served with coffee.

When it comes to meat, instinct and inclination guide diners in their choice of shredded beef cheeks in tomato sauce, crisp roast suckling pig served with potato salad in beet oil, sweet-and-sour shallots, headcheese (*soprassata*), supreme of pigeon—grilled, marinated in thyme and roasted, the thigh preserved in goose fat; or a trellis of potatoes grown in Mugello (an agricultural area north of Florence), accompanied with a slice of Tuscan bread dipped in red wine and sugar (a traditional local specialty often served to children as an afternoon snack). Depending on the season, there might also be tender kid served with white polenta and cabbage.

Also important are the cooked cheeses such as creamy Burrata, a buffalo mozzarella with a heart as tender as butter, served with a purée of fresh tomatoes with basil and fried beans. Desserts provide a chance to bring on a mellow Vin Santo. There are variations on chocolate, the crisp Gianduja biscuit filled with hazelnut cream and accompanied by a Tuscan *neccio* (a crêpe made with Garfagnana chestnut flour); a milky composition featuring a biscuit with mousse, vanilla Bavarian cream, ice cream and a delicate foam sauce. Or, the upside-down pie with pears in caramel jelly flavored with rosemary, the *zuccotto*, a semi-chilled chocolate concoction on sponge cake flavored with Alchernes, a sweet fruit liqueur.

This is peasant fare for lords of the manor, a feast fit for a king created by the hand of a zealous magician. Annie Feolde has the patrician, self-confident air of someone determined to demonstrate that Tuscan cuisine—her very own—is definitely one of the most refined and elegant in the world.

GIORGIO PINCHIORRI (BELOW LEFT), WHO LENDS HIS NAME TO THIS SMALL WINE SHOP, SUCCESSFULLY RUNS ONE OF THE BEST WINE CELLARS IN THE WORLD . ANNIE KEEPS A WATCHFUL EYE OVER HER KITCHEN STAFF AND IS ALWAYS HAPPY TO LEND A HAND WITH THE COOKING (FACING PAGE, LEFT). HER SPAGHETTI (BELOW RIGHT) AND SUCKLING PIG WITH SHALLOTS SERVED WITH A SWEET-AND-SOUR SAUCE (FACING PAGE, RIGHT) DEMONSTRATE HER FLAIR, WHICH COMBINES KNOWLEDGE, RUSTIC STYLE, AND CLASS.

ROAST SUCKLING PIG WITH SHALLOTS IN SWEET-AND-SOUR SAUCE

PREPARATION TIME: 45 MINUTES
COOKING TIME: 2 HOURS
INCLUDING 1 HOUR 15 MINUTES TO
MAKE THE STOCK THE DAY BEFORE
TO SERVE: 4

INGREDIENTS

For the pork and shallots
· 1 boned and rolled shoulder of suckling pig
· 4 racks of 3 ribs each
· 8 large shallots
· 1 cup (250 ml) red wine vinegar
· ⅔ cup (150 g) sugar
· 4 teaspoons (20 g) butter
· 1 tablespoon olive oil
· Salt and pepper

For the pork stock (optional)
· 8 ounces (250 g) pork bones
· 1 small onion, peeled and chopped
· 1 small carrot, peeled and chopped
· 1 stick of celery, chopped
· 3 ½ fluid ounces (100 ml) dry white wine
· 1 tablespoon olive oil
· Pepper

METHOD

Make the stock the night before. In a large skillet, sauté the bones for 10 minutes in the olive oil. Discard the fat in the pan and add the vegetables. Sauté them for 5 minutes. Pour off the grease and pour the white wine into the skillet. Cook until it has evaporated. Add 2 cups (500 ml) water, bring to the boil, skim, season with pepper, and simmer for one hour. Strain and reduce the liquid to ⅔ cup (150 ml). Keep cool. On the following day, remove the grease from the surface and set aside the broth. Peel the shallots and boil them in salted water for 3 minutes. Drain them and put them in a saucepan with the vinegar and sugar. Simmer uncovered for 15 minutes, or until the liquid is reduced by half. Drain the shallots and finish cooking them in butter until they are evenly browned. Keep warm. Heat the oven to 425°F (220°C). Season the meat. Pour the olive oil into a deep pot and sauté the shoulder and ribs, turning frequently, until lightly browned all over, in order to make the fat run and the crackling crunchy. Transfer the pot or casserole to the oven and cook, uncovered, for 15 minutes. Reserve the cooked meat in a warm place, covered with aluminum foil. Add the pork broth to the pot and cook for 2 minutes. Slice the racks into individual ribs and the shoulder into rounds.
Serve hot with the sweet-and-sour shallots and reduced cooking liquid.
This recipe can also be made with fully grown pork, the pieces of which are larger. Ask the butcher to make you a rack including 4 thick ribs, leaving the skin in place. After sautéing briefly, bake them for 25–30 minutes. The pork broth can be replaced by vegetable broth or a little water.

CHRISTINE FERBER

NIEDERMORSCHWHIR, FRANCE

THIS SUPREME CREATOR OF JAMS, CAKES, AND PRESERVES REIGNS IN THE HEART OF ALSACE. CHRISTINE FERBER'S DELICACIES HAVE MADE HER FAMOUS WORLDWIDE—SHE IS THE MUSE OF THE JAM POT, THE PRINCESS OF SWEET-AND-SOUR.

The road climbs past vineyards and scales the Vosges, bringing us to Niedermorschwhir in Alsace. At Christmas, the main street of the village, with its twisted spiral belfry immortalized by famed illustrator Hansi, fills with the spicy fragrance of gingerbread. One shop in particular, reminiscent of a fairy-tale gingerbread house, irresistibly draws passersby into its orbit.

It's called the Maison Ferber, and is a sort of pâtisserie/store where one can also buy newspapers and postcards. Christine Ferber is the store's presiding spirit, although her father Maurice and her brother and sister help out in the kitchen and behind the counter. Christine seems to be everywhere at once, and to have at least three arms and three hands—one used exclusively for answering phone calls from all over the world, and for writing books.

Le Larousse des confitures, La Cuisine des fées, and *Les tartes sucrées et salées*—these are just a few of the "how-to" bestsellers that Christine has written during her rare moments of free time in the winter. How much spare time? That would be hard to say, exactly, since Christine is always busy. She rises at dawn (5.00 a.m. on weekdays, 3.30 a.m. on Saturdays) so as to be the first to pick over new deliveries of fruit at the market, and to make sure her selections are perfectly fresh and free of blemishes. She spends the whole of the rest of the day in the kitchen, turning out chocolate, kugelhopf, sweet pretzels, and other delights.

The action never stops at Christine's. She sorts pans of blueberries and red currants, continuously checks and adjusts her recipes and sweet-and-sour mixtures—*and* conducts pre-Christmas tours of the premises for visitors. She holds "open house" with her painter and gourmet friends: Guy Untereiner (the Hansi of Siewiller), Raymond Emile Weydelich, who invented a picturebook character that appears in all his works, and Lydia Jacob—loyal friends who are always ready to pitch in and lend a helping hand in the kitchen.

Warmhearted Christine gives the impression of living at the nerve center of Alsace. The experimental kitchen, where she crafts her pastries and confectionery, serves as a kind of clubhouse for friends from all over the world. On Sundays, she prepares a convivial banquet for twelve or fifteen people on the premises, welcomes connoisseurs of every stripe, from businessmen to artists, and offers them ham in pastry or sushi, *baeckoffe* or roast baby chicken.

Christine Ferber is the "odd woman out" in this book, which was originally only going to include thirty-five woman chefs. She earned a place for herself through her kindness and

CHRISTINE FERBER IS NOT CONTENT TO BE JUST
THE QUEEN OF JAMS. SHE HAS GREAT INFLUENCE
OVER THE FOOD IN HER VILLAGE, NIEDERMORSCHWIR,
WHICH STANDS PERCHED ABOVE THE VINES OF THE VOSGES
(TOP LEFT). HER JAMS ARE FULL OF THE FLAVORS OF
NATURAL PRODUCE; CHRISTINE SELECTS THE BEST FRUIT
FROM THE SURROUNDING ORCHARDS, AND PETALS FROM
THE ROSE FIELDS (PAGE 66). THE WORK NEVER STOPS: POTS
OF JAM ON SALE IN HER SHOP (PRECEDING PAGE); COOKING
IN COPPER CAULDRONS (ABOVE); LADLING JAM INTO JARS
(TOP RIGHT); POTS OF QUINCE JELLY (FACING PAGE, TOP
LEFT); A SMILING CHRISTINE TOPS UP A JAR (FACING PAGE,
BOTTOM LEFT); GRATED APPLE TART WITH CINNAMON
STREUSEL (FACING PAGE, TOP RIGHT).

honesty, her talent and generosity, her vibrant ideas and her ability to bring people together. With her friend Hélène Darroze, who was born in the Landes region but moved to Paris, Christine is a linchpin among today's female chefs—some appearing in this volume—many of whom have fixed their sights on places outside of France, traveling as far as America to practice their art. Examples would be Christine's spiritual sister Ariane Daguin in New York, or Barbara Lynch in Boston.

"Queen of Hearts," Christine reigns supreme in the realm of sweets and preserves, although she might well have spent her life as the baker in a small village. "We're just bakers," her father used to remind her, "and don't you forget it." When she apprenticed with the great Peltier on rue de Sèvres in Paris, her fellow pupils used to hiss in her ear, "You're nothing but a *baker*." Nevertheless, after training at the École Nationale de Pâtisserie in Brussels, the youthful Christine soon mastered all the rudiments of her craft.

Christine got her start, paradoxically, because she never smiled. Her father thus assigned her younger sister to the shop, and set Christine the more difficult task of confecting bread and cakes in the kitchen. She eventually became an expert in chocolate, and a universally recognized artist in jams. It was Christine who invented the stunning and novel sweet/sour jams for garnishing meat, and especially game.

What is Christine's skill, exactly? It lies in her loving selection of perfect fruit, her ability to choose the best black cherries, ripest tangerines, and most succulent plums in season—skillfully combining them with raspberries and violets to enhance their respective flavors. She has spread the fame of her family's business worldwide, and, with her faithful assistants, keeps her copper pans bubbling with divine perfumes. She's a sight to be seen, dressed in a smock worthy of a laboratory scientist, stirring her concoctions with all her heart and limitless passion.

Some of her most popular inventions include pickles in honey, preserved cranberries, onions in caramel, Morello cherries with bay leaf, vine-ripened peaches in Pinot Noir, skinned tomato wedges with basil, and her blackberries with mace—the latter a kind of flavor poem that is perfect for accompanying tender roast meat. Her plum jam, apple jelly with walnuts, bitter orange with rhubarb, julienne of pears with vanilla, wild blueberries, Bergeron apricot and Alsatian blackcurrants—which can be eaten with a spoon like some divine compotes—are all well worth the trip, the price, and the time. And everything else here is just as good.

Ferber's ice cream is luscious, her pastries melt in the mouth, her cakes are unique marvels. Her kugelhopf is exemplary, her Black Forest gâteau an ode to central Europe, her chocolate macaroons peerless. Her chestnut *bûche de Noël* is a childhood dream. How could anyone not love Christine Ferber?

CHRISTINE FERBER'S RECIPE:

GRATED APPLE TART
WITH CINNAMON STREUSEL

PREPARATION TIME: 45 MINUTES
(INCLUDING 20 MINUTES TO PREPARE
THE DOUGH THE DAY BEFORE,
PLUS 30 MINUTES RESTING TIME)
COOKING TIME: 50 MINUTES
TO SERVE: 6

INGREDIENTS

For the tart
· 1 ⅓ cups (300 g) shortcrust
  pastry with praline and
  hazelnuts (see recipe)
· 1 ¼ cups (300 g) almond
  cream (see recipe)
· 1 cup (50 ml) thick heavy
  cream or crème fraîche
· 5 apples
· 4 teaspoons (20 g) flour
· 4 teaspoons (20 g) butter
· 2 tablespoons powdered
  (confectioner's) sugar

For the streusel
· 5 tablespoons (60 g)
  superfine (caster) sugar
· 5 tablespoons (60 g) chilled butter
· 2 tablespoons (30 g) ground
  almonds
· 2 tablespoons (30 g) all-
  purpose flour
· Three knife tips of ground
  cinnamon

EQUIPMENT
· Round pie pan, 10 inches
  (26 cm) in diameter and
  1 inch (3 cm) high (preferably
  with a loose bottom)

METHOD
The night before, sprinkle a
work surface with the flour
and roll out the dough into a
disk around 13 inches (34 cm)
in diameter, and 1/8 inch
(2.5 mm) thick. Butter the pan,
line it with the dough, and
press down lightly with the
fingertips on the base and sides.
Roll the edges with a rolling
pin to remove excess dough.
Prick the base with a fork.
Cover with plastic wrap and
refrigerate for at least 30
minutes. Preheat the oven to
350°F (180°C).
Make the almond cream.
Peel the apples, cut them in
half, core them, and grate them
on a coarse grater. Lightly mix
the almond cream, heavy cream
or crème fraîche, and the apples.
Spread the mixture over the tart
base. Bake for 40 minutes.
For the streusel: cut the butter
into very small dice and drop
them in a bowl. Add the sugar,
ground almonds, flour, and
cinnamon. Work the mixture
with your fingertips until the
mixture is the consistency of
breadcrumbs. When the tart is
lightly colored and has risen,
sprinkle it with the streusel
and bake for another 10
minutes or so until the edges
are golden and the streusel
crunchy. Unmold the tart onto
a cake rack and leave it to cool.
Sprinkle it with the powdered
(confectioner's) sugar before
serving with a homemade
custard, flavored with
cinnamon or with ground
cardamom.

ROSE GRAY & RUTH ROGERS

LONDON, GREAT BRITAIN

ITALIAN CUISINE FROM A TALENTED DUO ON THE BANKS OF THE THAMES
IN A BREATHTAKING CONTEMPORARY SETTING DESIGNED BY RICHARD ROGERS.

This is the story of two English friends: Rose Gray and Ruth Rogers. Their shared love of Tuscany takes them there every year to breathe the air of the hills. They will amuse themselves by picking out what's special about arugula from Naples and radicchio from Treviso, by reinventing Ligurian pesto in their own canny way. And they will bring back with them their favorite oils, fennel and garlic, borlotti beans, Sicilian peas, broccoletti, turnip greens (*cime di rapa*), and chickpeas from Puglia, to impress their friends. They love all that.

Away from the center of London, out west past Chelsea and Fulham, in the old dock area in Hammersmith, they created a restaurant dedicated to the food they believed in. And the building is no ordinary place: Ruth's husband, the renowned architect Richard Rogers (who designed the Centre Pompidou in Paris), has his offices next door. He dreamed up a generous, airy space full of natural light.

The tone is set in shades of white, with the broad aluminum counter, the chairs in metal and velum, and delicate ceiling lights, complemented by the greenery of the terrace. Directly opposite, on the other side of the river, are apartment buildings, and there is an incomparable view of the Harrods Depository, built in 1900. It feels like the countryside. And the two friends, Ruth and Rose, offer food that is bucolic yet refined: vegetables in season, handmade pasta, fresh salads, flavorsome sauces, and dressings to make you wish your hunger would last for ever.

The menu is changed daily, taking into account market availability, seasonal readiness, the catch off the Cornish coast and deliveries from Puglia or Campania. Today there will be puntarelle *alla Romana*, large endives cut into thin strips, with anchovies, peppers, capers and herb vinegar. Then the carpaccio of Yorkshire beef with artichoke, lemon, and parmesan. And more delights are in store after that, with the pasta and rice dishes.

Taglierini with sausage and peas, mint and thyme sauce; large ravioli stuffed with pigeon, veal and pancetta with butter and parmesan; seafood risotto with cuttlefish, shrimp, clams, tomato, parsley, and Pinot Grigio. The mood is that of great Italian cuisine, up the minute. Delicate and fresh, light and invigorating at the same time. The London in-crowd come to Hammersmith as if for a picnic. They start to relax; the jackets come off. They imagine themselves in a garden in Chianti, somewhere between Cerbaia and Gailoe.

Rose and Ruth are talking, explaining, discussing. Richard Rogers comes in on his own in a white collarless shirt and has the salad of the day. He drinks his glass of Sangiovese, reads *The Times*, and ignores the noise around him as attractive plates of food precede young and enthusiastic staff around the room. A piece of turbot on the bone with capers and marjoram, with an herb, arugula, and turnip green salad; the grilled sirloin served with delicate white borlotti beans.

The desserts are an Italian lesson in themselves. They could have been made by an English grandmother trained in Campania. The "chocolate nemesis," for example: a thin bitter-chocolate cake, positively eager to melt in your mouth; or the crunchy lemon tart, topped like a crumble with almonds and plums, and served with a caramel ice cream to die for. It is a joyous experience. The room bubbles as Ruth and Rose go round the tables. You can tell from the contented glances that they have made their customers happy.

HERE IN LONDON'S RIVERSIDE BOROUGH OF HAMMERSMITH, THE WORLD-FAMOUS ARCHITECT RICHARD ROGERS (FACING PAGE, TOP LEFT) CONVERTED AN OLD WHARF INTO OFFICES AND A RESTAURANT FOR HIS WIFE RUTH AND HER FRIEND AND PARTNER ROSE GRAY: THE BAR (BELOW) AND THE DINING ROOM OVERLOOKING THE THAMES (FACING PAGE, BOTTOM). MUCH OF THE CUISINE IS TUSCAN-INSPIRED, AS DEMONSTRATED BY THE ARUGULA, BEAN, AND MOZZARELLA SALAD (BELOW RIGHT), OR THE TURBOT WITH CAPERS (PRECEDING PAGE). ON THE OTHER HAND, THE CHOCOLATE CAKE, KNOWN AS "CHOCOLATE NEMESIS" (FACING PAGE, TOP RIGHT), IS WORTHY OF AN ENGLISH GRANDMOTHER.

ROSE GRAY & RUTH ROGERS'S RECIPE:
CHOCOLATE NEMESIS CAKE

PREPARATION TIME: 25 MINUTES
COOKING TIME: 30 MINUTES
TO SERVE: 6

INGREDIENTS
· 12 ounces (340 g) dark baking chocolate, broken into small pieces
· 5 eggs
· 1 ¼ cups (280 g) superfine sugar
· 2 sticks (225 g) softened unsalted butter
· 2 tablespoons (30 g) butter and 1 tablespoon all-purpose flour for the cake pan

METHOD
Preheat the oven to 300°F (150°C). Line an 8-inch (26-cm) diameter shallow cake pan 2 inches (5 cm) deep with nonstick baking paper, then grease it with butter and sprinkle with flour. Beat the eggs with one third of the sugar until the mixture quadruples in volume (this operation will require beating for around 10 minutes with an electric beater). Heat the rest of the sugar in a saucepan with 1 cup (250 ml) water until the sugar dissolves into a syrup. Add the chocolate pieces and the butter. Mix well. When smooth, remove from the heat and leave to cool. Pour the mixture over the eggs while it is still slightly warm and continue to beat gently until it is smooth (no more than 20 seconds). Pour the mixture into the prepared cake pan and place the pan in a roasting pan of hot water. The water must come right up to the top of the mold, so that the cooking is uniform. Bake it for 30 minutes in the oven until it has set. Check for doneness by gently placing the palm of your hand on the surface. If it is not set, continue cooking. Cool the cake in the pan before turning upside down to unmold onto a cake plate.

CATHERINE GUERRAZ

PARIS, FRANCE

SHE WAS DISCOVERED BY THE ÉLITE OF PARIS WHEN SHE MOVED
FROM AN OBSCURE STREET NEAR THE DEPARTMENT STORES ON THE RIGHT BANK
TO A MORE ATTRACTIVE SPOT JUST OFF THE CHAMPS-ÉLYSÉES. CATHERINE GUERRAZ
IS A DYNAMIC, SELF-TAUGHT CHEF FOR WHOM MAINTAINING TRADITIONS
IS SECOND NATURE — A WOMAN EAGER TO SHARE HER LOVE OF SIMPLE DISHES WITH OTHERS.

Until now, her name was known only to a small group of initiates, among whom it was an open secret. Gourmets whispered "Catherine," the way spies might whisper "007" or "Bond." In its original headquarters on rue de Provence, Chez Catherine boasted an amusing 1920s setting, featuring a zinc bar and leatherette banquettes, and served good, hearty, uncomplicated fare. But Catherine Guerraz finally tired of being Paris's "Miss Bistro" in her quiet backwater in the ninth arrondissement.

As the daughter-in-law of René Lasserre and a seasoned habitué of the fine restaurants she visits for her own pleasure, Guerraz eventually decided it was time to forsake an area famed primarily for the Printemps and Galeries Lafayette department stores—and for the ladies of the night who had taken to eating at her restaurant—and move to a more fashionable location near the Arc de Triomphe.

She's now firmly established in her new quarters, also called Chez Catherine. Here, she supervises a series of three interconnected dining rooms from the vantage point of her open kitchen. In the first, diners eat at a counter, as at Cipriani's in Venice. The second has a view of the kitchen, and the third—discreet and unobtrusive—resembles a private salon. Each separate dining room has its own distinctive charm, enhanced by the attentions of a waitstaff that has increased in numbers and honed its expertise.

Catherine's companion, Frédéric, is a wine fanatic and Catherine's most ardent supporter. Always impeccably dressed, he's attentive to the well-being of each diner, offering appropriate selections from the extensive wine list. He might, for example, choose a Côte Rôtie or a Clos Rougeard Saumur Champigny from Demars-Foucault to accompany the subtlety of Catherine's exquisite cuisine. He enlivens service in the dining rooms, creating an atmosphere that's warm and convivial. In fact, spectacle is an important part of the dining experience here. Although the cuisine is, of course, the first priority, the creation of just the right mood and tone can be a pleasure in itself.

What does one eat here? The very best contemporary cuisine, combined with some of the great classics. It's true what they say about Catherine Guerraz: she is indeed the gourmet "mother" of a newly emerging culinary tradition. With her charming style, lively personality, intriguingly freckled face, and her habit of updating old favorites without defying tradition, she continually enchants her discriminating diners.

Everything at Catherine's restaurant conspires to stimulate the appetite. To list just a few among many treats: the ramekin of Burgundy snails with chanterelle mushrooms, the pressed foie gras and crabmeat, the pheasant terrine with walnuts and crisp salad, the whiting *en papillote* with bourride sauce, the cod fillet baked in aromatic sauce, and the lightly cooked fillet of veal with horseradish. The kitchen staff has evolved over time, of course, and the restaurant's prices have climbed. The wine list, a kind of wish list for lovers of the divine bottle, exemplifies the new ambitions of the woman people refer to as "La Guerraz" in the same way they might say "La Callas."

However, her menu also includes fresh seasonal products and old favorites at reasonable prices—such as tripe *à la niçoise* with tomatoes and olive oil (a tribute to her grandmother, chef emerita of the old Comté). The tripe, like the andouillette (chitterling sausage) also featured on her menu, proves that Catherine hasn't entirely abandoned her old bistro background. Further examples, listed beside the more sophisticated fillet of red mullet with tapenade and artichoke mille-feuille, include a fillet of Salers beef with pepper sauce, and a rib of the same beef served with a marrowbone and tender potatoes. The desserts—which combine the traditional with the innovative—include an exquisite tarte tatin with tender, non-caramelized fruit and vanilla ice cream, a chocolate fondant, and a pistachio crème brûlée. They are all simply irresistible.

Of course you might be justified in complaining that there's nothing particularly revolutionary here, except for consistent good sense applied to dishes with varied appeal. On the other hand, in today's context, updated classics expertly executed are simply a joy for all, especially when served with a lively Château Brown white Graves from Bordeaux or a sumptuous Côte Rôtie by Gaillard de Malleval. The wines are chosen by a youthful, smiling wine steward who offers invaluable advice. Catherine Guerraz charms her customers and beguiles her supporters with unflagging verve. When she changed neighborhoods she extended her style, developed her methods, and proudly set her seal on the result. As you may have gathered, she is one of the new stars in the gastronomic firmament of Paris.

CATHERINE GUERRAZ IS DYNAMIC, CHEERFUL, AND NATURAL, KEEPING A TIGHT REIN ON HER MALE TEAM WITH GOOD HUMOR. HER TEAM ACCEPTS HER AUTHORITY WITHOUT COMPLAINT (TOP LEFT). HER CHOCOLATE DESSERT WITH CARAMEL AND LIGHTLY SALTED BUTTER (ABOVE), ROAST TUNA WITH SPICES AND DRIED FRUITS (FACING PAGE, BOTTOM LEFT), AND ESPECIALLY HER SWEETBREAD BROCHETTES WITH SALSIFY (PRECEDING PAGE) DEMONSTRATE THAT THIS MAGNIFICENT SELF-TAUGHT CHEF CAN EASILY MASTER ALL ASPECTS OF MODERN CUISINE. SUCH PROWESS IS EVIDENT IN THESE STOLEN MOMENTS FROM THE KITCHENS (TOP RIGHT AND FACING PAGE, TOP RIGHT). LUNCH IN THE DINING ROOM HAS ALL THE FEEL OF A CLASSY BISTRO IN THE EIGHTH ARRONDISSEMENT IN PARIS (FACING PAGE, TOP LEFT).

CATHERINE GUERRAZ'S RECIPE:

ROAST TUNA STEAK WITH SPICES AND DRIED FRUITS

PREPARATION TIME: 40 MINUTES
COOKING TIME: 35 MINUTES
TO SERVE: 4

INGREDIENTS

For the spiced tuna and purée
· 4 filleted tuna steaks weighing 4 ounces (120 g) each
· 1 ¾ lb (800 g) Jerusalem artichokes
· 1 cup (200 ml) light cream
· 1 tablespoon olive oil
· Salt and pepper

For the dried fruit paste
· 10 ½ ounces (300 g) dried apricots
· 7 ounces (200 g) gingerbread
· 1 dash ground cumin
· 1 dash ground cinnamon
· 1 pinch vanilla sugar

For the sauce
· 1 cup (250 ml) soy sauce
· 4 tablespoons honey
· 2 lemons

METHOD

To make the sauce, mix the soy sauce, honey, and juice of 2 lemons. Cook until the mixture has the consistency of a syrup (around 10 minutes). Cook the Jerusalem artichokes in salted boiling water for 20 minutes (slightly less if they are small). Drain them, peel them, and push them through a food mill. Add the light cream, season with salt and pepper, and reserve them in a warm place (over very low heat). To make the dried fruit paste, cover the apricots in boiling water and leave for 15 minutes until they are swollen and soft. Drain them well, then grind them in a food processor to a smooth paste with the gingerbread and spices. Season with salt and pepper. Make 4 balls of the paste. Season the tuna steaks with salt and pepper. Flatten the balls of paste into disks the size of each slice of tuna, and place one on top of each.

Heat a skillet and add 1 tablespoon of olive oil. Sauté the tuna for 2 minutes on the underside, then turn it over and sauté with the paste. Arrange each slice of tuna on warmed plates. Add two tablespoons of the artichoke purée and pour a ring of sauce around them. Serve immediately. For an attractive presentation, I add a few toasted slivered almonds, a sprig of dill, and a beet chip (thin slice of red beet fried in oil like a potato chip).

FATÉMA HAL

PARIS, FRANCE

CREATED IN HER RESTAURANT IN EASTERN PARIS, THE GREAT MOROCCAN CUISINE
OF FATÉMA HAL IS NOT JUST AN OEUVRE ASSEMBLED WITH PRECISION AND CERTAINTY,
BUT ALSO A LABOR OF LOVE DEDICATED TO THE PRESERVATION OF AN ANCIENT TRADITION.

Fatéma Hal is a woman unlike any other in her profession. Born in Oujda in 1952, today she's a
shining star in the culinary firmament, and a pioneer in the field of contemporary Moroccan cooking (*Les Saveurs et les gestes* is the title of her illustrated book dedicated to the "*dadas*," or women
chefs of Morocco). In the old days, when she was in her twenties, she assumed the course of her life
was set and would never change. She had married a "foreigner" when she was sixteen, and the couple had three children. The difference in her case—as compared to that of her mother, whose first
name is Mansouria—was that she had learned to read and write.

This accomplishment spurred her to go to university and pursue her studies further.
After gaining a degree in French literature at Paris VIII, she enrolled in the École Pratique
des Hautes Études. She published articles for UNESCO, and then won a post as technical
advisor to the Ministry for Women's Rights directed by Yvette Roudy. What did her mother
Mansouria make of all this? She thought it was a crazy idea—but it was one that continued
to develop over the next ten years.

To finance her growing ambitions as a chef, Hal offered shares in her future restaurant
to a group of acquaintances who believed in her. She collected 100,000 francs from her initial investors, and opened a no-frills restaurant near the Saint-Antoine hospital in Paris.
When Pierre Desproges, an early fan of her cuisine, publicized her enterprise on the radio
station Europe 1, people went out of their way to try out the new restaurant, congratulate
her, sample her marvelously spicy dishes, and listen to what she had to say.

At her restaurant she acts as a sort of ambassador for good food. Her efforts are supported by a loyal band of personal friends, and she also gives unstinting credit to her female
mentors. These include her mother, Jdaïni Mansouria, to whom her restaurant is dedicated;
her old neighborhood friend, Lalla Kheira—a repository of memories from Oujda who acted
as a surrogate grandmother, cook, and spiritual midwife to her; luminary dressmaker from
Tlemcen, Yamina Rabhi—a consummately elegant woman and guardian of the Dada Rabha
tradition, a cook from Fès with magic fingers.

Fatéma Hal will gladly offer to relate the story of her cuisine as others might offer to tell your fortune. She works with a team of cooks representative of Morocco's different regions. One is from her hometown of Oudja, near the Algerian border; another from the great modern metropolis of Casablanca; another from Fès, the capital of Moroccan gastronomy; and another from the port city of Marrakesh—capital of the country's Berber nomads. These diverse assistants each have their own distinctive way of sorting ingredients, of kneading and rolling out dough, and Fatèma sees to it that their recipes are written down for posterity.

This cooking is a convivial art based not on contemporary fusion, but on fidelity to the past. There's a ceremonial aspect to her meals, which feature such traditional dishes as "bridal fingers," made with warka paste shaped into crisp fingers; tangy shrimp spiced with coriander and ginger; pigeon *pastilla*; grilled sweet-pepper salad; eggplant *zaalouk*, and carrot and orange salad. Not to mention semolina rolled in saffron pistils and served with caramelized onions, and Fès-style raisins and almonds, with vegetables, or Oujda style, with cracked wheat.

Other works of art—and acts of love—produced by Hal include tagines made with prunes, chicken, raisins, and almonds; *briwates*—crêpes stuffed with onions and meat conserve that are similar to Indian samosas; her milk *pastilla*; and her honey *beghrir*, a kind of honeycomb crêpe.

"When you live far away from home," she explains, "cooking is the only thing you can take with you." We might also add that a woman like Hal is preserving a valuable heritage. Her recipe for *mourouzia*, a survivor from the seventeenth century, calls for at least twenty-six spices and consists of lamb that is first sautéed and then patiently simmered in a sauce combining honey, raisins, sesame seeds, and almonds. This dish, a relic from the past, provides ample proof that Moroccan cuisine is more varied than generally supposed.

For Hal, cooking is one thing, and talking about it another. This reflects the difficulty of translating the names for Arab dishes into French. Hal prefers the Arabic pronunciation of basic culinary terms. For example, she says "*kascsou*," not couscous, "*touagin*," not tagine. *Briouates* (stuffed with goat cheese and tender ground meat) are "*briwates*." *Pastilla* is "*bastella*" (or "*bestelle*" in Algeria). These variations reflect the fact that Oujda, a city close to the border of Algeria, is a human and linguistic crossroads.

Moroccan meals are also a prelude to the art of conversation, to convivial hours spent with friends while savoring shared delicacies served on vast platters. "Fatéma's table is a meeting place, a stage set where ordinary life is spiced with generous, simple, uncomplicated gestures. A place where friendships are forged and strengthened," writes her friend, the Moroccan author Tahar Ben Jelloun.

With her invigorating steamed shoulder of baby lamb, her fragrant stuffed and lightly spiced sea bream (cooked as it used to be in old Mogador), Hal demonstrates her skill in executing culinary treats of great delicacy. Accompanied by wines from Meknès and Oujda, a meal under her supervision, served in a setting reminiscent of a Moorish living room, has all the charm of a living past. At her restaurant, the *diffa*, a meal traditionally prepared to celebrate special occasions in Morocco, provides diners with a moment of pure bliss.

FATÉMA HAL'S RECIPE:

DRIED APRICOT AND ALMOND TAGINE

PREPARATION TIME: 35 MINUTES
COOKING TIME: 30 MINUTES
TO SERVE: 6

INGREDIENTS

· ⅓ cup (100 g) almonds
· 2 tablespoons peanut oil
· 6 pieces of shoulder of lamb
  or 2 pounds, 10 ounces
  (1.2 kg), i.e. 7 ounces
  (200 g) per person
· ¼ teaspoon ginger
· 1 pinch of saffron pistils
· 1 cinnamon stick
· 2 small onions, minced
· 1 teaspoon salt
· ½ teaspoon pepper

For the apricots

· 1 ¼ pounds (500g) dried
  apricots
· 1 cup (250 ml) water
· ⅓ cup (100 g) sugar
· 1 teaspoon cinnamon
· ⅓ cup (100 g) butter

METHOD

For the apricot mixture, wash
the apricots. Put the water,
sugar, cinnamon, butter, and
apricots into a saucepan and
bring to the boil. Cook over
low heat until the sauce
reduces to the consistency of
honey.
In another saucepan, bring
1 cup (250 ml) water to the
boil. Pour the almonds into
the boiling water and leave for
around five minutes. Remove
from the heat, drain, and
blanch them, i.e. remove the
brown skin covering them.
Dry them with a clean cloth.
Heat 1 tablespoon peanut oil
in a skillet and brown the
almonds.
Heat the rest of the oil in a
large pan and add the pieces
of lamb. Season with salt and
pepper, add the ginger, the
saffron pistils, and the
cinnamon stick.
Then add the minced onions
and pour 1 cup (250 ml)
water over the meat.
Simmer, covered, for about
30 minutes on low heat.
The lamb should be very soft
once the cooking is complete.
Arrange the meat and onions
on a serving platter or in an
earthenware tagine. Arrange
the apricot sauce around it
and sprinkle the meat with
almonds.

You can also serve this
delicious tagine with a sweet
potato purée flavored with
a little grated nutmeg or
accompanied by a sweet
couscous spiced with cinnamon.

ANGELA HARTNETT

LONDON, GREAT BRITAIN

A LIVELY NATIVE OF WALES WITH AN ABIDING PASSION FOR ITALY,
ANGELA HARTNETT EXERCISES HER TALENTS AT ONE OF LONDON'S MOST FAMOUS HOTELS,
WHERE SHE HAS SUCCESSFULLY REVOLUTIONIZED A CHERISHED BASTION OF THE BRITISH GENTRY.

Expectations were not high when Angela Hartnett assumed her post in the kitchens of the Connaught, the smallest and most exclusive of London's great hotels, and a traditional bastion of "British" style. However, when she was sent into the heart of Mayfair by Gordon Ramsay—who guides the culinary destinies of the Savoy Group and is the only man in the British capital who has three Michelin stars to his name—he immediately lit a fire under the venerable institution. In the old days, customers came to the great hotel's Grill Room to enjoy traditional fare such as cold turbot pâté served with a bland lobster sauce, Prince of Wales consommé, and sherry trifle.

Harnett's French predecessor, Michel Bourdin, had already set the new tone with an Escoffier-style Franco-British cuisine that might have been slightly dated but was perfectly executed. Angela Hartnett changed all that. The Connaught's customers had evolved. Men were no longer required to wear neckties, or even jackets. How shocking for such a venerable Mayfair landmark! But a new generation of rock-star patrons didn't believe in dressing up.

Angela Hartnett, who is strongly influenced by Italy, also changed the style of the kitchens. She specializes in rustic, Italian-accented dishes featuring southern flavors. For example: terrine of tomatoes and goat cheese with balsamic vinegar; a (superb) pumpkin tortelli with amaretto and sage butter in the style of her mentor Nadia Santini; tagliatelli with squid ink and crab; veal sweetbreads with Treviso chicory—all unequivocally evoking their Italian origins.

Under Hartnett's supervision, the Connaught is now resolutely turned toward Parma and Mantua, Bologna and Bari. London-born Angela's mother is Welsh, but her grandmother was Italian, and she has gradually returned to her ancestral roots. She's worked in England, Scotland, Barbados, and Dubai, but absorbed her culinary lore from her "nonna," and executed it in a modern version at London's Zafferano before setting out to train under Annie Feolde in Florence.

Gourmet London's gruff Scotsman Gordon Ramsay—who trained under Guy Savoy and Joël Robuchon, and at the three-star London restaurant on the Royal Chelsea Hospital Road—also serves as chief consultant to the Savoy Group, and is clearly Hartnett's inspiration. He trained her at Aubergine, a famous restaurant in Chelsea, and sent her for finishing to Petrus in London, and then to Amaryllis in Glasgow—which he directed from afar, subsequently assigning her to the very exclusive Connaught.

At the Connaught, Angela has been given a free hand to invent her own brand of cuisine, which is passionate, meticulous, and highly appealing. Nevertheless, the ham consommé with mixed minestrone, vaguely recalling oxtail soup, the vichyssoise with chive cream, raw mackerel escabèche, duck legs braised in corn and morel mushroom with port sauce, and breast of pork with pearl barley are all plausible variations on classic Franco-British cuisine.

Angela Hartnett—who directs thirty assistants (including six women) in her vast basement kitchens with an iron hand—consistently expresses her own tastes and imposes her own distinctive style. Although the herb risotto is served with English asparagus, it is also garnished with three-year-old Parmesan cheese. The sautéed sea bream may come from the North Sea or the English Channel, but it is served with an Italian-style gratin of eggplant and tomato splashed with virgin olive oil. For her turbot, Hartnett combines artichokes, baby leeks, and chicken broth with truffle oil. Her John Dory is accompanied by a bouillabaisse sauce. These dishes will give readers some idea of the new tone set by Hartnett.

The Connaught, which now boasts a summer terrace on Carlos Place (a novelty that might have shocked De Gaulle, who moved to London in 1940 and chose the Connaught—for its discretion—as his culinary outpost), now has its eyes firmly on the South. The settings of its two restaurants, the Menu and the Grill Room, are impressively elegant and patrician. The youthful and dynamic Anglo-Italian wait-staff is efficient and helpful. Lastly, the wine list offers a world tour of fine vintages that is truly stunning.

We might add that the desserts are splendid (for example, the semi-freddo chocolate praline, the figs poached in Muscat wine from the Loire Valley, and the rigorously classic chocolate profiteroles). Not to mention the dessert "appetizers," amusing mini-scoops of sorbet that are served separately. In other words, Ms. Hartnett—the new "Iron Maiden" of English cuisine, who was rapidly awarded a Michelin star—still has surprises in store for the creatures of habit making up the patrician clientele of that most "British" of great world hotels.

ANGELA HARTNETT'S RECIPE:

GREEK-STYLE MACKEREL AND VEGETABLE SALAD

PREPARATION TIME: 30 MINUTES
COOKING TIME: 15–20 MINUTES
TO SERVE: 4

INGREDIENTS

For the mackerel and vegetables
· 4 small mackerel, cleaned and gutted
· 2 medium carrots
· 4 small shallots
· 1 tablespoon olive oil
· ⅓ cup (100 ml) frying oil
· Flour
· Salt and pepper
· 2 sprigs fresh coriander
  (cilantro), chopped
· 2 sprigs basil, leaves chopped

For the marinade
· ½ cup (75 ml) olive oil
· ½ tablespoon white wine vinegar
· ½ tablespoon balsamic vinegar
· 3 coriander seeds, crushed
· 3 white peppercorns, crushed
· 2 star anise
· 1 clove

METHOD

Combine all the marinade
ingredients in a saucepan and bring
to the boil. Remove from the heat
and leave to cool.

Prepare the vegetables by peeling
and thinly slicing the carrots and
shallots.

Heat 1 tablespoon of the olive oil
in a frying pan and sauté the
carrots for 2 minutes. Add the
shallots and continue cooking for
2 minutes but do not let them turn
color. The vegetables should be
slightly crunchy. Transfer the
vegetables to a bowl and season
with salt and pepper. Add the
marinade and leave to cool.

Season the mackerel with salt and
dust them very lightly with flour
on both sides. Heat the frying oil
to hot and fry the mackerel for
3 to 4 minutes on each side,
depending on size, then drain
them.

Gently heat the vegetables in
the marinade. Add the basil leaves
and coriander leaves. Serve with
the mackerel.

Accompany with a salad of fresh
herbs.

MARIE-CHRISTINE KLOPP

ROYE, FRANCE

SHE IS THE *GRANDE DAME* OF PICARDY CUISINE. HER NAME IS MARIE-CHRISTINE KLOPP,
AND SHE PLIES HER CRAFT WITH TALENT, MAKING USE OF PRODUCTS FROM THE MARQUENTERRE
MARKET GARDENS IN THE MARSHLAND AROUND AMIENS TO CREATE A GOURMET FEAST.

She's the doyenne of northern cuisine. Modest, disciplined, and—like many of the women featured in this book—self-taught. Did she have to struggle more than the others to succeed? It's true she was originally destined to become an executive secretary. But then her father, a talented pastry-cook and caterer, died young. He had earned a star shortly after the opening of his restaurant in Roye, just off the expressway, some 70 miles (about 110 kilometers) from Paris.

She began by taking charge of her father's dining room. However, discouraged by an ever-changing roster of chefs, she quickly decided to fill the breach in the kitchen herself, proving with her daily stubborn enterprise that a Parisian with roots in Luxembourg can become the deftest of all Picardy chefs. Marie-Christine Klopp is a magician all right, a self-effacing wizard who cooks products from the Somme bay with peerless dexterity.

Her takes on the eels, frogs, and snails from the Marquenterre area are luscious. Other treats—such as leeks prepared according to a local recipe, rhubarb in brown sugar, and produce from the marshland market gardens around Amiens—are prodigious. Diners immediately sense that something great is happening behind the Art Deco walls of Roye's central square.

Her restaurant, located only a mile from Paris, is something of a surprise. For example, the somewhat austere façade conceals an invitingly warm, wood-paneled interior with carefully laid tables. The lively Gérard Borck, a maître d'hôtel of the old school with enthusiasm to spare, makes his guests feel right at home, skillfully suggesting appropriate wines, eloquently describing his latest discoveries, explaining the day's specialties, and vaunting the qualities of the fresh fish he brings back from the Rungis wholesale market in his pickup truck, which also serves him on "wine-hunting" expeditions to Alsace and Bordeaux.

Gérard Borck presents Marie-Christine's dishes, which reflect the season, the tides, and the weather, with the dedicated faith of a true believer. Marie-Christine is truly a magician, a kindly spirit who creates her dishes as instinctively as a bird sings. Today's menu features sautéed frogs with roughly mashed potatoes, grated horseradish, and baby beans served in a spicy cream; crisp eggplant with marinated eel in brown sauce accompanied by selected baby vegetables in season.

Variations on the snails raised by Monsieur Brener include a creamy winter-cress velouté with fritters, and chanterelle mushrooms *à la grècque*, in garlic cream, a mild tapenade, or stuffed vegetables. Light olive-oil garnishes for vegetables add a subtle Mediterranean touch to this great cuisine from the north. Everything is just right, uncomplicated, savory, and digestible. Diners do not pick at this food; they wolf it down with delight.

We haven't forgotten the John Dory in sorrel purée with a conserve of milk onions; the little suckling pig with its crisply caramelized skin; the delicious cheeses that are the specialty of friend Philippe Olivier in Burgundy; the triangle of bitter chocolate served with a semolina crust; and the "sushi" combining rice pudding, rhubarb, and muesli—this chef's definitive "cubist" masterpiece.

Depending on the season of the year and the inspiration of the moment, offerings might also include a magnificent flamiche with leeks; a puff-pastry almond tart; plump scallops with endive accompanied by a delicious and unusual mango and ginger chutney; wild duck with laurel, beets, onions, and prunes; or the splendid calf's head in Covert beer accompanied by a stunning purée of potatoes and gingerbread. Readers will immediately understood that, here, the cuisine of the north invites diners to enjoy a festival of gastronomic delights.

Strong beer, endives, and herring, and game from the nearby marshes blend naturally on the plate. The meal ends with a chocolate truffle frosted with Maragogype (a variety of coffee), a hot soufflé seasoned with Houlle juniper, or molded oranges with pepper—all reflecting their strong local roots. Anyone who has tried this restaurant will tell you that on the beach road to Roye, where the Picardy countryside is still unspoiled, there's a wonderful surprise in store for adventurous gourmets. Marie-Christine Klopp's nothern France is truly lovely!

MARIE-CHRISTINE KLOPP (FACING PAGE, LEFT) WANDERS THROUGH THE CROP FIELDS AND ALONG THE CANALS (BELOW LEFT) OF HER REGION IN ORDER TO COLLECT THE BEST INGREDIENTS. HER COOKING MAKES USE OF THE BEST PRODUCE THAT MARQUENTERRE AND THE AMIENS REGION HAS TO OFFER. HER CUISINE IS IN THE TRADITIONAL PICARDY STYLE, AS SHOWN BY HER SIGNATURE DISH, FLAMICHE WITH LEEKS (FACING PAGE, RIGHT), BUT ALSO MODERN IN TERMS OF HER USE OF LOCAL PRODUCE, AS WITH HER MILK CHOCOLATE TRIANGLE LACED WITH LOCAL GIN (BELOW RIGHT). THIS NORTHERN FRENCH STYLE OF COOKING IS LIGHT BUT REQUIRES MUCH SKILL. A PERFECT EXAMPLE IS TANDOORI BABY BACK RIBS WITH POTATOES AND BABY PURPLE ARTICHOKES (PRECEDING PAGE).

MARIE-CHRISTINE KLOPP'S RECIPE:

FLAMICHE WITH LEEKS

PREPARATION TIME: 40 MINUTES
COOKING TIME: 35 MINUTES
TO SERVE: 6

INGREDIENTS

· 1 ¼ pounds (500 g) leeks, washed and drained
· ⅓ cup (100 g) salted butter
· ⅔ cup (150 ml) heavy cream
· 6 rounds shortcrust dough made with butter, measuring 5 inches (12 cm) in diameter
· 6 rounds shortcrust dough made with butter, measuring 6 inches (14 cm) in diameter
· 2 egg yolks beaten with 1 tablespoon water
· Salt and pepper

METHOD

Slice the leeks thinly with a sharp knife. Use all of the white part except the part closest to the roots.

Melt half the butter in a heavy-based saucepan. As soon as it splutters, add the sliced leeks. Season with salt and pepper. Cook on very low heat, adding a little water from time to time. Cut the rest of the butter into small pieces and add it gradually. When the leeks are a soft mixture without liquid, add the heavy cream and stir with a wooden spoon.

Rinse a cookie sheet and place the 6 smaller rounds of dough on it. Put a teaspoon of the leek mixture in the center of each. Dip a pastry brush in water and brush it round the edge of the dough rounds, then cover with the larger pastry rounds, and press down well to seal the two rounds of dough together. Brush the tops with the beaten egg yolks, and make a little design on each traced with a knifepoint. Bake in a preheated 350°F (180°C) oven for 10 minutes then reduce the temperature to 300°F (150°C) for 20 to 25 minutes.

After the first 10 minutes of cooking time, it is a good idea to lightly cover the flamiches with aluminum foil to prevent burning.

The pastry should be golden and crisp.

Serve piping hot.

To make a large flamiche for 6 people, make a pastry round of 11 inches (28 cm) and 12 inches (30 cm) diameter respectively and roll out the dough so it is not as thin.

LÉA LINSTER

FRISANGE, LUXEMBOURG

EVER SINCE SHE SNATCHED THE BOCUSE D'OR TROPHY FROM HER MALE COMPETITORS,
THE GREAT LÉA LINSTER HAS REIGNED AS UNCONTESTED STAR OF HER TINY DOMAIN.
WE VISIT LUXEMBOURG'S SECRET WEAPON.

Léa Linster—known for her ruddy complexion, strong personality, and "big mouth"—is the universally recognized doyenne of Luxembourg cuisine. Ever since 1989, when she won the international Bocuse d'Or trophy in Lyon, the great lady of Frisange has been a star. She's the first—and so far the only—woman ever to be awarded a culinary trophy in international competition.

But don't worry: the great Léa has remained faithful to the source of her reputation, a restaurant located in an area of Thionville, just off the main road, beside one of this flat country's canals. With stunning elegance, she completely redecorated her Flemish mansion in subtle shades of beige and gray. People flock there for a few hours of calm and the enjoyment of a gourmet meal. A road sign points the way to "Léa Linster, chef," underscoring that this leading-light of the Grand Duchy has remained an exemplary "artisan."

Léa is obviously no ordinary chef. She's neither a "*mère*" in the old Lyon tradition of women who opened traditional but excellent bistros, nor a trendy cover-girl type like Ghislaine Arabian—the Belgian chef who built up a big media following in Paris. Léa has remained loyal to her peasant roots. This former law student is a determined woman who abandoned university, took over from her parents at their rustic roadside inn, and transformed the premises into a shrine of discreet luxury. At Léa's there's no glitz or phony sophistication, just a continuous quest for authenticity. Her poultry comes from a neighboring farm near Lorraine, her cream has an old-fashioned taste, her wine is grown at her own vineyard in the Moselle valley.

Her hallmark is classic chic, a basic style that—although it may appear to change when she changes assistant chefs—is actually immutable. "Simple, but Brilliant" (*Einfach und Genial*), as the title of her German-language recipe collection claims. Connoisseurs come here to sample the famous dishes that made her reputation and won her the famous Bocuse d'Or— a reflection of her restaurant's increasing fame and her own talent for keeping pace with the times, seeking out trendy new products, and using southern ingredients and exotic spices.

Clever and dynamic, Léa has become a sort of adoptive daughter to the great Paul of Collonges, and consistently features timeless classic such as soup made with VGE truffles

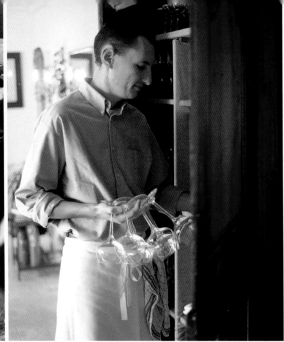

(based on Paul Haeberlin's truffle Souvaroff), sea bass in pastry with Choron sauce, and roast Bresse chicken with macaroni au gratin. One of Léa's standard summer offerings is a "*Bocuse d'Or*" menu, featuring a simple chilled soup of seasonal vegetables (on a recent visit, this was a divine tomato soup with goat cheese). Other treats include foie gras in aspic with supreme of chicken and a salad of winter cress, lobster salad with a delicate tarragon sauce, shellfish accompanied by zucchini stuffed with shellfish mousse in a foamy shrimp broth seasoned with lemongrass.

Then there's the poached supreme of free-range pigeon served with a confit of pigeon thighs and green vegetables cooked in the poaching liquid; or the celebrated saddle of lamb in a potato crust (a first-prize winner in Lyon); the crème brûlée in the style of "Uncle Paul" of Collonges, and the tempting selection of desserts. Nothing strange, no weird inventions, just an anthology—as it were—of fine savory products used in flawless dishes garnished with simple sauces.

To this are added classics such as shredded rib steak served with superb Pont Neuf potatoes, and sea bass cooked in an impressive salt crust and carved at the table before being served with an extraordinarily light sauce of fennel and olive oil. These dishes prove that even classics can be light as a feather. To round out the meal, there's a gamut of old-fashioned desserts updated to suit modern tastes—a soup plate of hot cherries topped with orange and lemon peel and accompanied by yogurt ice cream; chocolate tart with caramel and raspberries, and chilled lemon soufflé. A range of treats demonstrating that classicism executed with this kind of sensitivity reflects a virtuoso talent.

Worthy of note is the highly elegant, off-white, Zen-style dining room, with a teak terrace extending into the countryside, and the "panoramic" view of the kitchen that offers a continuous and fascinating spectacle. And, lastly, the youthful French servers who fulfill their task with cheerful professionalism, and enthusiastically explain the excellent wine list, featuring vintages produced in the Grand Duchy (most notably, those from her own vineyards, and Mathis Bastian's Rieslings and Pinot Noirs). To sum up, this is a truly great restaurant that obviously deserves all the prizes and stars it has won.

LÉA LINSTER'S RECIPE:
WAXY POTATOES
WITH DUCK FOIE GRAS

PREPARATION TIME: 25 MINUTES
COOKING TIME: 25 MINUTES
TO SERVE: 4

INGREDIENTS
· 4 tablespoons (60 ml) balsamic vinegar
· 6 medium waxy potatoes
· 1 pound (450 g) duck foie gras
· ¼ cup (60 ml) strongly flavored duck stock
· 2 pinches sea salt
· 2 pinches Szechuan pepper

METHOD
On medium heat, cook the balsamic vinegar until it is reduced to around 1 tablespoon. Steam the potatoes in their skins for around 25 minutes. Leave them to cool, then cut them in half lengthwise. Slice the foie gras into 12 slices around ½ inch (1.5 cm) thick, ensuring they have the same shape as the potatoes. Arrange the potatoes on a cookie sheet and sprinkle with a few grains of salt. Place the foie gras slices on them, season lightly again with salt and bake in a preheated 400°F (200°C) oven for around 6 minutes or until the foie gras is lightly cooked. Arrange the foie gras and potatoes on a plate. Heat the duck stock and coat the foie gras with it, adding a trail of 1 teaspoon of the reduced balsamic vinegar around the potatoes. Sprinkle with a few grains of sea salt and the Szechuan pepper. Serve immediately.

JOCELYNE LOTZ-CHOQUART

BESANÇON, FRANCE

SHE IS THE BEST COOK IN HER ADOPTED REGION. THIS SELF-TAUGHT,
TOTALLY COMMITTED PARISIAN SUCCUMBED TO THE CHARM OF THE FRANCHE-COMTÉ
SEVERAL YEARS AGO, AND HAS NOW FINALLY WON THE RECOGNITION SHE DESERVES.

Her story could be a fairy tale, a novel by Victor Hugo or Hector Malot. Imagine a little girl from a deprived area of Paris, whose father was a plumber and whose mother was a concierge; a little girl who was not given much attention, although she did attend school in Belleville. Her parents died when she was still very young; she married, gave birth to a child, and worked at various odd jobs—secretary during the day, hatcheck girl at the Paris restaurant L'Atelier Maître Albert in Paris at night.

While doing a temporary job at Le Mercure Galant, she met the man of her life, Gérard Lotz, who was the maître d'hôtel there at the time. The young couple decided to travel. Gérard was already familiar with sub-Saharan Africa, so they opted for Port-au-Prince, in Haiti, where they opened a restaurant. When they returned to France they settled in Belfort, where their son Gérard was born. They began to look around Besançon, the lovely capital of the Franche-Comté region, for a suitable restaurant, and found one near the Doubs River, naming it after the eighteenth-century explorer, Mungo Park, whose writing had inspired them, and decorating it with souvenirs of their travels.

Jocelyne and Gérard ran the restaurant together but, when their chef fell ill, Jocelyne was forced to fill the breach. Supposedly filling in only temporarily, she soon discovered a real love for the work. She served a brief apprenticeship with their Alsatian neighbor Dominique le Stanc, one of the great chefs of the time, who was then working on the Côte d'Azur. After this experience, Jocelyne knew that her preferred place was behind the stove.

Jocelyne has made a vocation of promoting products from the Franche-Comté, updating them, presenting them without unnecessary sauces or frills, relying on refined and sometimes astonishing combinations to create impact. Her style is a mixture of artfully honed rusticity and a certain local chic, executed with a finesse and daring that brings out the true nature of each ingredient. Examples include her delicate scalloped-potato mille-feuille with Morteau sausage and creamed morels, and her carp with sage on a Comté-cheese pancake. Dishes like this, along with the ice milk topped by a pear poached in Macvin (a bitter, walnut-flavored blend of Savagnin wine and grape must) make up a unique menu entitled "Passing Time."

She has decorated her house in tribute to an African traveler (above), understands the art of shopping (top left), and works with produce from her adopted region of Franche-Comté, such as morels (top right). All of Jocelyne Lotz-Choquart's cuisine is first tasted by Gérard, who is also responsible for service in the restaurant (facing page, bottom). Her cooking is a perfect illustration of the region's rich flavors, even though some of the more refined and delicious ingredients may come from elsewhere—Burgundy snails with spinach, pink radish cream with horseradish (preceding page) or John Dory with pickled lemons and gnocchi (facing page, top left). Her gingerbread with rhubarb in old Pontarlier (facing page, top right) is a delicious treat.

Jocelyne gives poetic names to her original gourmet dishes. Her menus list treats with titles such as "Joyous Cuisine," "Evening Pleasure," "Sources," "From the Earth," "Gastronomic Journey," and "Playing Hooky." Through them, she recounts the story of her adopted region's highways and byways. Her snails in a nest of greenery served with tiny creamed radishes and horseradish; her crayfish broth with chestnuts in a bay-leaf sauce; her fricassee of cep mushrooms and green lentils flavored with licorice and Savagnin in a turban of puréed parsnips are all divine moments of pleasure, crafted in the new style of Franche-Comté cuisine.

And then there's the braised pike perch in oxtail broth with morel mushrooms and ribs of Swiss chard; the supreme of Bresse chicken in the local dry white, "Vin Jaune," with foie gras and morel mushrooms, a sauce of stunning simplicity, and a polenta cake—all executed with a precision that never fails to enchant. Jocelyn's inventiveness never flags; her dishes are as pretty as pictures. It's as though she'd read some old magic books that inspired her to give a fresh slant to traditional products from the Franche-Comté by blending them in carefully arranged "marriages."

Diners also love the crayfish bisque made with aged Pontarlier wine; the delicate leek tart with farmhouse bacon in oxtail broth; the strip of pollack spiced with fried Morteau sausage and a green-tinged purée of ramson (wild garlic). Or the glazed pork cheeks with cardamom, shredded cabbage, and a pasta-thin julienne of white mushrooms flavored with licorice and pine buds.

All of these dishes evoke the poetry of distant and enchanted woodlands. As with Jean-Paul Jeunet, the great chef of the Arbois region, or Marc Veyrat, the madman of the Alps in Savoie, the terrain sets the tone, infusing everything with its spirit and traditions. This chef with the calm exterior, smooth features, blonde hair, and bright blue eyes sets her mark on everything she does with talent, lightness, and authority.

Local cheeses like Morbier are served warm and crusty, accompanied by a vinaigrette of beets and green apricots. Desserts are just as enchanting. They include rhubarb compote with Fougerolles Morello cherries and ice cream, blended with gentian and served with *sèches*, which are thin butter wafers; warm walnut cream and Vin Jaune caramelized in brown sugar and accompanied by a pot of wine ice cream or a light, lemon-flavored ice cream with crushed cherries and a mango and Morello cherry sauce. It's a treat just to read the mouthwatering menu.

The wines, described with precision by Gérard, are drawn from a range of great Comté vintages: the lively Chardonnay from the commune of Pupillin, a white Savagnin Jaune with a hint of walnut from Puffeney the Poulsard red with a raspberry bouquet from Rolet, and the great Vin Jaune from Montigny-les-Arsures are all incentives to travel down the cherished Loue to Courbet. The magic to be found at Jocelyne Lotz-Choquart's table is wonderful indeed.

JOCELYNE LOTZ-CHOQUART'S RECIPE:

CHOCOLATE GINGERBREAD CAKE WITH VIEUX PONTARLIER AND RHUBARB PRESERVE

PREPARATION TIME: 45 MINUTES
COOKING TIME: 1 HOUR 15 MINUTES
TO SERVE: 6–8

INGREDIENTS
For the cake
· 3 ounces (80 g) semisweet dark chocolate
· 8 ounces (250 g) gingerbread (pain d'épices)
· 2 cups (100 ml) milk
· 2 cups (100 ml) Vieux Pontarlier
· ¾ cup (175 g) butter plus 4 teaspoons (20 g) for the mold
· 8 egg yolks
· ½ cup (100 g) sugar, plus 1 tablespoon for the mold
· 4 tablespoons (50 g) ground almonds
· 4 egg whites

For the rhubarb preserve
· 1 pound, 2 ounces (500 g) rhubarb
· 1 scant cup (200 ml) cane sugar syrup
· 4 tablespoons (50 ml) fir tree liqueur
· Small pot of Fougerolles sour cherries

METHOD
To make the chocolate gingerbread cake, melt the chocolate in a bain-marie or double boiler. Cut the gingerbread into large cubes. Combine the milk and Vieux Pontarlier, then soak the gingerbread in it and process in a food processor. Preheat the oven to 325°F (160°C).
Cut the butter into small cubes and put it in the bowl of a mixer. Process on slow speed, add the egg yolks, sugar, ground almonds, melted chocolate, and the gingerbread mixture. Continue to process for 10 minutes at the same speed. Beat the egg whites into stiff peaks and fold them into the mixture.
Butter a 26-cm (10-inch) cake pan, sprinkle it with sugar, and add the mixture. Bake for 1 hour in the preheated oven, covering it with buttered aluminum foil if it browns too quickly. Unmold it on a cake rack and leave to cool. In the meantime, trim and skin the rhubarb and cut into 1-inch (3-cm) pieces. Combine it with the cane sugar syrup and fir tree liqueur. Cover and cook until soft, around 15 minutes. Remove the lid and cook, stirring constantly, until it has the consistency of a thick preserve. Add sugar during the cooking if necessary, as the rhubarb may be rather acidic. Drain the sour cherries and pour the alcohol in which they were preserved into a saucepan. Cook to reduce it by half then put the sour cherries in it to coat them well. Slice the cake and bake the slices in a preheated oven, 350°F (180°C) until they are crisp. Serve with the rhubarb preserve and sour cherries.
Vieux Pontarlier is a liqueur flavored with anise and flower fragrances. It can be replaced by an aniseed-flavored liqueur.
Fir tree liqueur is obtained by macerating the new shoots. It can be replaced by 4 to 5 candies that will dissolve during cooking.

GISÈLE LOVICHI

SARTÈNE, CORSICA

GISÈLE LOVICHI IS CORSICAN CUISINE'S LEADING LIGHT. A STUBBORN
AND SELF-EFFACING LONER, SHE NIMBLY JUGGLES THE UNIQUE PROPERTIES
OF THE ISLAND'S PRODUCTS AT HER RESTAURANT BELOW THE PRETTY TOWN OF SARTÈNE,
JUST A STEP AWAY FROM THE MAJESTIC GULF OF VALINCO.

It's a long hike to the foot of the hill, but the view of the slender, tall, cramped houses above
is worth it. According to the writer Prosper Mérimée (1803–1870), this cluster of gray
dwellings, huddled like a flock of sheep at the foot of the mountain, is "the most truly
Corsican of all Corsican villages." It boasts steep winding streets and a triangular terraced
square that affords a spectacular view of the valley.

Visitors come here for a taste of authenticity. One shop sells three varieties of local wine
(red, rosé, white), salami from the mountains, and strong sheep's-milk cheese. Another displays handcrafted soap, olive oil, and lavender—all of which are prepared right in front of
customers' eyes. And the highlight of the visit? The Auberge Santa Barbara, indicated on an
otherwise unadorned sign two kilometers down the road that runs along the sea and the
majestic Gulf of Valinco.

This is where you'll find Gisèle Lovichi, the great lady of Corsican cuisine. Lovichi has piercing blue eyes, wears an immaculate apron and a white scarf knotted around her head, and greets
visitors with a broad smile as she explains the menu and makes delectable suggestions. Her daily
offerings subtly and unobtrusively vaunt traditional local dishes—thick, spicy white-bean soup,
fine mountain charcuterie, stuffed roast lamb, zucchini with brocciù cheese, a platter of
Corsican cheeses, and crisp, freshly made fruit salad. But this list hardly scratches the surface.

Gisèle Lovichi's menu is an anthology of the island's flavors and traditions, dishes cooked
slowly, using products from Corsican vegetable gardens and the sea. Lovichi's daughter, the
lovely brunette Marie-Pierre, reminiscent of Mérimée's Colomba, maintains a lively con-
versational patter as she serves the divine plates of vegetables with just a hint of olive oil
and vinegar, traditional soups enlivened by a hint of chopped garlic, and delicate tripe prepared in the Sartène manner with a dash of tomato juice. It doesn't take new arrivals long to
realize that Gisèle has a real gift, and that her work, despite its apparent simplicity, is the
fruit of long and painstaking effort.

Customers with time to spare linger for tours of the garden tended by Lovichi's grandfather (who is almost ninety), and of the tidy house's interior. It soon becomes abundantly clear that this unpretentious house with the tile roof, overnight accommodation in a new annex, and tables with a view over the Sartène, is an alluring gourmet outpost on the island.

And here comes Marie-Pierre herself, bearing brocciù cannelloni and pigeon garnished with the myrtle that grows wild in the garden; it is also used for making a pungent after-dinner cordial. Diners rarely leave a single crumb on their plates, and gladly volunteer their conviction that everything served here is an act of love.

After the rack of lamb with herbs, be sure to save some room for the French toast with pears and honey, the warm puff-pastry apple tart, or the frozen nougat with honey. The wine to drink is—of course—a Sartène rosé. The modest check comes as a pleasant surprise after this feast fit for a king. Many thanks are due to Gisèle Lovichi for maintaining a restaurant of such exemplary good taste.

In winter, she takes up her pilgrim's staff and carries the good word of Corsican gastronomy abroad, to a luxury foreign hotel in Thailand or Korea for a prestige gourmet week. She also operates a clothing store in the old town, just above her inn. When spring returns, so does Gisèle, taking up the pots and pans once more to bewitch us.

Gisèle Lovichi is unique in Corsica, although the *Michelin Guide* has never awarded her a star. But she's our special star, a pilgrim's beacon, faithfully followed by all who admire her efforts to understand and restore, without fuss or pretension, everything that is honest and fine in the local cuisine.

ACCORDING TO PROSPER MÉRIMÉE, SARTÈNE IS "THE MOST CORSICAN OF CORSICAN VILLAGES." AT THE FOOT OF THE HILL UPON WHICH THE VILLAGE PERCHES, LIES GISÈLE LOVICHI'S RESTAURANT. SHE IS THE GUARDIAN OF CORSICAN CUISINE. SHE TAKES CARE OF HER ESTATE AND TASTES THE LOCAL VIN DE PAYS IN THE COMPANY OF WINEGROWERS, SUCH AS SIMON ANDRÉANI (BELOW LEFT), WHO RUNS THE FIUMICOLI ESTATE. SHE ALSO CREATES A WIDE RANGE OF DISHES THAT ENCOMPASS THE TRADITIONS OF CORSICA, INCLUDING SQUAB WITH MYRTLE (FACING PAGE, RIGHT), TRIPE SARTÈNE-STYLE, PEARS POACHED IN WINE WITH SPICES (PRECEDING PAGE), AND VEGETABLE TIAN (FACING PAGE, LEFT). ON SUMMER EVENINGS, IT IS A DELIGHT TO DINE IN THE GARDEN (BELOW RIGHT).

GISÈLE LOVICHI'S RECIPE:
SQUAB WITH MYRTLE

PREPARATION TIME: 40 MINUTES
COOKING TIME: 15 MINUTES
TO SERVE: 4

INGREDIENTS
· 4 squab
· 2 tablespoons oil
· 1 small onion, thinly sliced
· 2 garlic cloves, minced
· 1 carrot, peeled and diced
· 3 bay leaves, 3 sprigs thyme, and 1 bunch parsley
· 2 cups (500 ml) red wine
· ¼ cup (50 ml) Armagnac
· 6 tablespoons (75 g) chilled butter
· 2 ¼ pounds (1 kg) ceps (porcini) or portobello mushrooms, thinly sliced
· A few myrtle berries
· Salt and pepper

METHOD
Quickly flambé the squab by searing them in a flame. Cut off the wing-tips and cut out the backbone, leaving the breast whole. Pour the onion into a sauté pan and heat it. Add the squab and brown them all over with the sliced onion, garlic, carrot, bay leaves, thyme, parsley, salt and pepper. When the squab are nicely browned, light the Armagnac and pour it over them, then add the red wine. Leave to reduce on a low heat. Season the squab with salt and pepper and transfer them to a preheated 400°F (200°C) oven. Bake for 15 minutes. Remove them from the oven, leave them to rest, discard the excess fat and pour the remaining cooking liquid into a sauté pan. Add a third of the butter and all the mushrooms and cook, stirring, until the mushrooms are soft. Strain the liquid, add the myrtle berries, and simmer the sauce on low heat, gradually beating in pieces of the rest of the butter. Sprinkle the squab with the mushrooms before serving. Serve with polenta and coat with the heated sauce.

JOHANNA MAIER

FILZMOOS, AUSTRIA

CONNOISSEURS TRAVEL FROM SALZBURG, VIENNA, AND MUNICH
TO SAMPLE THE CUISINE PRODUCED BY A WOMAN WHOSE RESTAURANT IN THIS SMALL
MOUNTAINTOP VILLAGE IS THE MOST HIGHLY RATED IN AUSTRIA.

We're in the rugged mountain country near Salzburg, an area that has managed to retain its unique flavor. The autumn bounty is celebrated here from the end of August through the end of October, a period during which the local inns vie in showing off their treasure trove of traditional recipes. Farms hold open house for visitors, and each village vaunts its own specialties. These might include organic vegetables, fresh cheese, wholewheat country bread with cumin, aged Tomme cheese, and mild, light brandies—such as the celebrated Vogelbeer, made from mountain ash and as crisp as a morning breeze, or Holler (elder), which has a distinct flavor of the berry and a subtly bitter aftertaste.

The reigning monarch of this land is a vibrant fifty-year-old woman named Johanna Maier. Her parents had a laundry not far from Filzmoos that was subsequently taken over by her sister. When Johanna was very young she fell in love with the tall and spirited Dietmar, whose parents ran the Hubertus inn, located in the heart of the village. This couple's story is the stuff of which legends are made. They embarked on such escapades as secretly leaving for Paris, traveling on two different trains leaving two different stations. She intended to work as an au pair, but ended up as a waitress in the Montparnasse restaurant where Dietmar had found a slot for himself as a cook.

They stayed for two years before making their idyllic partnership official, and eventually giving birth to three boys and a girl. When her mother-in-law died, Johanna assumed the post of kitchen assistant. "She finally took over entirely," notes Dietmar with a laugh. Suave, lively, and elegant in his Tyrolean jacket, this Cary Grant in the Salzburg style now acts as an attentive greeter and experienced maître d'hôtel, while Joanna—wearing her amusing white cap—reigns like a queen bee over her six permanent and three temporary assistants.

She's a sight to be seen in her spotless kitchen—wearing her immaculate but unusual (for a chef) uniform featuring the traditional Austrian dirndl skirt—as she chops vegetables, shells shrimp, scatters a little lettuce over a plate or straightens a chive. This female executive, who is ever alert and never misses anything, artfully deploys her charm, authority, and finesse in

HUBERTUS IS LOCATED IN FILZMOOS. IT IS AN ANCIENT LODGE,
WHERE A NINETEENTH-CENTURY ATMOSPHERE BLENDS
SEAMLESSLY WITH A MORE RESERVED AND CONTEMPORARY
STYLE. THE DINING-ROOM WINDOWS LOOK OUT ONTO THE
GREENERY OUTSIDE (BELOW); THE CHAIRS ARE DECORATED
WITH A TRADITIONAL HUNTING DESIGN (LEFT).
DIETMAR (PICTURED WITH JOHANNA MAIER, FACING PAGE,
RIGHT) IS HER COMPANION, DEFENDER, AND THE MOST VOCAL
SUPPORTER OF HER CUISINE. SHE MOVES DEFTLY AND
SKILLFULLY TO FINISH A DISH (FACING PAGE, LEFT).

a traditional cuisine of peerless lightness. And this is why (as he'll be the first to tell you) the head of the *Gault-Millau Guide* for Austria—a local benchmark for the past twenty-five years—awarded her the highly prized rating of four chefs' hats.

Although Maier is a totally self-taught chef who learned her first lessons by watching her husband and mother-in-law, she also admits to having been influenced by her eminent Werfen neighbors Rudi and Karl Obauer. "When I watched them work, I realized what it was that I really wanted to do in life," she recalls. She also benefited from advice from these famous colleagues. Her imposing hotel, located in central Filzmoos and decorated with carvings and bay windows, combines the style of a nineteenth-century chalet with modern comfort, and belongs to the prestigious Relais & Châteaux chain.

Johanna, who today has forged firm friendships within the chain, received valuable tips from those of her peers specializing in Germanic cuisine: for example, her Baden neighbor Dieter Müller, three-star German chef Bergisch Gladbach, and Tyrolean Hans Haas—star of the fine-food firmament in suburban Munich, and headquartered at the Tantris. Not to mention Alsatian Jean-Georges Vongerichten, who went on to a successful career in New York.

She listened to everything these mentors had to say, but still has her own way of doing things. Her specialties feature authentic tastes, lightness, and fine-tuned flavors reflecting "the best of everything." This sums up the philosophy of a pantheist who claims to find God "everywhere in nature, rather than just at church," and who practices yoga, takes two days off from work per week to renew her inspiration, and believes that fine cuisine is an end in itself. However, this relaxed attitude doesn't prevent her from working obsessively with local products from mountain and river—and from other sources as well. Her medley of foie gras (mousse, cream, and parfait in blackcurrant or litchi aspic), her lobster salad with mushrooms and lemon thyme, and her turbot with basil risotto are standards in her kitchen—as are the char (a freshwater fish) with crayfish ravioli, the "Schnitzel"-style lamb chops, venison, pigeon, and veal presented (with explanations) two ways. "The best of . . ." might be the motto of this evangelist of the kitchen, who is never happier than when explaining, demonstrating, discussing, and illustrating her theories in practice.

Veal is represented by sweetbreads, cutlets, and fillets; venison by fillets, chops, and roasts; pigeon by thighs or fillets that are roasted, braised, sautéed, or breaded in the Viennese style. The lavish traditions of the Austro-Hungarian empire, as practiced under the beloved Franz Josef, are still alive here. Desserts—including elderberries and raspberries in aspic, fruit and ice cream, and delicacies combining apricot and fresh cheese, or chocolate with passion fruit—prove that Johanna Maier, who wins hearts with her cooking, hides considerable versatility behind her charming exterior.

Now known universally as "Empress" Maier, this woman—who doesn't claim to have revolutionized contemporary cuisine, but merely to have lightened traditional dishes and placed new emphasis on basic flavors—charms diners with her concern for authenticity, and wins them over to the idea that, in cuisine, the only valid yardstick is quality. In the land of the Hapsburg Empress Sissi, Filzmoos has found its empress of the table.

THE BEST PRODUCE THAT AUSTRIA HAS TO OFFER ARE COMBINED TO MAKE JOHANNA MAIER'S CUISINE A DELICATE AND MOUTHWATERING EXPERIENCE: ELDERBERRIES MIXED WITH STRAWBERRIES (PAGE 103). BELOW LEFT: BREADED LAMB CUTLETS; FACING PAGE, RIGHT: FILLETS OF VEAL IN A ZUCCHINI COATING. HUBERTUS IS A QUIET LODGE ON THE BANKS OF THE RIVER AND ACTS AS A BEACON FOR THE VILLAGE (BELOW RIGHT). JOHANNA REMAINS CONSTANTLY FOCUSED ON EVEN THE SMALLEST DETAILS (FACING PAGE, LEFT), ENSURING THE COMPLETE SATISFACTION OF HER GUESTS.

JOHANNA MAIER'S RECIPE:

FILLET OF VEAL IN A ZUCCHINI COATING WITH CHANTERELLE MUSHROOMS

PREPARATION TIME: 35 MINUTES
COOKING TIME: 25 MINUTES
TO SERVE: 4–6

INGREDIENTS
· 1 fillet of veal, fat and fibers removed
· 1 sprig of rosemary
· 2 pinches salt and freshly ground black pepper
· 4 to 6 zucchini or small yellow squash
· 5 tablespoons (45 g) butter
· 1 shallot
· ½ cup chanterelles
· 3 tablespoons (80 ml) chicken stock
· Small bunch of parsley
· Salt and freshly ground black pepper
· Plastic wrap and aluminum foil

METHOD
Season the meat all over with salt and pepper.

Pull the rosemary leaves from the stem and sprinkle them all over the veal fillet. Roll up the veal fillet very tightly in plastic wrap so that it is the same thickness throughout and then roll it up again in a sheet of aluminum foil.

Bring a large saucepan of salted water to the boil. Put the veal fillet in the boiling water; it should remain wrapped in the aluminum foil. Cover the pot and remove it from the heat.

Leave it to rest for 20–25 minutes then broil for 3 to 4 minutes under broiler at 150°F (60°C).

Finely chop or grind the zucchini or yellow squash. Season with salt and pepper. Melt 1 tablespoon (15 g) butter in a skillet. Cook the zucchini or squash on high heat.

Remove the aluminum foil and plastic wrap from the veal and slice it. Garnish it with the zucchini or squash.

Slice the shallot thinly. Heat the rest of the butter in a skillet, sauté the shallots, add the chanterelles, and cook for a few minutes. Add the chicken stock and leave to reduce.

Mince the parsley and sprinkle it over the meat before serving.

FLORA MIKULA

PARIS, FRANCE

THIS NATIVE OF NÎMES, WHO BEGAN HER CAREER IN LONDON
AND THEN NEW YORK BEFORE "MAKING IT" IN PARIS, ADORNS HER TABLE
WITH TREATS THAT BURST WITH SOUTHERN SUNSHINE.

Her name is Flora Mikula, and she worked as Alain Passard's assistant at Arpège before open-ing her own restaurant on the Left Bank, to which she gave the evocatively Provençal name of Les Olivades. She then moved to the Right Bank, where she now—with verve and style—runs Le Carré d'Or on the Champs-Élysées. Here is a woman from the south who also draws on her Polish heritage. She's a hard worker who likes bright colors, who creates a cuisine emphasizing olive oil, anchovy paste, and tapenade.

Her hallmark are sun-drenched dishes with a strong yet subtle impact. Deploying rare talent, she constantly renews her culinary palette. Her restaurant is located in a former shirt factory that still boasts its British-style fireplace, impressive light fixtures, white walls, and moldings. Her premises are like a private club where "Flora's friends" gather to enjoy her fresh ideas and new inventions.

Produce from earth and sea, from the garrigue and the Mediterranean, are the inspira-tions for this skillful and determined technician. Flora Mikula first worked at Le Comptoir in New York, then in London—mainly at Le Meridien, under the supervision of Jean-Michel Lorain—before breaching Parisian outposts such as La Manufacture d'Issy, run by Jean-Pierre Vigato, and L'Avenue, the gourmet brasserie that launched Joël Robuchon and Jean-Claude Vrinat and continues to thrive under the direction of the Costes brothers.

This record proves that Mikula can set her hand to anything, that she's at home with any style, adeptly manipulating products, regions, and seasons. Physically, she's a typical flaxen-haired northerner—as was the brilliant Ghislaine Arabian, once the only two-star female chef in Paris. But Mikula reaffirmed her southern roots when she opened her first restaurant. Les Olivades was a declaration of love dedicated to the land of olive oil and cicadas, of sun-drenched vegetables (tomatoes, zucchini, peppers, eggplant), and to seafood from every coast. She has a passion for the flavors of the south, in the broadest sense of the term.

FLORA MIKULA, WITH HER ALL-FEMALE KITCHEN STAFF (TOP LEFT), KNOWS HOW TO LOOK ON THE BRIGHT SIDE OF LIFE. SHE CARRIES OUT HER DAILY ACTIVITIES WITH GREAT JOY; FOR EXAMPLE, SHE ADDS SOME FINISHING TOUCHES TO HER SOLE (ABOVE). SHE ALSO WORKS WITH AMAZING PRECISION, STIRRING A FRAGRANT PAN OF CALAMARI (TOP RIGHT). PRECEDING PAGE: A HINT OF THAI CUISINE MINGLED WITH MEDITERRANEAN INGREDIENTS: GOAT CHEESE PASTRIES WITH ICED TOMATO SOUP. FACING PAGE, BOTTOM LEFT: BAKED PEACHES WITH A RED GRANITA. THE UNDERSTATED DINING ROOM LOOKS OUT OVER AVENUE GEORGES V (FACING PAGE, TOP). SHE GREETS HER "FANS" ACCOMPANIED BY HER HUSBAND (FACING PAGE, BOTTOM RIGHT), WHO SUPERVISES THE SERVICE.

Flora's inherent verve remained undiminished when she moved from the Left Bank to the Right, although at her new location in the heart of Paris's "*Carré d'Or*," she might easily have yielded to the temptation to create an international or fusion cuisine, Champs-Élysées style. She did just the opposite, further honing her own work, doing things her own way, emphasizing quality raw materials in artful combinations. Her personality has become even more distinctive, attracting a clientele of passionate fans who don't scrutinize the bill too closely.

On the fringes of the most famous avenue in the world, she has created her own niche, a kind of club where she rings changes on seasonal products, provided they are of the highest quality. She doesn't appear in the dining room until late, leaving to her dedicated team the task of extolling the virtues of a constantly changing menu. Flora experiments with flavors and products, giving them new life. The voyage to the south that she offers is indeed a special one.

Diners appreciate her variations on the theme of shrimp and crab, served in a chilled consommé with baby vegetables and basil, her semi-cooked tuna served with eggplant caviar in a *pissaladière* (a Mediterranean tart with tomatoes and anchovies), and her tuna on glazed avocado. Her fresh fish of the day might be sea bass accompanied by grilled vegetables, garnished with spices and crushed almonds, or grilled fillet of John Dory with stuffed artichokes, Provençal-style, and a few gnocchi with lemon conserve. Divine, and a touch Italian . . .

The Pyrenean lamb is roasted with lemon thyme and served with pimiento del piquillo sauce and smashed potatoes with olive oil. The pigeon comes with baked peaches and a few chanterelle mushrooms. Desserts—following lessons learned from Maestro Passard, who was a pastry cook before becoming a chef—are one of the house's strong points. Favorites include baked apricots on pistachio-flavored sponge cake served with apricot-strawberry sorbet. Or the dish of cherries with cream cheese and verbena sorbet, garnished with a tiny, Pastis-flavored baba. Or summer fruit and melon in season, served with hibiscus syrup and red-wine granita.

This fresh cuisine, which ravishes and enchants, would no doubt have found favor with the sensualist Colette. She was born in Puisaye, far from the vineyards, in the heart of rural Burgundy, but she found a new life and new gastronomic joys in Saint-Tropez, where she wrote *Les Vrilles de la vigne* and *Prisons et paradis*. Surely Colette would have found simple but sensual words to describe the cuisine produced by Flora, who knows how to be both creative and beguiling, rigorous and amusing, technically adept and appealing. The design and decor of her restaurant are Parisian, to be sure, but its spirit is definitely rooted in Provence.

BAKED PEACHES WITH RED GRANITA
AND PANNA COTTA

PREPARATION TIME: 35 MINUTES
COOKING TIME: 2 HOURS 10 MINUTES
INCLUDING 2 HOURS THE NIGHT
BEFORE FOR BAKING THE PEACHES
TO SERVE: 8

INGREDIENTS

For the peaches
· 5 vine peaches
· 4 tablespoons honey
· Juice of 1 lemon
· Juice of 1 orange

For the granita
· 1 ¼ cups (300 ml) water
· 2 tablespoons (30 g) sugar
· 4 tablespoons peach or
  blackcurrant pulp

For the panna cotta
· 2 cups (500 ml) light cream
· ¼ cup (50 g) sugar
· ½ vanilla bean (pod), split in half
· 2 leaves unflavored gelatin,
  softened in cold water and
  squeezed

METHOD

The day before, preheat the oven to 200°F (90°C). Combine the honey and citrus juice. Pour the liquid into an ovenproof dish add the whole peaches and bake for 2 hours, basting occasionally with the cooking liquid. Remove from the oven, peel the peaches, cut them in half and remove the pit. Dice two of the halves and reserve them; refrigerate the rest.

To make the panna cotta, combine the cream, sugar, and split vanilla pod. Stir and bring to the boil. Remove from the heat. Add the unflavored gelatin. Stir until the gelatin has dissolved completely, then add the cubed peaches. Distribute the panna cotta between sundae glasses. Refrigerate until required. The next day, make the granita 3 hours in advance. Boil the sugar in ¼ cup (300 ml) water for 5 minutes. Remove from the heat and add the peach or blackcurrant pulp. Mix well and pour into a mold. Leave to cool, then freeze for 20 minutes. Stir the mixture to break up the crystals, then stir twice more at hourly intervals. To assemble the dish, put half a peach on each sundae glass of panna cotta and top with the granita.

OLYMPE

PARIS, FRANCE

THE FIRST WOMAN CHEF TO BE RECOGNIZED BY BOTH MEDIA CRITICS AND DISCRIMINATING CONNOISSEURS FOR HER TRAILBLAZING WORK DURING THE 1970S AND 1980S, CREATIVE AND ORIGINAL OLYMPE IS BACK AGAIN, THIS TIME ON RUE SAINT-GEORGES. SHE IS JUST AS NEWSWORTHY AS EVER, AND DEFINITELY DESERVES TO BE REDISCOVERED.

She was the queen of the 1970s, the first woman chef to win a star in Paris. To be sure, there had always been such leading culinary lights as Mère Brazier at the Col de la Luère in Lyon; Paulette Castaing at the Beau Rivage in Condrieu, and Solange Gardillou at the Moulin du Roc in Champagnac-de-Belair. But these women were traditional chefs working in the provinces, each in their own way exemplifying a long tradition of culinary "*mères*" at the stove—women who opened traditional-fare bistros with great success.

Olympe (alias Dominique Versini) was the first of a new breed. She came to her vocation indirectly, and started from scratch. Her first love was the theater, and she enrolled at the age of thirteen in a drama school where she studied for four years. However, when she failed the competition for admission to the prestigious institution on rue Blanche, she accepted temporary work with her lawyer sister. On her occasional breaks she visited her father and mother, who ran a small rural Provençal restaurant in Méoune called the Auberge de la Source.

"A former lawyer who took up cuisine when he was over fifty, Papa faithfully copied Ali-Bab [pseudonym of celebrated French chef Henri Babinski who traveled the world in the early 1900s, collecting recipes of the food he loved and compiling a gastronomic encyclopedia]. After being separated for twenty years from my mother, who had founded a restaurant but did not cook herself, he returned to the kitchen." Olympe has vivid memories of what happened next. One day in March 1968, when she was taking a stroll near Notre Dame with her sister, she met Albert Nahmias, who had just completed a degree in sociology and was working for the Iolas gallery. She married Nahmias in 1972, and in October 1973 they opened the first Restaurant d'Olympe, on rue du Montparnasse. What was this initial experience like? It was woven of a love story, a culinary vocation, and plenty of nerve. This was her period of daring and experimentation. The restaurant's setting was minimalist, and so were its portions—although there was nothing minimalist about the prices. As only luxury products were used, no apologies for the high prices seemed necessary.

Albert is a seasoned intellectual who reinvented himself as a self-taught Amphitryon. A sociable man with a gift for promotion, he has an instinctive sense of current trends and knew exactly

A SOLITARY COOK IN HER SMALL AND INTIMATE DINING
ROOM (ABOVE), DOMINIQUE VERSINI HAS NOT ABANDONED
HER INDIVIDUALITY BY SETTING UP A SMALL RESTAURANT
IN THE NOUVELLE ATHÈNES QUARTER OF PARIS. NOTHING
ESCAPES HER: SHE GRABS THE BEST PRODUCTS AT THE
MARKET, FOR EXAMPLE THESE PORCINI MUSHROOMS (LEFT);
SHE DRAWS UP A NEW SPECIALS BOARD EVERY DAY (FACING
PAGE, BOTTOM LEFT) AND HAS A SPECTACULAR CHOICE OF
WINES, ALL SERVED BY A SKILLED WINE WAITER (FACING
PAGE, TOP). HER LOGO, PAINTED ON THE WINDOW,
WAS INSPIRED BY A SERIES OF THRILLERS (FACING PAGE,
BOTTOM RIGHT).

what he wanted. Never at a loss for words, he quickly set the restaurant's distinctive tone. Olympe, meanwhile, turned out to be a natural chef with a touch of genius. Early media reviews from specialists such as La Reynière, Philippe Couderc, and Henri Gault were fulsome, and the restaurant's dining room soon filled with Parisian socialites eager to catch the crest of the new wave.

Connoisseurs relished the restaurant's seven versions of crayfish—Olympe offers both the white- and red-clawed varieties—including La Cardinal, a divine concoction with spiced tomatoes that is still a favorite today. Olympe was awarded three *Gault-Millau* chefs' hats and a *Michelin* star. Just before the birth of her daughter, Sarah, she was invited to appear on Bernard Pivot's *Apostrophes* television program to discuss her cookbook in the company of eminent chefs such as Paul Bocuse and Paul Haeberlin. As the junior member of this exclusive club, and a heavily pregnant woman willing to be exposed on the small screen, she gained immediate recognition and admiration throughout France.

Nerve, daring, character, and determination have always been Olympe's defining characteristics—and protection against the uniformity around her. She gave recipes to *Le Figaro* and was a guest on French television's *La Une* channel (subsequently *TF1*), appearing on "*Le Regard des Femmes*," and on France-Inter radio with Eve Ruggieri. Her culinary specialties include duck ravioli, spicy tripe, tuna with bacon, and an airy millefeuille.

At her own restaurants, first on rue du Montparnasse and then (in 1979) on rue Nicolas Charlet—in an understated Art Deco setting that is more spacious and very "nightlife," very *Orient Express*—she dared to stay open on Sunday nights (a rarity for fine Parisian restaurants), and welcomes a merry band of celebrity diners there. Guests have included Francis Ford Coppola, Robert de Niro, Diane Dufresne, Henri Salvador, Eddie Barclay, and Jean-Louis Trintignant. Gourmets and just plain hungry people from the world of show business are regulars, and should almost have their own napkin tucked into a little drawer.

At this point Olympe separated from Albert and became a consultant for Virgin, running the restaurant on the top floor of the Champs-Élysées Megastore. Her image was somewhat tarnished by this venture, which lasted five years. She then quietly opened a new restaurant under her own name at the former Casa Miguel, originally a low-cost eatery where elderly ladies could buy a square meal for just five francs. Behind an amusing façade, copied from the covers of French thrillers, Olympe reappropriated her real name, Dominique Versini, and opened for business.

Her set menu is artfully modest (an astute and reassuring strategy), served in an antique stucco setting that is decorated with pleasant paintings evoking an idealized Provence. Murano-glass light fixtures add a touch of distinctive charm. Olympe's regulars have remained faithful to her, and sometimes a film producer will book both small, crowded dining rooms just for himself and his team.

Old-fashioned expertise, subtle magic, skilled methods, and an instinct for fine products are still the bywords here. The Olympe working in the Nouvelle Athènes quarter today is serene and philosophical. Although the Saint-Georges area boasts many fine restaurants, its denizens quietly flock to this one when they want something a little special.

The crowded tables don't exactly facilitate private conversation, but the culinary offerings are flawless. Exhibiting tireless talent and enthusiasm, Olympe presents dishes without superfluous frills that are impeccable, straightforward, and precise. The marinated sardines, vegetable casserole with bacon, and chestnut pancake with poached egg are centerpieces of a rare and original menu.

For example, the duck foie gras, pressed fish roe with fennel, and fabulous herring caviar—as good as Sevruga—served with meltingly delicious potato cakes and creamed cauliflower are all irresistible. Other delights include pike perch in juniper-flavored mustard sauce, tuna and bacon with onions, strips of hind brisket sautéed in coriander, and the much-appreciated roast Sisteron shoulder of lamb for two, served with scalloped potatoes.

Not to be missed are the divine crayfish Cardinal in season, nor, when it comes to desserts, the homemade ice cream (ah, that "real" pistachio!), the fruit crème brûlée and the Paris-Brest cream pastry. For wine, try the unpretentious chilled Côtes du Vivarais, served in a Lyon-style half-bottle, and drink to the beautiful, newfound Olympe.

IN CASA OLYMPE THE CLIENTELE STILL ENJOY A HEARTY MEAL (FACING PAGE, BOTTOM LEFT) AND THE CHOICE IS DIFFERENT EVERY DAY (BELOW LEFT). OLYMPE'S CREATIONS INCLUDE CRUNCHY BLACK PUDDING WITH MIXED GREEN SALAD (BELOW RIGHT), CRAYFISH WONTON (FACING PAGE, TOP), AND ALMOND MILK PASTILLA (PAGE 113).

CRAYFISH WONTON

PREPARATION TIME: 40 MINUTES
COOKING TIME: 2–3 MINUTES
TO SERVE: 6

You can prepare the ingredients 4 to 5 hours before cooking them. You can also replace the crayfish with lobster, cutting the raw flesh into small pieces.

INGREDIENTS

- 28 large crayfish
- 4 tablespoons peanut oil
- ½ medium onion, peeled and sliced
- 1 large tablespoon tomato paste
- 2 tomatoes, washed and coarsely chopped
- 4 teaspoons (20 ml) Cognac
- 3 large pinches of cayenne pepper
- 6 cups (1.5 liters) light cream
- 1 egg yolk
- 2 packages wonton wrappers
- 2 ripe tomatoes, peeled, seeded, and chopped
- ½ bunch chervil, washed, leaves removed
- 3 tablespoons heavy cream
- 1 small piece fresh ginger root, peeled and chopped
- Coarse salt
- Table salt

UTENSILS

- 1 pastry brush
- 1 3-inch (8-cm) cookie-cutter and (nonstick) baking paper

METHOD

Remove the heads and tails of the crayfish and put them to one side.
Pour the peanut oil into a large saucepan, then add the onion, tomato paste, chopped tomato, and crayfish heads. Fry the mixture on medium heat for 3 to 4 minutes. Remove from the heat and crush the crayfish heads as finely as possible in a mortar with a pestle. Return the saucepan to the fire, add the Cognac and set it alight. Season with the coarse salt. Add the cayenne pepper and all of the light cream. Cook on low heat for 30 to 35 minutes until the cream thickens, but do not let it boil. When the cream has thickened, rremove the pan from the heat and blend using a stick blender. then strain and reserve this sauce.
In a small bowl, mix the egg yolk with 1 tablespoon water. Reserve this mixture which wil be used to seal the wonton. Make the wonton. In the center of each square wrapper, place 1 crayfish tail, 2 to 3 pieces of tomato, 1 pinch of table salt, 1 chervil leaf, and 1 knifepoint of heavy cream. Brush round the edge of the wonton square with the egg yolk mixture. Cover the wonton wrapper with another wrapper. Cut out the wonton thus formed with a cookie cutter and gently press it between your palms to expel the air and seal it. Repeat the operation to obtain 7 wontons per person.
Refrigerate them on a dish covered with nonstick baking paper.
A few minutes before serving, bring a large pot of salted water to the boil.
Meanwhile, reheat the sauce over low heat, adding the chopped ginger.
Add the wontons to the boiling water and cook for 2 to 3 minutes.
Drain and arrange the wonton in individual heated shallow bowls. Coat them with the heated sauce.
Serve immediately.

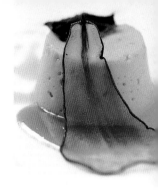

AGATA PARISELLA

ROME, ITALY

THE MATERNAL, GENTLE, AND UNASSUMING AGATA PARISELLA
IS AN OUTSTANDING PIONEER OF CONTEMPORARY ROMAN CUISINE. HER WORK
WITH CHEESE IS ADMIRABLE, AND SHE CREATES A SALTIMBOCCA
THAT CAN ONLY BE DESCRIBED AS A MASTERPIECE.

She presides like a mother hen over the Esquilin quarter of Rome. This neighborhood, in the south-east corner of the Eternal City, is notable for two landmarks: the basilica of Santa Maria Maggiore, and the Agata e Romeo restaurant. The person who originally stood behind the counter here was Romeo Caraccio's mother. Today, her place has been taken by the wholly self-taught Agata Parisella, a woman with a natural talent for the culinary arts, who faithfully replicates all the traditional skills. Agata has reigned for the past thirty years over the restaurant and the house, a state of affairs that is accepted without complaint by the innately conservative connoisseurs of Rome.

The restaurant runs smoothly, as if the gentle Agata had been on the job forever, following her mother-in-law's guidance as to the proper way of doing things. It is notable that this self-effacing woman, who rarely raises her voice, lets her husband do the boasting and her daughter explain the day's specials—as well as the latest offerings from the market—to her customers. She has adopted as her own the staples of a rustic tradition, to which she adds a touch of lightness and modernity, a taste for sweet-and-sour combinations, subtle blends, and imaginative work with classic cheeses.

Her favorite hunting grounds? The market that sells produce from Latium and its surrounding area. The gentle and discreet Agata is particularly skilled at using the homemade pastas available locally, artfully combining them with various fruits and vegetables. Examples include her famous pecorino flan garnished with pear sauce and acacia honey, and her potato and mille-feuille torte layered with goat cheese.

Pasta is naturally a featured staple. Two of the finest examples are Agata's spaghetti with black pepper and Piacentinu cheese—strong but not too strong—and paccheri, an oversize, thick, macaroni-like pasta with a large hole in the middle, cooked *all'amatriciana* with bacon and tomato, creating a subtle treat in the refined rustic mode.

The house's signature dish is a culinary classic that Agata produces with peerless mastery, the famous saltimbocca *alla romana*, a dish featuring finely shredded veal and Parma ham with

AGATA, THE QUEEN OF THE KITCHEN, MARIA-ANTONIETTA, THE MULTILINGUAL HOTEL MANAGER, AND ROMEO, THE EXPERT WINE WAITER (ABOVE LEFT), FORM A MAGNIFICENT TRIO AT THIS CHARMING ROMAN RESTAURANT (FACING PAGE, TOP RIGHT). WHILE ROMEO CARACCIO TENDS HIS WINE CELLAR (ABOVE RIGHT), AGATA PARISELLA PUTS THE FINISHING TOUCHES TO HER PASTA ALL'AMATRICIANA, WITH BACON, TOMATOES, AND PECORINO CHEESE (ABOVE CENTER) AND HER MILLE-FEUILLE (FACING PAGE, TOP LEFT). AGATA TAKES A FINAL LOOK AT THE RESERVATIONS BOOK (FACING PAGE, BOTTOM LEFT). PRECEDING PAGE: FOSSE CHEESECAKE WITH FIG SAUCE AND CHESTNUT HONEY. PAGE 118: SPAGHETTI WITH PEPPER IN ONE HAND AND STRONG CHEESE IN THE OTHER.

a hint of butter and a sage leaf. This subtle masterpiece combines the paper-thin slices of meat and mouthwatering organic baby vegetables (lovely tender carrots). Here, chef Agata has updated a timeless classic often massacred by others in Rome's trattorias.

Agata Parisella, who would rather show you how she does things than explain it in words, stands on the frontier between modernity and tradition. Quality raw materials, used with discretion and delicately flavored, enhanced with butter or oil but nothing more; these are the linchpins of today's cuisine. Agata's saltimbocca is a lesson in good eating, emblematic of Latium, and worthy of inscription on a Roman flag.

Although she excels in products from both land and sea, serving fish and shellfish in season, Agata also has a magical way with sweets. For example, her creamy mille-feuille is a light, delicate nest of airy soufflé. The names given to apparently simple dishes can be surprising, as their brilliance may not be obvious amid all this simplicity. Perhaps this explains why Agata Parisella, who cooks as naturally as a bird sings and has done so in exactly the same way for three decades, had to wait almost twenty years before earning her first star.

To accompany her delicate, feminine, light cuisine, Agata offers superb, carefully chosen wines—not only from Latium, but also with a nod toward nearby Tuscany and its neighbor Umbria. Her selections include the noble Piemontese and appealing Venezia. Wines are a passion with the voluble Romeo Caraccio. Leaving his wife to rule the kitchens, Romeo holds long discussions with their customers, suppliers, and friends—who are often one and the same. He mixes easily with his customers, whether they are dining alone or in groups, infusing life into the attractive manor house with the high vaulted ceiling that's a kind of cozy haven of wood and stone located in a corner of the Roman ramparts. Not all of the wines here are expensive. There are some fine bottles at reasonable prices—not only the light Fontana Candida white, but also a range of highly respectable Orvietos. In addition, the wine list is breathtakingly extensive.

It is also important to note that this is a family operation; that the attentive Franco-Italian service is under the charming supervision of Agata and Romeo Caraccio's gracious elder daughter, Maria-Antonietta, who is the epitome of smiling efficiency. Maria-Antonietta is this house's secret weapon.

AGATA PARISELLA'S RECIPE:

FOSSE CHEESECAKE WITH FIG SAUCE AND CHESTNUT HONEY VINEGAR

PREPARATION TIME: 30 MINUTES
COOKING TIME: 25 MINUTES
TO SERVE: 6

INGREDIENTS

· 3 ½ tablespoons (25 g) butter
· 3 ½ tablespoons (25 g) all-purpose flour
· 1 cup (250 ml) milk
· 14 ounces (400 g) fosse cheese, grated
· 3 eggs
· 1 pinch grated nutmeg
· 7 ounces (200 g) figs
· ⅓ cup (100 ml) chestnut honey vinegar
· 1 pinch salt

METHOD

First make a bechamel sauce by melting the butter on low heat. Add the flour and mix well for 2 minutes. Incorporate the milk and a pinch of salt. Simmer for 4 to 5 minutes on low heat. Add the grated fosse cheese and mix well. Then incorporate the eggs and and add a pinch of grated nutmeg. Pour the mixture into a greased springform pan and bake in a preheated 350°F (180°C) oven for about 25 minutes. When the cake is ready, let it cool completely before unmolding. Meanwhile, macerate the figs in the chestnut honey vinegar for around 10 minutes. Grind the figs and liquid in food processor to obtain a sauce and spread it on top of the cake. Serve immediately.

Contrary to popular belief, figs are not high in calories. The fruits consist of 80 percent water and 12 percent sugar. Dried figs, on the other hand, are much higher in calories. Fresh figs can be used in tarts, pies, cakes, or ice cream, and can be eaten as is as a dessert, accompanied by heavy cream or whipped cream or macerated in sugar and a liqueur.

Cheese known in French as "*de fosse*" (from a trench) is obtained by aging cheeses made of the milk of cows and ewes (or sometimes just ewes) for three months in trenches cut into sulfurous tufa rock in a little village in Italy called Sogliano sul Rubicone.
The trenches are bottle-shaped and are around 10 feet (3 meters) deep. The cheeses are stored in white canvas sacks and are piled on top of one another to prevent the air getting to them. When the ditch is full, wooden planks are placed over the sacks, and these are covered with sand. When the sacks are removed from the trench, a strong odor permeates the whole village. A miracle of nature has been accomplished! These cheeses are, of course, jealously guarded.

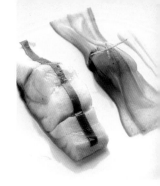

ANNE-SOPHIE PIC

VALENCE, FRANCE

Her great-grandmother started out at the Auberge de la Côte du Pin in Ardèche, on the other side of the Rhône. Now, under Anne-Sophie Pic—eponymous heir to the famed family restaurant located on the legendary French Nationale 7 highway—a great institution has risen from its ashes.

The Pic family's venerable tradition is currently being perpetuated by a diminutive woman, as self-effacing as a cat, who has nonetheless dared assume the daunting, legendary, cast-iron legacy left by her father and grandfather before her, successfully incorporating it into her own distinctive style.

This is the unique and fascinating story of one family's return to its roots. Anne-Sophie's great-grandmother, whose first name was also Sophie, ran the Auberge du Pin at Saint-Péray-en-Vivarais in the Ardèche, on the other side of the Rhône. This ancestress, Sophie Sahy, was a native of Saint-Sylvestre-en-Vivarais. When she married landowner Eugène Pic, she became the unwitting founder of an eminent culinary dynasty. Her own specialties were dishes simmered for hours in a cast-iron pot, whose aromatic fragrances entranced her son André, born in 1893. When André moved the family restaurant to Valence, on the mythical Nationale 7 highway, he drew his inspiration from memories of these maternal masterpieces when filling the plates of his delighted customers. His gratin of crayfish won him three stars in 1934, and his reputation grew in tandem with those of other contemporary gastronomic luminaries—Point in Vienne and the Dumaine in Saulieu.

The torch was taken up by André's son Jacques, born in 1932, who added his famed sea bass with caviar to the house's repertoire, and produced sumptuous dishes based on foie gras, truffles, and lobster. He also inaugurated the fabulous "Rabelais" menu, a gargantuan version of the tasting menus offered in modern settings today. When Jacques died, his son Alain took his place behind the stove, contributing his own layered beef and foie gras dish to the Pic heritage.

With the death of Jacques, however, the restaurant lost its third star. Was its reputation too heavy a burden for his heirs to carry? Did Alain—who inherited from his father another Pic-family characteristic, painful shyness—feel that he was not up to the task? Whether or not that was the case, Alain retired from the family business and, under his own name, inaugurated

Anne-Sophie Pic and her husband David Sinapian have renovated her grandfather André's traditional residence. The dining room (below) is in glorious shades of dark red. The new façade is in the timeless style of a neo-Provençal lodge (facing page, right). Anne (facing page, left) smiles as she displays a basket of the best strawberries from her supplier. The wonderful recipes: wakamé steamed sea bass with oysters and sweet-and-sour cucumber (preceding page) and abalone in parsley sauce with salsify and pomegranates (left).

a more modest establishment at Montbonnot-Saint-Martin, near Grenoble. It was at this point that the tiny and deceptively fragile-looking Anne-Sophie decided to fill the breach.

What motivated this academic specialist in economics to take up the challenge in her turn? "It was in the stars," she says, adding, "I always knew it would be that way." She served her apprenticeship at home, learning every aspect of running a restaurant kitchen. Although "blackballed" at one point by the Maîtres Cuisiniers de France, she donned chefs' whites and set out to restore order to her kitchen. She assigned the task of renovating the premises to her husband David Sinapian, who did so under the approving eye of Maman Pic.

Today the house has taken on new life, and now also boasts elegantly bright and cheerful bedrooms that are fresh and contemporary. There is new staff in both the kitchens and dining room, although head wine waiter Denis Bertrand—a fixture at the restaurant for the past thirty years—is still on hand to give diners the benefit of his extensive expertise in both great classics and fine local vintages. Anne-Sophie has taken charge of the stoves, inventing a new style. Although she has pruned the menu and lightened the house's traditional offerings, she continues to serve such traditional fare as sea bass with caviar, crayfish au gratin, and layered beef and foie gras, forging new links in a "father-to-daughter" tradition proudly noted on the restaurant's attractive menus. She has kept the "Rabelais" menu, and emphasizes seasonal ingredients, seafood, and—in the fall—game. Here is a woman who, although resolutely contemporary, has not rejected her roots.

The family lineage includes her grandfather André, whose specialty was truffle turnovers. Then came her father, bon-vivant Jacques, who shifted the emphasis to olive oil, black truffles, eggplant, foie gras, and succulent fish. And, today, there's Anne-Sophie: modest and gracious, but determined to do things her own way. Her style features delicacy, subtlety, sweet-sour contrasts, translucent aspics, a light touch, finesse, and a contemporary slant.

On her menu are succulent, quick-sautéed prawns, stuffed with crab meat and sprinkled with tart kiwi vinaigrette; sea bream baked in the skin and served with cockle broth and a contrasting slice of acid citrus fruit; tiny squid filled with the miniature round pasta known as *puntines* and garnished with two purées and basil-flavored pistou soup; thick lamb chops with fresh sheep's-milk cheese and herb cannelloni; pigeon wings in walnut pastry served with a delicate turnip tart; ice creams flavored with pistachio, chestnut, or vanilla, and a crisp Caribbean wafer for lovers of strong chocolate, and her concentrated fruit juice: this is the new take on Pic for the twenty-first century.

There's nothing superfluous on the plain, unadorned plates—just the pure taste of perfect and authentic products. Additional joys are provided by a wine cellar containing all the great vintages grown on the northern slopes of the Côte du Rhône region, from the Hermitage en Cornas to the Crozes Saint-Joseph suggested by the excellent wine steward; by the charming and elegant bedrooms; by the attractive indoor terrace; and by the inn annex bearing the name of the great-grandmother—a special tribute. To add to these are the relaxed dining style and snug, well-lit salons under vaulted white ceilings. Thanks to the dedication of this young woman, a great and legendary house has been restored to life for the pleasure of discriminating gourmets.

A MOMENT'S REST IN THE MORNING FOR ANNE-SOPHIE: TIME TO HAVE A COFFEE AND READ THE NEWSPAPER BENEATH A GIANT PRINT OF TAMARA DE LEMPICKA AT CAFÉ VICTOR HUGO (BELOW LEFT), VALENCE'S ANSWER TO PARIS'S LA COUPOLE. A FRESH AND LIGHT DESSERT (BELOW RIGHT): POACHED APPLIES IN CREAMY LEMON SAUCE.
FACING PAGE, LEFT: ANNE-SOPHIE PERCHED ON THE WALL OF THE ANCIENT AUBERGE DU PIN ON THE SAINT-PÉRAY COAST. THIS WAS WHERE HER FAMILY ORIGINATED.
FACING PAGE, RIGHT: SADDLE OF VENISON.

ANNE-SOPHIE PIC'S RECIPE:

SADDLE OF VENISON WITH CHESTNUT POLENTA AND QUINCE PRESERVES

PREPARATION TIME: 50 MINUTES
COOKING TIME: 3 HOURS, 20 MINUTES
INCLUDING 3 HOURS FOR THE QUINCES
TO SERVE: 4

INGREDIENTS

For the saddle of venison
· Two fillets of a saddle of venison (see below)
· 4 tablespoons (50 g) butter
· 4 tablespoons (50 ml) poivrade sauce
· 12 raisins in brandy
· 1 heaping tablespoon mixed nuts (hazelnuts, pistachios, almonds)
· 1 heaping tablespoon almond pralines
· 1 heaping tablespoon chocolate-coated almonds
· Salt and pepper

For the preserved quinces
· 4 quinces
· Juice of half a lemon
· 2 pounds, 7 ounces (1.1 kg) sugar
· 12 cloves
· 2 tablespoons (30 g) butter
· 1 pinch of saffron

For the polenta
· 5 tablespoons (55 g) fine, quick-cooking cornmeal
· 4 tablespoons (50 g) celery purée, defrosted
· 1 cup (250 g) unsweetened chestnut purée
· 4 tablespoons (50 ml) light cream
· 4 teaspoons (20 g) butter
· Salt and pepper

METHOD

At least 3 hours before, prepare the quinces. Wash them, leaving the skins on, quarter them, discard the core and seeds, and sprinkle with lemon juice to prevent the flesh turning brown. Combine the sugar with 3 quarts (3 liters) water, add the cloves, and bring to the boil. Add the quinces, reduce the heat, and simmer for 3 hours. Drain the quinces, reserving the poaching liquid. To make the polenta, combine in a saucepan the celery purée and chestnut purée and season with salt and pepper. Place in a bain-marie and cook, stirring for 10 minutes. Pour onto a damp, cold work surface or cookie sheet, spreading it with a spatula to a depth of ½ inch (1 cm). Refrigerate it until it has set. Lightly sauté the quinces in a saucepan in the butter until they color. Drain off the grease, add a little of their cooking liquid and a pinch of saffron.

Cut the polenta into small rectangles measuring around 1 x 2 inches (2 x 5 cm). Melt 4 teaspoons (20 g) butter in a nonstick skillet and sauté them on each side until they color. Warm the raisins in a little of their alcohol and drain them. Coarsely chop or grind the dried fruits, pralines, and chocolate almonds.

Season the venison fillets with salt and pepper. Heat the butter in a large skillet until it foams, then sauté the fillets on high heat all over for 3 minutes. Reduce the heat and cook for another 2 minutes. Degrease the pan, cover it with aluminum foil, and leave to rest for 5 minutes. Then cut into thick rounds. Reheat the poivrade sauce.

Arrange the rounds of venison on heated serving plates and sprinkle with the nuts

Serve with the polenta, quinces, raisins, and poivrade.

The saddle of venison iconsists of two fillets on either side of the spinal column. Once boned there should be 3 pounds, 5 ounces (1.5 kg) of meat. The fillets are small and they cook quickly because venison, with its short fibers, should be served very rare.

VALERIA PICCINI

MONTEMERANO, ITALY

IN TUSCANY, WHERE THERE ARE LANDSCAPES REMINISCENT OF FRANCE'S CAMARGUE,
VINEYARDS BY THE SEA, UNSPOILED COUNTRYSIDE,
AND STORYBOOK VILLAGES, LIES THE RESTAURANT RUN BY VALERIA PICCINI.

In southwestern Tuscany, just an hour from Rome and two hours from Florence, stands an isolated village named Montemerano. Surrounded by natural parkland, it features a breed of cattle characterized by long, slender, lyre-shaped horns, wild boars, and an spoiled, swampy terrain guarded by mounted *Butteri*—the local cowherds who wear long leather coats rubbed with linseed oil. In the background stand lovely hills dotted with impressive cliff-side villages, Etruscan tombs (similar to those at Poggo Prisca near Sovan), vineyards, and the Saturnia hot springs.

This is walking country. The roads are winding, the many hills steep, and the paths tortuous. The villages—such as Pitigliano, Sorano, or Scansano (a medieval outpost with a fine wine museum)—are perched like fortresses on spurs of volcanic rock. The gourmet capital of the region is the city of Monterano near the Gorello hot springs, where the cure takes place outdoors in huge, petrified vats containing therapeutic waters that reach temperatures of 98.6°F (37°C).

Crooked streets rise upward into the town center, to the church of Sano di Pietro, with its polyptych, and the many fine-food shops around it. The town baker produces delicious, fresh, unsalted breads—some containing black olives—that fill the street with fragrance every morning. The town's star attraction is definitely the restaurant run by Valeria Piccini, a culinary monarch in her vigorous mid-forties who, for more than twenty years past, has stood behind her mother-in-law's stove courageously learning and then practicing, on her own, everything the latter had to teach—and more.

Her restaurant is called Da Caino—a tribute to her father-in-law, Maurizio Caino. Welcoming guests to the restaurant is the task of Piccini's husband, an enthusiastic wine expert. He created a fantastic wine cellar in cavities dug out of sheer rock, where his regal wines— some of the best vintages in the world (Krug Clos du Mesnil, a Spanish Vega Sicilia Unico, French Châteaux Margaux, Latour, and Petrus, plus a rare Le Pin Merlots from Chili and the fine new vintages from California)—share shelf space with select regional Tuscan vintages. All of them are stored in generous numbers.

Valeria Piccini and her husband Maurizio (facing page, top) have turned Da Caino into the place to be in southwestern Tuscany. Top: Valeria with local cattle. This former chemical engineer now creates subtle dishes that just melt in the mouth. Examples include her splendid lamb chops (facing page, bottom) and pecorino tortelli being prepared (above) and completed (preceding page).

There's a wine merchant called Per Bacco offering regional vintages such as a fruity Ansonica white or a ruby red made from Sangiovese rootstock, a Cabernet from the Parrina estate, and a highly appealing Morellino di Scansano red from the lovely Elisabetta Geppeto of La Fattoria le Pupille. Also available are homemade jams and condiments, olive oils, and gourmet coffees such as Jamaica Blue Mountain—sold freshly ground in either mild or strong versions.

The premises also offer guests a choice of three bedrooms, all tastefully decorated with antique furnishings and fine fabrics, and the kind of reading room you might find in a friend's country home—all of which lend unique charm to a deceptively simple setting. Lastly, there are two tiny dining rooms accommodating some twenty people (no more), who are treated to a festival of fine taste.

Six assistants work in silent concentration beside Valeria Piccini in her small but tidy culinary laboratory, visible behind a glass picture window. The best products from Tuscany—from the coast, the hills, and elsewhere—are brought together here for the confection of wonderful dishes.

The fact is that Valeria (who originally studied chemistry) came by chance—or inclination—to the world of cuisine, in which she didn't actually have any formal training. On the other hand, she's an enlightened traveler who, in the company of her perspicacious companion Maurizio, has been everywhere and seen everything. She's an attentive diner herself—knowledgeable, thoughtful, and eager to be impressed—retaining useful lessons, avoiding pitfalls, fleeing false chic like the plague, seeking genuine tastes and pure flavors for the creation of her special brand of cuisine.

Some of her unique dishes are inspired by Tuscany, of course; others by trips to Catalonia. The latter include her fantastic cod tripe with beans and bacon in an emulsion of tiny Sicilian Pachino tomatoes, which boasts a frank, uncomplicated taste. The ideas for her dishes reflect the local style—nothing pretentious, very few sauces, a pronounced penchant for variety meats, and a gift for the kind of unambiguous flavors that are obviously the result of a scientific combination of exact tastes with no false notes.

Depending on the time of year and the season, offerings might include a ricotta mousse with a meltingly delicious garnish of tomato and pesto; sautéed veal sweetbreads with asparagus tips and balsamic vinegar; cannoli stuffed with kid and served with a purée of peas and ham; papardelli with mild garlic, rosemary, Parmesan cheese, and minced guinea hen; and lamb chops delicately combined with cockscombs and larded with bacon, served with a purée of leeks, artichokes, and beef marrow. Or, again, "severed" pigeon with a "shroud" of chives and port sauce; boar larded with taggiashe olives, and pecorino tortelli with beans and foie gras in a broth of stewing chicken and artichokes.

Readers will have understood by this time that there's never a dull moment at this restaurant run by the imaginative Valeria Piccini—who's nonetheless careful to remain rooted in local tradition. Her one touch of elegance are the elaborate desserts that seem almost out of place as part of this wonderfully great and simple Italian cuisine. For example, the ginger parfait with grated grapefruit rind; the frozen almond and walnut praline with shredded apples and raisins marinated in rum, and the many variations on crunchy bitter or sweet chocolate—as mousse, ice cream, with Amarena sauce, with Cognac cream and yogurt sorbet, or with candied oranges and Grand Marnier.

We rest our case and withdraw. But before we go, we must say a word about the fine Maremma wines skillfully presented by Maurizio and the couple's son, Andrea. This father-son team does ample justice to the culinary expertise of the great Valeria Piccini.

LAMB CHOPS WITH LEEK PURÉE
AND BEEF MARROW

PREPARATION TIME: 1 HOUR
COOKING TIME: 90 MINUTES
TO SERVE: 6

INGREDIENTS
· 3 tender lamb chops
· 2 carrots
· 2 white onions
· 2 celery stalks
· 1 cup (250 ml) strong dry red wine
· 3 leeks
· 3 ½ ounces (100 g) goose foie gras
· 6 cockscombs
· 2 red onions
· 18 thin slices Cinta Senese guanciale
· 6 pieces beef marrow
· Extra-virgin olive oil
· 4 ounces (125 g) lard
· Salt and black pepper

METHOD
Have the butcher bone the loin of lamb (the upper part of the chine) and reserve the chops. Use the bones to make a broth, using 1 quart (1 liter) water, 1 carrot, 1 white onion, 1 celery stalk, and the red wine. Cook for 30 minutes. Trim and thinly slice the white part of the leeks and blanch them for 15 minutes in water on low heat. Season with salt. Cook the foie gras for 3 minutes on each side in a skillet. Blend in a food processor with the leeks. Remove and keep warm. Blanch the cockscombs in a traditional vegetable stock made with the rest of the vegetables. Thinly slice the cockscombs and add them to the broth. Cook for 30 minutes then slice the cockscombs and add them. Slice the red onions into 18 rounds. Heat 2 tablespoons oil in a skillet and sauté the onion. Season them with salt. In a cast-iron pan, heat 12 tablespoon oil and cook the beef marrow until browned. Remove from the pan and keep warm. Season the lamb chops with salt and pepper. Cook them on high heat on a skillet for a few minutes, or until browned. Complete the cooking in a preheated 400°F (200°C) oven for 5 minutes. Cut the Cinta Senese guanciale slices into pieces about 1 inch (2–2.5 cm) thick. Cover them with thin slices of the lard. Arrange three rounds of red onion on one side of a serving platter, then add the leek purée and place a slice of marrow on top. Pour the sauce containing the cockscombs in the center of the disk. Slice the lamb chops and arrange the slices on top.

CORNELIA POLETTO

HAMBURG, GERMANY

LATIN FANTASY AND GERMANIC RIGOR COMBINE IN RECIPES
THAT BRING THE BEST OUT OF FINE DAILY MARKET PRODUCE.

She's blonde, bubbly, and beautiful, and Hamburg born and bred. She spent two years with Heinz Winkler, the triple-starred South Tyrolean chef in Aschau in Bavaria, learning all the tricks of modern cuisine. She fine-tuned her skills for three years back home, working with Anna Sgroi at Anna e Sebastiano. Then Cornelia Poletto set up on her own, working with the shrewd, clever Remiggio, her handsome Italian husband from Udine.

Their partnership—one product of which is their little girl, Paola—is a union of water and fire, Germanic rigor and Latin extravagance. And that is just what we find in the sober restaurant opened under their name in 2000. Its two rooms are all dressed in white. There is a pleasing Germano-Franco-Italian atmosphere, evocative of whatever was best at the daily market, transported enthusiastically and skillfully onto the plates. The desserts may provoke recollections from childhood—particularly the famous quenelles of rhubarb semolina with smooth vanilla ice cream. The love for fine produce from both sides of the Alps is evident.

Cornelia Poletto, née Diedrich, is thirty-three years old and full of drive. She plays wonderfully at combining clean, pure flavors. Her cooking is all about finding concentrations of freshness, mischievousness, and lightness. She will often come out into the restaurant to say as much, to explain the thinking behind a starter, or carve a fish, like the splendid sea bass baked in salt with a cauliflower or fennel purée, as dictated by her thought for the day.

The fashionable district of Eppendorf has been colonized by latterday yuppies, antique shops, and interior decoration boutiques. Hamburg's successful businessfolk—or *Pfeffersäcke* ("sacks of pepper")—have a reputation for being severe, Lutheran, and in too much of a hurry to stop for lunch. Cornelia has managed to get them to come into her restaurant. Her lunch menu changes every day. This morning, for instance, she came up with a little monkfish saltimbocca with lentils and balsamic vinegar, slices of milk-fed veal with cabbage, and a *fromage blanc* iced mousse, which she will serve with freshly stewed rhubarb. Simplicity itself, and it goes down a treat.

They will all be wanting to come back this evening, for the poached veal fillet with marinated white asparagus, or pan-fried scallops with diced mango, or warm liver with apple and a salad with white truffle dressing. As for pasta, either agnolotti or tortelloni carbonara with a delicate egg sauce and the South Tyrolean *speck*. Or risotto with asparagus, mint and wild prawns. The baby chicken with ceps and celeriac in a Barolo sauce is a dish which sums her up: typical produce from the north of Germany, "seasoned" with Italian flavors.

Nobody could be blonder than Cornelia, save her daughter Paola. Nobody could be more charming, in an Italian way, than the handsome Remiggio, with his silvery temples. He talks volubly in any language—he once worked for a top London hotel when the city was in its gourmet infancy. He is delighted to see Italian food triumphing everywhere today, particularly in northern Europe.

Of the few stars to be awarded to women by the German *Michelin* guide, this one, bestowed only two years after it opened, is undeniably deserved by this charming and discreet place, located under a yellow façade in a busy avenue. Who couldn't love the Polettos?

THE ATTRACTIVE GERMAN WOMAN AND HER ITALIAN HUSBAND (BELOW) HAVE MADE THIS RESTAURANT, WITH ITS PALE-COLORED DECOR (FACING PAGE, BELOW AND TOP RIGHT), FAMOUS EVEN THOUGH IT'S A LONG WAY FROM THE HAMBURG CITY CENTER. THE CUISINE IS A MIXTURE OF GERMAN, FRENCH, AND ITALIAN, SUCH AS THIS ASPARAGUS AND WILD SHRIMP RISOTTO (BELOW RIGHT), TORTELLINI ALLA CARBONARA (FACING PAGE, ABOVE LEFT), AND THE TYROLEAN VARIATION OF STRAWBERRY ICE CREAM WITH RHUBARB (PRECEDING PAGE, TOP).

CORNELIA POLETTO'S RECIPE:
HOMEMADE TORTELLINI ALLA CARBONARA

PREPARATION TIME: 30 MINUTES
COOKING TIME: 3 MINUTES
RESTING TIME: 1 HOUR
TO SERVE: 4

INGREDIENTS
For the pasta dough
· 1 cup (125 g) farina (cream of wheat)
· ⅔ cup (75 g) all-purpose flour
· 2 eggs
· Pinch of salt

For the filling
· 8 egg yolks
· 4 tablespoons (50 g) grated pecorino cheese
· 2 tablespoons whipped cream
· 1 egg white, lightly beaten
· Salt, freshly ground pepper, and grated nutmeg

Pancetta sauce
· 4 slices salted pork belly (pancetta)
· 1 shallot
· 1 garlic clove
· 4 tablespoons (50 g) butter
· 2 tablespoons (30 ml) dry white wine
· ⅓ cup (100 ml) chicken stock
· 2 tablespoons chopped flat-leaved parsley
· 2 tablespoons grated Parmesan cheese
· Salt and freshly ground black pepper

METHOD
Combine all the ingredients for the pasta dough and knead until smooth.

Wrap the dough in plastic wrap and leave to rest for at least one hour in the refrigerator.

To make the filling, beat the egg yolks in a double-boiler or bain-marie until they are foaming. Remove from the heat and continue to beat until they have cooled. Add the pecorino cheese, season with salt and pepper then add the whipped cream. Refrigerate until required.

Roll out the pasta dough as thinly as possible in a pasta machine and form 3-inch (8-cm) squares. In the center of each square place a teaspoon of the filling. Brush the edges with beaten egg white, then fold over the square and shape into tortellini.

Slice the pancetta into strips. Peel and coarsely chop the shallot and garlic. Melt the butter in a skillet and sauté the pancetta, then add the shallot and garlic. Deglaze the pan with white wine and reduce it lightly. Add the stock. Bind with a little butter, then add the chopped parsley. Season with salt and pepper.

Poach the tortellini in salted boiling water for 3 minutes, then add them to the pancetta sauce and arrange on plates. Sprinkle with Parmesan cheese before serving.

MARIE-FRANCE PONSARD

BELLEVILLE, FRANCE

ALTHOUGH SHE IS THE KIND OF PERSON WE NATURALLY ASSOCIATE WITH LYON,
SHE WAS BORN AND BRED IN LORRAINE. AT HER RESTAURANT, LOCATED BETWEEN
NANCY AND METZ, SHE EXEMPLIFIES TODAY'S FEMALE CHEF—THE KIND CUSTOMERS
TAKE INTO THEIR HEARTS. A FUNDAMENTALLY MODEST WOMAN, DESPITE HER MICHELIN STARS,
SHE OFFERS A CUISINE THAT IS REGIONAL AND TRADITIONAL.

Self-effacing and unassuming, she's too often forgotten when people describe the delights of her region. And yet, she's the *Mère* Brazier of Lorraine. Her name is Marie-France Ponsard, she's the daughter of a pork butcher in Pont-à-Mousson, and has lived and worked for over a quarter of a century in Belleville, where she delights natives and visitors alike with her original ideas, her taste for glowing simplicity and premium products, and her seasonal takes on fish, vegetables, and poultry.

People stopping long enough to sample a meal at her Bistroquet, just a step away from the Moselle, are treated to an object lesson in how to do things right. Her foie gras, Meuse pigeon, braised Challans duck, fresh fish from Brittany, wild winter cress, Mirabelle plum brandy (from the local distiller in Lucey); her fabulous mixed warm tripe platter (calf's head, foot, and tongue in a *ravigote* sauce), and her Croisic shrimp ravioli with chervil—all constitute definitive statements on tradition and how it can be subtly modernized.

Cooking seems to come naturally to this inspired self-taught chef, who belongs in the company of colleagues who make a point of exploiting what's best in the market at any one time. Like her famed predecessors Mère Brazier at Lyon and the Col de la Luère; or Jean Ducloux, Dumaine's jovial successor at the Greuze in Tournus, she offers only what is listed on her extensive and meticulously detailed menu. Here is food that, as Bocuse would put it, "doesn't have to be decoded."

An additional asset in the dining room is the deft and entertaining Jean Ponsard. Like an actor performing in a culinary commedia dell'arte, he confides knowing asides to diners on the riches of the day's market and the menu. With his broad smile and luxuriant mustache, Jean Ponsard is indeed the house's presiding majordomo, its deus ex machina. It was he who redecorated the somewhat rudimentary 1900s bistro in the Montmartre-eclectic retro-chic style, and it is also he who serves as an expert maître d'hôtel, transforming his dining room into a

MARIE-FRANCE PONSARD IS THE DAUGHTER OF A CHARCUTIER WHO NOW LIVES ON THE BANKS OF THE MOSELLE. SHE HAS REMAINED TRUE TO HER LORRAINE ORIGINS. HERE SHE CAN BE SEEN LOOKING AFTER DUCKS AT THE BREEDER'S (FACING PAGE, TOP) AND IN HER KITCHEN (TOP RIGHT). PIKE PERCH IN RED WINE (ABOVE) OR WITH POTATOES (FACING PAGE, BOTTOM) AND SOUFFLÉ WITH LORRAINE MIRABELLE PLUMS (PRECEDING PAGE) ARE JUST TWO OF THE DELICIOUS DISHES THAT DELIGHT HER SATISFIED CLIENTELE, WHO COME TO CELEBRATE IN HER LOVELY DINING ROOM, WITH ITS ART DECO FEATURES (TOP LEFT).

delightful work of performance art. He also helps with the desserts, which can be classic or modern but are always brilliant and delicious. They add en extra dimension—sweet but not too sweet—to this restaurant where everyone feels right at home.

What are some of the outstanding items on Marie-France Ponsard's menu? Scallops fresh from the shell, marinated in olive oil and seasoned with ginger; an appealing cod and lobster combination in a savory broth; and duck with firm yet juicy sour cherries accompanied by delectable baby turnips. Here are meals of infinite finesse, often featuring appealingly light, vinegary sauces that appear to aid digestion even as you eat.

Knowing such treats are in store, diners are eager to make their selections from the carefully orchestrated wine list: a Condrieu de Cuilleron with a bouquet of peach and apricot; or another great Médoc, Palmer's Alter Ego; a Laffitte Carruades, or a Dame de Montrose.

The extensive gourmet menu provides an accurate idea of what to expect, boasting a judicious combination of the modern and the classic: scallops with Avruga seeds; Lorraine-style foie gras with mildly spiced caramelized potatoes; freshly caught fish with beurre blanc and spring vegetables. The meal ends with uncured Meuse goat cheese and bacon, followed by a selection of peerless desserts.

Something not to be missed is the hot soufflé with Mirabelle-plum brandy: light and airy, it's a model of its kind and represents a nod to regional traditions. However, no one should ignore the day's specials, which—depending on the inspiration of the moment—might be a round of mango topped with chocolate and garnished with a purée of passion fruit; or a Piedmont hazelnut crust with caramelized bananas, amber Java milk chocolate, and caramel butter.

At the conclusion of this bravura performance, diners offer heartfelt thanks to host Jean, and kiss Marie-France on both cheeks. As they leave, many remark that Lyon itself would be hard-pressed to boast a culinary "*mère*" of this caliber. Lorraine is indeed blessed in having the Ponsards.

MARIE-FRANCE PONSARD'S RECIPE:

PIKE PERCH FROM THE LOIRE WITH POTATO SCALES AND WHITE BUTTER SAUCE

PREPARATION TIME: 35 MINUTES
COOKING TIME: 15 MINUTES
TO SERVE: 4

INGREDIENTS
· 1 large pike perch
· 3 tablespoons (40 g) clarified butter, melted
· 2 tablespoons (30 ml) white butter sauce (see below)
For the potato scales
· 4 small potatoes
For the white butter sauce
· 1 shallot, minced
· Several sprigs tarragon
· 6 tablespoons (80 ml) white wine
· 6 tablespoons (80 ml) white wine vinegar
· 6 tablespoons (80 g) butter, cut into pieces
· Sea salt and pepper

METHOD
Wash the pike perch and remove the skin and bones. Cut the fillets into 4 large portions. Season them with salt and pepper.
Wash the potatoes and slice them lengthwise on a mandolin slicer to a thickness of 1/16 inch (2 mm).
Boil the salted water in a saucepan and add the sliced potatoes. Cook for 2 minutes. Cover the fish fillets with the potato slices, and brush them with melted clarified butter. Lightly butter an ovenproof dish and place the pike perch in it. Bake in a preheated 450°F (230°C) oven for about 15 minutes.
Meanwhile, prepare the sauce. In a sauté pan, cook the shallot, tarragon, sea salt, pepper, white wine and white wine vinegar for 15 minutes on high heat. When the liquid has reduced, gradually incorporate the pieces of butter. Remove the fish fillets from the oven and coat them with the butter sauce.

CARME RUSCALLEDA

SANT POL DE MAR, SPAIN

ON THE COAST SOME TWENTY-FIVE MILES (FORTY KILOMETERS) NORTH OF BARCELONA,
SPAIN'S OUTSTANDING WOMAN CHEF—THE DISCREET AND CHEERFUL
CARME RUSCALLEDA—PRODUCES A TECHNICALLY ACCOMPLISHED CUISINE
THAT PROUDLY REFLECTS ITS NATIVE ROOTS.

This slender woman with short hair, whose facial expression can be simultaneously serious and smiling, cuts an unusual figure among her peers. An explosive presence in the company of Europe's great chefs, she boasts the only three-star rating in Spain where, when it comes to fine restaurants, prejudice against women is still the rule. Apart from Ruscalleda, only one other woman chef in Spain can boast a star at all: Toni Vicente of Santiago de Compostela in Galicia, at the other end of the country, has one. Does this mean that, on the Iberian peninsula, women confine their culinary expertise to the home, and never work professionally? Or that they're inhibited in the exercise of their technical prowess, their instinct for innovation, and the imaginative combination of rare and perfectly matched flavors?

Carme Ruscalleda, the wholly self-taught daughter of farmers who are still active as pork butchers in the little seaside village of Sant Pol de Mar, executes a highly personal brand of cuisine—delicate, light, resourceful, technically expert. She's not afraid of challenging established traditions, even though she rarely comes right out and says so. On the other hand, although she continues to use local products—fish, of course; and also meat and game from the surrounding hillsides, she has abandoned the old-fashioned custom of lengthy simmering.

Catalonia—native land of artists such as Salvador Dalí, Antoni Tapiès, and Ferran Adria— is home to the El Bulli restaurant, where culinary genius Adria has revolutionized ideas of what fine cuisine should be in the twenty-first century, and drawn on the local penchant for using artistic creativity and novelty as a weapon accessible to all. Here is an unusual woman who, in 1998, at a modest seaside hotel with a tiny garden wedged beside a branch railway line in Sant Pol, around forty kilometers (twenty-five miles) from Barcelona, tentatively opened a small "family" restaurant. Sant Pol (population 2,400) boasts a few unpretentious houses and some more modern ones along the coast and the beach. Carme, who of course comes from a family of farmers, is married to Toni Balam, whose people are fishermen. When she first opened her little

CARME RUSCALLEDA IS EVERYWHERE AT ONCE.
PAGE 140: ON THE SEA SHORE, WITH A FRESHLY CAUGHT
SCORPION FISH. SHE CHOOSES THE VEGETABLES FROM HER
SUPPLIERS (TOP), ADDS A FINISHING TOUCH TO A DISH
PREPARED BY ONE OF HER KITCHEN HANDS (ABOVE), AND
SKILLFULLY PRESENTS HER CRAYFISH RAVIOLI (FACING
PAGE, TOP). HER DELICIOUS CATALAN CUISINE CAN BE
ENJOYED ON THE TERRACE, WHICH HAS A SEA VIEW (FACING
PAGE, BOTTOM), AND HER SURPRISING CHEESE PLATTER IS A
HIT (PRECEDING PAGE).

restaurant, she limited service to the evenings. Now, fifteen years later, she has won three stars, the recognition of her peers, and acclaim from Spanish restaurant critics.

Despite her success, Carme Ruscalleda continues to practice craftsmanship on a manageable scale. Twenty-three people working in the kitchen serve a maximum of thirty-five diners, no more. The restaurant does not therefore turn a large profit, but its labor-intensive quality is beyond dispute. The youthful waitstaff, dressed in uniforms with white collars and black buttons, serve diners a cuisine reflecting the tides and the seasons.

The dining room is small but well lit, with a view of the sea and the dark blue benches in the garden. In the vast laboratory of the efficiently organized basement kitchen, Ruscalleda's assistants go quietly about their work, scaling just-caught fish, plucking poultry, preparing fresh, seasonal vegetables. The restaurant's handsome white plates are delivered to their destinations as if they were precious gems. First come the appetizers, mini-portions of chicken galantine in aspic with almonds and salad; smoked porgy with lentils, honey, and mustard; quail fillets with dried apricots, raisins, pine nuts, and salty nougat, garnished with preserved tomato and orange.

And then begins the serious part of the meal. This phase starts off with pigeon consommé and stuffed pig's tail garnished with vegetable chips and fresh truffles. This is followed by scallops with artichokes and tender potatoes, and then the meal's centerpiece—which might be a masterly and aromatic blend of flavors from land and sea: transparent ravioli stuffed with prawns, mixed herbs, spinach, port, and Stilton. Next? Sea cucumbers (known here as *espardenyes*) with smooth mashed potatoes, zucchini, pesto, prawn tails, and artichokes presented three ways—with salt cod and egg yolk, with quince and currents, and lastly with a loin of rabbit with pepper sauce and potatoes *brunoise*.

The cheese board is an exercise in style executed against an illustrated backdrop featuring five types of raw-milk cheese, each with its respective accompaniment. Cheese made from the milk of Asturian cows is served with bread, young wine and sugar; aged Mimolette with a milkshake flavored with breadfruit and toasted hazelnuts; goat cheese with beeswax; Mignon des Ardennes with sorbet and escarole; Irish blue cheese with Banyuls aspic. Dessert begins with a selection of figs, honey, walnuts, and olives, inspired by a traditional Catalan song. These introductory treats are followed by lemon cream, a delicate mille-feuille with angel hair, licorice crunch, and white chocolate flavored with raspberries, or dark chocolate flavored with orange.

Creativity is expertly controlled; flavors retain all of their inherent personality. The wines, which come from the region between Penedès and Tarragona, provide a lusty counterpoint to the food—just like Carme herself, who appears at the end of the feast she has conducted like a savory symphony to ask if everything was all right. The sea stretches out below. The railway line stands nearby, waiting to whisk diners directly back to Barcelona. But, for the time being, no one's thoughts are on the city. They could stay right here forever.

CRAYFISH RAVIOLI
WITH CRISPY NOODLES

PREPARATION TIME: 1 HOUR, 30
MINUTES

COOKING TIME: 55 MINUTES

TO SERVE: 4

INGREDIENTS

For the ravioli
· 16 crayfish (tails shelled,
  heads and shells reserved for
  the oil and noodle broth)
· 4 sheets lasagne
· ⅓ cup (100 g) fresh sheep's
  milk cheese
· 2 tablespoons fennel seed
· 2 tablespoons basil
· 2 tablespoons minced shallots
· ⅔ cup (150 g) preserved
  tomatoes
· ⅔ cup (100 g) fresh spinach
· 2 small garlic cloves
· 4 teaspoons (20 g) butter
· Salt and pepper

For the spiced oil
· Heads of 8 crayfish
· 4 small hot chili peppers
  and 1 dried chili pepper
· 2 tablespoons Cognac
· 1 scant cup (200 ml) olive oil

For the noodles
· 6 ounces (150 g) spaghetti
· Head and shells of 8 crayfish
· 4 tablespoons olive oil
· 4 tomatoes, skinned and crushed
· 2 garlic cloves, crushed
· ⅔ cup (150 ml) sherry
· 2 sprigs of parsley

For the sauce
· 1 ⅓ cup (150 g) Parmesan cheese
· 1 ½ cups (350 ml) light cream

METHOD

Shell the crayfish, refrigerate
the tails, and save the heads.
To prepare the spiced oil,
sauté the 8 crayfish heads in a
little olive oil, stirring and
crushing them. Seed and chop
the dried chili pepper and
fresh chili peppers and add
them, together with the
Cognac and olive oil.
Continue to cook on low heat
for around 10 minutes. Pour
off the liquid and strain it.

To make the broth for
cooking the noodles, sauté the
rest of the heads and shells in
4 tablespoons olive oil. Add
the crushed tomatoes, garlic
cloves, sherry, and parsley.
Cook for 10 minutes, then
add 3 quarts (3 liters) water,
and cook for 20 minutes.
Season with salt and pepper,
then strain. Pour the liquid
into a saucepan and use it to
cook the spaghetti for
5 minutes more than the
normal cooking time
indicated on the package.
Drain and leave to cool to
room temperature.

To make the ravioli, mash
the fennel seed, basil, and
shallots into the sheep's milk
cheese. Grind the preserved
tomatoes in a food processor
with three-quarters of the
spiced oil. Cook the lasagne
sheets for a little longer than
indicated on the package.
Preheat the oven to 375°F
(190°C).

To make the sauce, mix the
Parmesan cheese in a pan with
the light cream and bring to
the boil. Trim the fresh
spinach leaves and cook them
on high heat in the butter.
Season with salt. Cover the
lasagne sheets, first with a
layer of spinach, then with
the spicy tomato, and finally
with a layer of sheep's milk
cheese. Take the salted and
peppered crawfish and season
with the rest of the spiced oil,
and the chopped garlic cloves.
Close each ravioli into a
package and bake for
3 minutes.

Meanwhile, heat the olive oil
and fry the noodles to make
them crunchy.

Remove the ravioli from the
oven, and arrange them on
the hot Parmesan sauce.
Serve with the crispy noodles.

REINE SAMMUT

LOURMARIN, FRANCE

THE KITCHEN OVER WHICH SHE REIGNS SUPREME IS IN THE LUBÉRON.
IS SHE A NATIVE OF PROVENCE? NOT AT ALL. BUT SHE HAS FITTED SO NATURALLY
INTO THE AREA, EVERYONE NOW CONSIDERS HER THE BEST REPRESENTATIVE OF THE REGION.
THIS IS THE PORTRAIT OF A FAMILY.

The culinary star of Provence? A diminutive native of Lorraine from Frison, who's sensitive, timid, self-taught, and was raised in the depths of the Vosges forest. Because her father was a customs inspector, she was constantly on the move between the Moselle and Sarre regions—but if you meet Reine Sammut, don't ask her whether she spent her childhood between Sarreguemines and Sarralbe in Alsace. When she married, she fell under the benign influence of her in-laws, who were half-Maltese and half-Tunisian, although her basic style is Provençal. When she joined forces with her friend Fulvio Pierangelino, it didn't take her any time at all to decide to leave with him for Italy, where he works wonders in Tuscany at Gambero Rosso, the celebrated two-star restaurant in San Vincenzo. It was there she developed her wonderful ideas for such treats as tomato ravioli and shellfish risotto.

And, to tell the truth, no one has been more successful than this newcomer in capturing the spirit of southern cuisine, in producing dishes emblematic of the area's culinary highpoints. Her cool head, modest demeanor, and cheerful smile suit her perfectly. With her Mediterranean chef's hat clamped firmly on her head, this solid and skillful technician—who learned everything she knows from her mother-in-law and then honed what she had learned on her own—practices a cuisine typical of the provincial south with ease.

She artfully manipulates the mysteries of her craft, delighting both regular and chance customers with squilla, shellfish, fine seafood, baby squid, herb-flavored braised meat, and luscious desserts reflecting a return to native roots. No doubt about it, this active and inquisitive queen of the kitchen has gold in her fingertips.

At her restaurant, husband Guy plays the role of bubbling Amphitryon, boasting the persona of a 1960s rock star who refuses to age, enthusiastically promoting Reine's menus. The Lubéron region finds expression here in ways that are both rustic and sophisticated, with dishes reflecting the color of the days, the seasons, and the markets of Pertuis, Apt, and Cadenet. Fine Lauris asparagus, Tricastin truffles, Cadenet almonds, veal gizzards, and herbs and vegetables from local truck farmers are right at home at La Fenière.

GUY AND REINE SAMMUT (ABOVE RIGHT) HAVE ACHIEVED
THEIR DREAM: THEY HAVE MOVED THEIR BISTRO,
LA FENIÈRE (ABOVE LEFT), FROM THE CENTER OF
LOURMARIN TO A GREEN ESTATE ON THE ROAD TO
CADENET. IT IS A JOY IN SUMMER TO RELAX IN THE
GARDEN, HAVE A LEISURELY RURAL MEAL WITH A GLASS OF
WINE AND THE LOCAL PAPER (FACING PAGE, LEFT).
CRUNCHY CHICKEN WINGS WITH GARLIC IN ASPIC (ABOVE
CENTER), FILLETS OF TUNA WITH PRESSED MULLET ROE
(FACING PAGE, RIGHT), AND CRUNCHY BROUSSE CANNOLI
WITH LEMON PEEL (PRECEDING PAGE) ARE JUST SOME OF
THE NEW-WAVE PROVENÇAL DELICACIES PERFECTED BY
REINE SAMMUT.

To experience perfect bliss, all you have to do is check into one of the establishment's simple but attractive, plain but colorful bedrooms, and then wander down to a table on the delightful, sunny terrace. Choices for dinner might include pea velouté with morels and creamed bacon; baby zucchini with stuffed zucchini flowers and garnished with a chive cream; fried pressed eggplant with sweet peppers; tomato conserve with sardine fillets in olive oil. And, of course, the countrified breaded spiced tripe to savor with cumin-flavored puréed chickpeas before going on to a risotto of spring vegetables or tiny cuttlefish with saffron.

And then there's the baked sea bass with candied lemon, stewed kid with delicate white semolina, and brochette of giblets; or the iced calissons (sugar-coated confectionery, a specialty of Aix-en-Provence) with apricot purée and bitter almonds—proving that something great is happening in this light, uncluttered house opening on to the lavender fields, the Lubéron mountain range, the nearby valley of the Durance, the Calavon, and the Aiguebrun. Youthful and attentive servers are enthusiastic partners in this endeavor, enhancing the dining experience with their verve. Wines from Provence, the Rhône Valley, and neighboring Ventoux and Var—plus the new Lubéron whites, reds, and rosés—provide a piquant counterpoint to the meal.

This sun-drenched cuisine harmoniously combines regional ingredients that, for Reine, are musical instruments of rare quality and subtlety. The flavors of Provence—with a nod at neighboring Italy, the taste of the Mediterranean in all its majesty, traditional dishes that have been updated and energized—all that and more can be found on the terrace, bathed in sunshine and with a lovely view, or in the well-lit dining room with its contemporary decor.

The seafood bouillabaisse; ricotta tortellini with squilla shrimp; medley of lamb including a roast rack of ribs, kidneys, braised sweetbreads, and truffled trotters; truffled brocciù, and salad of winter cress and endive; each have their gourmet tale to tell. To follow come wonderful desserts recalling childhood delights, such as the admirable baked Alaska—a traditional dessert in Lorraine, here enhanced with the addition of local truffles and flamed Provençal brandy. Then there's the puff-pastry fougasse griddle cake, with orange-flower-flavored fruit, or the subtle compote of apples and pears with cinnamon—all lessons in unpretentious lightness.

The best Lubéron wines (such as the noble and glowing red vintage that is the local equivalent of Côte Rôtie) and those from Provence and the Rhône Valley, are ideal accompaniments for a first-class cuisine that is nevertheless accessible, universally appreciated, and experienced as a friendly and supportive gesture of good fellowship. Here, happiness is the warm Lubéron sunlight celebrated by the poets.

REINE SAMMUT'S RECIPE:

TUNA FILLET WITH PRESSED MULLET ROE AND HERBS

PREPARATION TIME: 25 MINUTES
COOKING TIME: 2–3 MINUTES
TO SERVE: 4

INGREDIENTS

· 1 pound, 5 ounces (600 g) tuna fillet
· 1 scant cup (200 ml) olive oil
· ⅓ cup (100 g) baby octopus
· ⅓ cup (100 ml) aged wine vinegar
· 2 tablespoons (30 g) gray mullet roe (bottarga), thinly sliced
· 2 tablespoons (30 g) mixed herbs (dill, chervil, chives), washed, drained, and chopped
· Salt and pepper
· Sea salt and mignonnette pepper

METHOD

Heat some of the olive oil in a skillet and sauté the tuna fillet for 2 to 3 minutes on both sides. Then leave to rest and cool. Cut the octopus into strips and blanch them in boiling water for 2 minutes. Sauté them in the rest of the olive oil and season with salt and pepper. Make a dressing with the aged wine vinegar, salt and pepper. Cut the tuna into slices about ¼ inch (5 mm) thick. Arrange 5 slices on each plate. Arrange a slice of roe on each tuna slice. Arrange the octopus on either side of the tuna and add the herbs. Season with the dressing and sprinkle the tuna with sea salt and mignonnette pepper.

NADIA SANTINI

CANNETO SULL'OGLIO, ITALY

THREE-STAR ITALIAN CHEF NADIA SANTINI IS RECOGNIZED BY HER PEERS
AS "THE BEST COOK IN THE WORLD." WITH SANTINI BEHIND THE STOVE, TORTELLI DI ZUCCA,
GUINEA-HEN RAVIOLI, AND OTHER ITALIAN DELICACIES BECOME
THE STUFF OF WHICH EXPERIENCED GOURMETS DREAM.

The tiny village is called Runate and contains just a few lonely houses perched between the plain of the Po River and the green fields around the rice paddies. Between Cremona and Parma, Verona and Mantua, lie numerous little historic towns built around small public squares boasting crenellated towers and skilled craftsmen who turn out marvelous products.

Nearby Zibello is a village famous for its Culatello, the most luscious ham in the world. This is where Parmesan cheese joins hands with its Lombardy cousin, Grano Padano, and where the local almond biscuits known as Sbrisolona are highly prized. In other words, wherever you go here, you discover culinary treasures—and the best one of all is in an ivy-covered mansion with a gate leading straight to paradise. This is Dal Pescatore (Home of the Fisherman).

The house's salons are filled with a disparate collection of books, bibelots, antique tools, and worn skis that make new arrivals feel they're visiting old friends. And there's more: a gleaming parquet floor, pale yellow walls, a colonnaded terrace overlooking an interior garden, comfortable tables for just thirty diners, and affable service. The restaurant's maître d'hôtel, Antonio, is a generous-spirited host, and a good Samaritan attentive to his diners' welfare. Back in the kitchen, his wife Nadia—assisted by Antonio's mother Bruna and the couple's son Giovanni—stands behind the stove concocting wonderful dishes.

This has always been a family business. It was founded by Antonio's grandfather in the 1920s and awarded four knives and forks in the Italian *Michelin Guide* for charm, unpretentious luxury, and comfort in addition to the coveted three stars for cuisine. Only four Italian chefs, including Nadia, have won this honor: Luisa Valazza at Soriso (see p. 164), Annie Feolde (see p. 60), who won hers at the imposing Enoteca Pincchiori in Florence, and, lastly, Alajmo du Calandre in Rubano, near Padua.

Antonio and Nadia Santini exhibit all the enthusiasm and culinary expertise typical of Italy. They direct the Pescatore with a combination of personal charm and seriousness of purpose. Their experience is atypical, however. They were originally students of political science in Milan, where Nadia had also acquired a diploma in food science. They then joined forces to take over the inn run by Antonio's mother Bruna. The latter continues to work in the

Always focused when the going gets hot (below), Nadia Santini is the undisputed star of Italian cuisine. Left: in wooden containers, the different varieties of pasta await the daily service. The bread is ready (facing page, left). A young apprentice brings vegetables, picked to order from the kitchen garden (facing page, right).

kitchen today, demonstrating her characteristic discretion, discipline, and professionalism, punctuated by her legendary silences. Bruna makes all the restaurant's pastas. The self-effacing Nadia—who barely raises her eyes when you speak to her—has taken over everything else, successfully accentuating and extending the house's distinctive style.

In the attractive Runate house, the kitchen was traditionally a woman's domain. Bruna herself replaced Teresa, the wife of grandfather Antonio—a fisherman whose given name has been adopted by today's Antonio. Bruna's husband Giovanni provided the link between dining room and kitchen. Today, the age-old habits of the past endure. A highly gifted and inspired self-taught chef, the divine Nadia relies instinctively on tradition, bringing fresh life to the methods of the past—hand-cut pasta, perfectly timed sauces, short cooking times, carefully calibrated seasonings.

Customers gladly opt for the suggestions of the day, trusting absolutely in the man who calls the tune. Antonio describes the wines perceptively, and discusses the day's specials with precision, familiarizing his guests with the house style. He might suggest as a starter—for example—the celebrated Parmesan-cheese wafers that have gone around the world. And it is not hard to recall the remarks made by Paul Bocuse, who spent three days here, when he was asked what he did. "I ate," he answered, without elaborating—adding only that this is the "best restaurant in the world."

This particular day, there's a salmon and lobster terrine with virgin olive oil and a hint of caviar; eel cooked in its skin and flavored with orange; snail and porcini-mushroom soup with Norcia black-truffle curls. Then there's the fettuccine combined with crisp baby squid and seasonal vegetables, or the risotto flavored with saffron pistils and served with fried Puglian artichokes. Not to mention the tortelli stuffed with buffalo ricotta and country Parmesan cheese flavored with white Alba truffle.

This is truly mouthwatering fare. Diners eagerly look forward to sampling this menu of peasant specialties adapted for noble lords—or the other way round. With the affability of a jovial squire, Antonio suggests a Friuli Sauvignon, a torte from Montevertine in Tuscany, the Barolo Sperss from Gaja in Piedmont or, for dessert, a noble Anselmi Capitel Foscarino Soave from the Veneto region. But first come an array of dishes, including baked sea bass and glazed veal knuckle seasoned with oregano and served with yellow polenta and a mini-purée.

The feast draws to a close with a range of hot and cold desserts: a raisin flan *"fragolino"* with seasonal fruit sorbets, or a crisp, tender, exquisite variation on raw Venezuelan chocolate from the specialist Amadei. This is more than a meal, it's a moment of pure bliss, a succession of dreams, a mellow Lombardy symphony composed by a deft hand in Emilia-Romagna, at a tranquil mansion located in the heart of the Po River plain.

ACCOMPANIED BY BRUNA, HER MOTHER-IN-LAW, NADIA CHECKS THE QUALITY OF THE PASTA, FRESHLY MADE HERE EACH DAY (BELOW AND FACING PAGE, BOTTOM). THE PASTA CONTRIBUTES TO THE MAGNIFICENT QUALITY OF THE HOUSE DISHES. TIME FOR A QUICK DRINK IN THE PARLOR (FACING PAGE, TOP LEFT) BEFORE ENTERING ONE OF THE ELEGANT DINING ROOMS OF THIS BEAUTIFUL COUNTRY HOUSE. TASTE THE PIKE, FRESHLY CAUGHT FROM THE RIVER BEHIND THE HOUSE (FACING PAGE, TOP RIGHT), OR FRUIT WITH A BERRY SAUCE (PAGE 149).

NADIA SANTINI'S RECIPE:

LAKE GARDA PIKE IN OIL WITH PARSLEY, ANCHOVIES, AND SALINA CAPERS

PREPARATION TIME: 20 MINUTES
COOKING TIME: 25 MINUTES
TO SERVE: 4

INGREDIENTS
· 4 slices pike weighing around
  5 ½ ounces (150 g) each
· Juice of half a lemon
· 1 celery stick, sliced
· ½ fennel bulb, sliced
· Salt
For the parsley and caper sauce
· 2 small bunches flat-leaved
  parsley, chopped
· 1 teaspoon chopped capers
· 1 garlic clove, chopped
· ½ salt anchovy, rinsed,
  drained, and chopped
· ⅔ cup (150 ml) extra-virgin
  olive oil from Lake Garda

UTENSILS:
· 1 fish kettle
· 1 saucepan

METHOD
In a skillet, place the slices of
pike and cover with cold water.
Add the lemon juice, celery,
and fennel. Season with salt
and bring to the boil, then
remove from the heat. Leave to
cool while you make the sauce.
In a saucepan, combine the
chopped parsley and capers,
garlic clove and anchovy. Cover
with the extra-virgin olive oil
and bring to the boil. Remove
the pan from the heat as soon
as it boils and pour the contents into a sauceboat to stop
the cooking and retain the
bright green of the parsley.
Remove the pieces of pike from
the cooking water. Remove any
visible bones from the flesh,
using tweezers.
Serve the pike with the sauce
and broiled polenta.

153

ANNA SGROI

HAMBURG, GERMANY

A SICILIAN WHO HAS BROUGHT HER COUNTRY'S CUISINE
TO THE INHABITANTS OF HAMBURG.

She was the first Italian woman chef to be awarded a star in Germany, while at Anna e Sebastiano, located in a very classy part of North Hamburg. Now she has moved closer to the center, set up on her own, and earned another of those rare emblems of excellence. From Sicily—she was born in Alcamo near Palermo—Anna Sgroi has come to breathe life back into Lange Reihe, not far from the station and the Kunsthalle.

Anna's first job was as a hairdresser in Milan. There she met a musician called Sebastiano (now her partner) and also realized that cooking was her true passion. When Sebastiano had to go to the north of Germany to stay with a musician friend, she went along with him. Together they set up Anna e Sebastiano, a stylish and modern restaurant which quickly met with success.

Her thorough knowledge of modern Italian cooking was gleaned from family, friends, and her own intuition. She was set to complete a two-week training course in Milan with Marchesi, the first three-star chef in Italy. She only stayed for three days. From then on Anna has worked alone in her small, modern, eponymous establishment in Lange Reihe. She rarely comes out of the kitchen to see the diners, delegating the task to her sole German waitress.

The space holds about fifteen tables; the odd window looks out onto a small square. It is a clean, white, unfussy setting, with its marble floor, wooden tables, and walls devoid of unnecessary ornamentation. In the evenings there is a crush to get a table at Sgroi. She sets the most delicious menus: seafood salad here, vegetables grilled in olive oil there, risotto *alla trevisana*, spaghetti *alle vongole veraci*, delighting the clientele who come to their table for a trip abroad.

Everything—the oil, the vegetables—is sent from Italy. "Except the potatoes," she points out with a laugh, admitting that German producers have made great progress: her veal comes from Schleswig-Holstein and her poultry from a farm near the Baltic Sea. Hamburg now apparently boasts over two hundred Italian restaurants. "But only five or six are authentic," Anna stipulates, explaining that a great number of her fellow citizens who have emigrated to Germany simply "do pasta in tomato sauce and pizzas, and claim to be making proper Italian food."

The success of that proper Italian food all over Germany—witness the ex-two-star Da Gianni in Mannheim, and several ex-one-stars such as La Vigna in Salzburg, Osteria Enoteca in Frankfurt, Grissini in Mannheim—seems to reflect a need for escape in a country which, after all, is somewhat lacking in sunshine.

Completely self-taught, Anna works in the kitchen with three helpers (German, Finnish, and Sri Lankan). She uses the best ingredients—vegetables, olive oils, seafood, white meats and poultry—from Italy or nearer at hand, and has the finest Italian wines served at the few tables, which quickly fill up in this simple, modern setting. Octopus carpaccio marinated in onions and white wine; Ligurian rabbit ravioli with olives and potatoes; an aromatic and superbly al dente radicchio risotto; ravioli filled with foie gras and spinach; Umbrian *strozzapretti* in a guinea-fowl ragout; fillet of sea bass with fork-mashed potatoes and cress: these are just some of the dishes made possible by her agile approach.

Add to that scallops wrapped in lettuce leaves and seasoned with balsamic vinegar; a delicate turbot with artichokes; crispy duck with polenta—the high-flyers are there too. And in accompaniment, white wines such as Vernaccia di San Gimignano, the Sicilian Regaleali, or reds like a Tuscan Montepulciano or Dolcetto d'Alba from Piedmont. The classic desserts (rich Sicilian cannoli, candied almond tart, lemon mousse with strawberries, figs in red wine with vanilla ice cream, pear and apricot pastry with walnut ice cream) are in tune with the rest: not excessively creative, but rhythmical, delicate, and precise.

Anna has brought Italy to the German restaurant-going public. Their appreciation is made clear in the eager attention Hamburg pays her every evening, in its enthusiasm for international food.

ANNA SGROI IS COMPLETELY SELF-TAUGHT AND IS NEVER AS MUCH AT HOME AS SHE IS IN HER KITCHEN (FACING PAGE, TOP RIGHT). THE SETTING IS CLEAN, WHITE, AND WORKMANLIKE (BELOW LEFT), AND THE CIGAR-AND-LIBRARY CORNER (FACING PAGE, BOTTOM) IS AN AMUSING IDEA. THREE OF HER RECIPES ARE SCALLOP SALAD WITH RED WINE SAUCE (PRECEDING PAGE), PEAR TURNOVER (BELOW RIGHT), AND OCTOPUS CARPACCIO WITH ASPARAGUS AND OYSTER MUSHROOMS (FACING PAGE, TOP LEFT).

ANNA SGROI'S RECIPE:
PEAR AND APRICOT TURNOVER

PREPARATION TIME: 30 MINUTES
COOKING TIME: 35 MINUTES
TO SERVE: 4

INGREDIENTS
· 10 ½ ounces (300 g) puff-pastry dough
· 14 ounces (400 g) Bartlett pears
· 14 ounces (400 g) apricots
· 1 ½ tablespoons sugar
· Juice of 1 lemon
· ⅓ cup (100 ml) Prosecco (sparkling dry Italian wine)
· ⅓ cup (100 ml) custard
· 4 teaspoons slivered almonds
· 2 egg yolks, beaten
· Flour

METHOD
Peel and dice the pears and apricots. Add 4 teaspoons of the sugar, the lemon juice, and the wine. Cook on low heat for 10 minutes then drain. Combine the fruits with the custard and almonds.

Preheat the oven to 425°F (220°C).

On a floured work surface, roll out the dough into a rectangle. Place it on a nonstick or buttered cookie sheet, then brush with egg yolk. Arrange the fruits over one half, fold the other half over them, seal the edges, and brush the top with the rest of the egg yolk. Bake for around 25 minutes or until the top is nicely golden. Remove from the oven and sprinkle with the rest of the sugar.

Serve with almond ice cream.

SUZEL

RINGENDORF, FRANCE

This isn't just a restaurant, it's a dream-come-true. And Suzel isn't just a chef, she's a magician who has created a world that is hers and hers alone. Gourmets should flock to explore this idyllic spot in the lovely Alsatian region of Hanau, just a short distance from Strasbourg.

Suzel's Farm is in an idyllic spot, nestled among the vineyards, green hills, and wildflower-strewn paths around the northern Vosges mountains, with its colorful, picturesque houses and high, half-timbered walls. We're in a picture-postcard setting thirty kilometers (some eighteen miles) northwest of Strasbourg. Don't be confused by the similarity between the names Ringendorf and Ringeldorf, two adjacent but very different villages. Also nearby is the village of Kirrwiller—famous for the Adam Meyer music hall, a rural equivalent of the Moulin Rouge.

As its name implies, Ringendorf ("*ring*" plus "*dorf*," or village) features a system of ring roads and—so visitors won't lose their way—a series of signs announcing La Ferme de Suzel. And here it is! The complex includes a main building with old-fashioned rooms, a balcony, wood paneling, parquet floors, a little veranda, and an outbuilding scheduled to become a guesthouse. The most striking feature of the house is its profusion of Alsatian decoration. It's almost like a counterpart or annex of the Strasbourg Alsatian Museum located seven kilometers (around four miles) away in nearby Bousewiller, or the one in Haguenau.

The decor features cupboards painted in intricately flower-patterned red; hats and veils in display cases; old-fashioned dresses, scarves, and toys; fine Hannong and Sarreguemines faïence; valuable Hartzwiller and Portieux crystal, kelsch fabrics (the familiar blue and red striped fabrics typical of Alsace). Clearly, this is the home not only of fine cuisine, but also of an intriguingly theatrical decor.

The "stage manager" is a woman fascinated by traditional Alsace. A native of Sarraguemines whose roots are Russian, Suzel is an impassioned fan of the culture native to the Vosges and the Rhine—Erckmann-Chatrian's tales, Hansi's drawings. Her first venture was the successful Suzel tearoom located in the historic Petite France area of Strasbourg. So successful, in fact, that people began to call her by her trade name, forgetting that she's really called Odette Jung.

She earned her reputation confecting traditional fruit, chocolate, streusel cakes, divine soft meringues, and delicate whipped cream. She then gradually added more substantial fare

ODETTE JUNG, KNOWN AS SUZEL, RUNS BOTH THE KITCHEN AND THE DINING ROOM. SHE SERVES A POUSSIN EN COCOTTE (BELOW), AND VERIFIES THE QUALITY OF THE PRODUCE (LEFT AND FACING PAGE, LEFT) TO ENSURE THE SATISFACTION OF HER GUESTS. VISITORS DELIGHT IN THE DISCOVERY OF HER ATTRACTIVE, RENOVATED FARMHOUSE IN THE HEART OF THE VILLAGE OF RINGENDORF (FACING PAGE, RIGHT).
PRECEDING PAGE: QUAIL WITH PORCINI MUSHROOMS.
LEFT: AN ASSORTMENT OF DELICIOUS INGREDIENTS: CARROT SEEDS, MUNSTER CHEESE, AND RADISHES.

to her offerings—serving hot smoked salmon, potatoes with dill and fresh herbed cheese, casseroled chicken. Eventually she was able to sell her Strasbourg house and open the restaurant of her dreams in the picturesque farm in the Hanau area.

What does Suzel's Farm look like? It reflects an idea developed in cooperation with Bernard Demay, a specialist in polychrome wood whose works can be admired in his Zutzendorf studio, where he works with his wife Christine, and at the La Cour Renaissance gallery in Strasbourg. He uses old wood, wood paneling, and parquet flooring. Suzel's contribution to the decor is her extensive collection of local pottery, cake tins, paintings, carafes, objets d'art, and knicknacks.

At this fairy-tale farm, the kitchen is a sort of cherry on the cake, producing a series of odes to delectable old-fashioned treats. In an effort to impress her grandmother, Odette (or Suzel) originally learned her craft on her own, confecting exquisite treats invented by her active culinary imagination. Some of these include a lightly cooked foie-gras terrine seasoned with Cumberland sauce; fresh sautéed mushrooms with sour cream and poached egg; supreme of guinea hen with sauerkraut; summer salad with sautéed shellfish, and winter game.

This range is extended with lukewarm pressed pig's feet accompanied by pickles and tiny onions; pike perch and sorrel *en papillote* served with wild rice and a flan of seasonal vegetables; poached trout with butter and almonds, and sea bass in a Gewürztraminer sauce. Except on weekends, meals are served only in the evening. Both dining rooms are always full of satisfied diners who can also eat in the garden during fine weather.

ON HER IDYLLIC FARM, SUZEL (FACING PAGE, LEFT)
HAS CREATED A SMALL MUSEUM OF ART AND POPULAR
TRADITIONS, INCLUDING COSTUMES AND BOWLS (ABOVE
LEFT AND RIGHT), LOCAL FABRICS, TABLECLOTHS, AND
REDISCOVERED WOOD PANELING. SHE USED TO RUN A
TEAROOM IN THE PETITE FRANCE DISTRICT OF
STRASBOURG, AND HAS RETAINED A TASTE FOR DELICIOUS
PATISSERIE, INCLUDING HER GRANDMA'S SHORTCAKE
(FACING PAGE, RIGHT).

The clientele is made up of initiates who've discovered the secret of this restaurant—it's not listed in the *Michelin Guide*. Diners sit at carefully set, well-separated tables where they can savor snails cooked in garlic butter and served unshelled in a salt crust; chicken-liver terrine and sautéed mushrooms with poached egg; blood sausage *en papillote* with potatoes; unskinned salmon with sorrel; casseroled pullet with cream and noodles; old-fashioned blanquette de veau, and baked trout from the Petite Pierre pond—timeless classics updated with a light touch by an accomplished culinary wizard who pulls them out of her hat as if by magic.

Suzel, who works these marvels with the assistance of a small, exclusively female team, adds a little raspberry vinegar with a touch of cream to her sauerkraut—which may seem heretical, but actually creates a zesty contrast between the creamy and the tart in the royal dish of Alsace. The homemade desserts (strawberry, raspberry, and blueberry tarts, tender meringue with fruit and lightly whipped cream, *vacherin* meringue cake with vanilla ice cream and mangoes) will take you back to your childhood. The wines are a celebrations of fine Alsatian vintages: a heady Sylvaner, a patrician Riesling, opulent Gewürztraminer, rich Tokay, crisp Muscat, cheerful Pinot Blanc, and peerless, fruity Pinot Noir.

Time flies by in this setting. Or is it in fact that, here in the Hanau region, at the heart of traditional Alsace, time comes to a standstill. Here, you will have realized, is a restaurant that captures the heart.

GRANDMA'S SHORTCAKE

PREPARATION TIME: 45 MINUTES

COOKING TIME: 1 HOUR,

PLUS 4 HOURS TO REFRIGERATE

THE CUSTARD

TO SERVE: 6

INGREDIENTS

For the shortcake dough
· 6 eggs
· 1 ¼ cups (150 g) all-purpose flour
· 4 tablespoons (50 g) cornstarch
· 1 cup (250 g) superfine sugar
· 2 packages of vanilla sugar (about 4 teaspoons [20 g])
· 1 package baking powder (about 2 teaspoons [10 g])
· 2 tablespoons (20 g) butter

For the custard
· 2 cups (500 ml) fresh milk
· 1 vanilla bean (pod)
· 5 very fresh egg yolks
· ½ cup (100 g) sugar

For the topping
· 4 cups (500 g) mixed berry fruits (gooseberries, strawberries, raspberries, blackcurrants)
· 3 sprigs mint

METHOD

Preheat the oven to 300°F (150°C). To make the shortcake, first separate the egg yolks from the whites. Sift the flour and cornstarch through a sieve and reserve. Beat the yolks and sugar energetically until you have a pale, foaming, creamy mixture. Add the vanilla sugar and baking powder. Beat the egg whites into stiff peaks. Fold in—alternately—the egg yolk and sugar mixture, and then the mixture of flours, to keep the mixture light. Butter a shallow sponge-cake pan and pour in the batter. Bake for 1 hour. Unmold it onto a cake rack and leave to cool.

While the shortcake is baking, make the custard. Split the vanilla bean in half, add it to a saucepan containing the milk, and bring to the boil. Remove from the heat, cover, and leave to infuse for 10 minutes. Add the sugar to the egg yolks and beat well until they turn pale. Gradually beat in the milk. Pour the mixture into a saucepan and cook, stirring constantly with a wooden spoon, making sure it does not boil. When it is thick enough to coat the back of a spoon, pour it into a terrine mold and leave to cool. Then refrigerate for at least 4 hours.

To prepare the topping, clean the fruits, rinse them, and pat them dry before trimming them and removing the stalks. Slice the shortcake and serve it with the berries and custard. Decorate it with the mint sprigs. The custard, which can also be accompanied by vanilla ice cream, is much better if served the next day. Before chilling it, strain it to eliminate any small impurities in the egg yolks. Leave the vanilla in the custard right up until you serve it.

163

LUISA VALAZZA

SORISO, ITALY

IN A SECLUDED CORNER OF PIEDMONT, JUST A STEP FROM LAKE ORTA—ONE OF THE SMALLEST
BUT MOST APPEALING OF ALL THE ITALIAN LAKES—STANDS A PEACEFUL INN WHERE
A SELF-TAUGHT CHEF HAS CLIMBED TO THE PINNACLE OF GASTRONOMIC EXCELLENCE.

Although we obediently followed all the road signs as we traveled northeast from Milan, we repeatedly lost our way. We took the exit at Borgomanero and headed in the direction of Lake Orta. The road appeared to finish in a dead end, but actually wound toward the Piedmont foothills, a hill, and a patch of forest. Yes, the village really is there, at the end of the road, perched on a hilltop near the mountain peaks. The balconies of the houses are decked with flowers, the inn a welcome sight indeed.

This is Sorriso ("smile" in Italian, spelled with two r's for the inn and only one for the village), the latest three-star restaurant in Italy. The first thing visitors notice at the Sorriso is the cheerful demeanor of host Angelo Valazza, who confirms the clichéd image of what a typical Italian maître d'hôtel should be. He has worked in Switzerland, for Kulm at Saint-Moritz; in Frankfurt, Germany, at the Frankfurter Hof and—to improve his English—in Yorkshire.

It's quite an experience to observe him running his small (thirty-seat) dining room, conversing in a dozen languages, miming what he can't explain, like a seasoned commedia dell'arte actor who happens to have a special expertise learned at Lausanne's catering school. His daughter Paola handles the wines, which range from a Del Bosco Chardonnay marketed by Maurizio Zanella, to a Lombardy Franciarcota (both as good as a French Puligny) and a Soave Capitel Foscarino d'Anselmi—as mellow as the noblest of vintages—or a stunning, well-rounded Bartolo.

The kitchen reflects all the experience, finesse, and rare delicacy possessed by Luisa, a youthful mamma with the face of a Madonna, who artfully prepares such treats as her green ravioli with goat cheese and country butter, and her spinach gnochetti with Parmesan cheese. If we were to compare her culinary creations to music, we might immediately think of Mozart—another creative genius who was inspired by the Italian Renaissance. Or to an instrument? A Stradivarius from the hand of Cremona's famed instrument maker.

This is not an exaggeration. All five senses are stimulated by this cuisine, which features the flavors of alpine flowers, white truffles, and tender sage. Each dish is pretty as a picture,

LUISA VALAZZA PUTS THE FINISHING TOUCHES ON HER RAVIOLI (ABOVE RIGHT AND LEFT). OTHER DISHES INCLUDE EGG FETTUCCINI WITH ZUCCHINI AND MUSHROOMS (FACING PAGE, TOP RIGHT) AND RISOTTO WITH PARTRIDGE IN CREAM SAUCE (FACING PAGE, BOTTOM LEFT). SHE ENJOYS WORKING WITH WHITE TRUFFLE, AND HER HUSBAND (FACING PAGE, TOP LEFT) IS IN CHARGE OF SERVICE "WITH A SMILE" IN THEIR CHARMING RESTAURANT (ABOVE CENTER). PRECEDING PAGE: FIG FRITTERS AND SORBET WITH BLUEBERRY SAUCE.

crisp and tender. You almost hate to break the spell by taking a bite, but the beguiling music continues to resonate in the mouth.

Among Luisa's many treats are tomato mousse with basil and raw porcini mushrooms; warm Lombardy foie gras accompanied by puréed peas and grenadine sauce—an admirable sweet-sour combination; prawns and white beans, puréed with bacon bits and a light pesto; the miraculous baked potato skin stuffed with mashed potato and egg yolk and sprinkled with Alba truffle (a combination that naturally enhances the flavor of the bland potato); and, to help digestion along, a porcini mushroom consommé.

Customers rave about the *fassone*—the famous Lombardy beef with Barolo wine. The beef is the best meat in the world, the most tender, from huge pampered animals that are leaner and more flavorful than even the legendary Kobe variety. To end the meal, a little mint sorbet coated with chocolate that leaves the spirit free and the digestion at rest, ready for a new gastronomical adventure.

Lake Orta lies nearby, with its miniature port, its romantic San Giulio Island emerging from the water, its basilica and gardens, its shaded café terraces facing the boats. Adjacent Soriso stands almost forgotten in the unspoiled countryside. This explains the miracle of such a great restaurant and its warm hospitality. People make excursions to it for the day, for short stopovers, for a country weekend, or just to sample a new experience in a quiet setting. They find a low-key style, restful surroundings, and the infinite possibilities offered by the surrounding countryside for hiking and walking tours. The restaurant's table offers a host of pleasures featuring local products such as truffles and fassone veal, vegetables from nearby gardens, and fresh fish from the lakes. Tonight, for example, the menu includes layered potatoes and eggplant, with a squid gratin flavored with white Alba truffles, guinea hen *en casserole* with rhododendron honey and peach marinade, followed by chocolate tart with Piedmont almonds, or a sabayon with Muscat grapes.

The wines are amazing, the restaurant's atmosphere warm and inviting. Luisa Valazza is totally self-taught—something everyone knows and yet never tires of talking about. This woman with a degree in Italian literature decided twenty years ago to shift her emphasis from books to the stove. She did it to please her husband and also because, when they first settled in her native village, they couldn't afford to pay a chef. Here's a delicious miracle, Italian-style. Gourmets from Piedmont and elsewhere never tire of it.

LUISA VALAZZA'S RECIPE:

FRESH FETTUCCINI WITH ZUCCHINI AND CHANTERELLE MUSHROOMS

PREPARATION TIME: 25 MINUTES

COOKING TIME: 5 MINUTES

TO SERVE: 4

INGREDIENTS

· 1 shallot
· 1 very small garlic clove
· 2 tablespoons olive oil
· ⅓ cup (100 g) chanterelles
· 2 zucchini, sliced
· ⅓ cup (100 ml) tomato sauce
· 1 scant cup (200 ml) meat stock
· 4 teaspoons (20 g) pine nuts, toasted
· 4 or 5 basil leaves, torn
· Salt and pepper

For the egg pasta
· 1 ¼ pounds (500 g) durum wheat flour
· 6 egg yolks
· 2 whole eggs
· 1 tablespoon olive oil
· Table salt

METHOD

Make the dough by pouring the flour onto a work surface and making a well in the center. Break the eggs into the well and add the oil and salt. Mix the ingredients until smooth. If the dough is too dry, add a little olive oil. Roll out the dough and run it through a pasta machine in order to get a strip of pasta 12 inches (30 cm) long. Cut into ribbons ½ inch (1 cm) wide and leave to rest for around 1 hour.

Finely chop the shallot and garlic. Heat the oil in a skillet and sauté them, adding the cleaned and sliced chanterelles and zucchini. Add the tomato sauce and simmer for 5 minutes. If the mixture is too dry, add a little meat broth. Add the toasted pine nuts and torn basil leaves. Cook the pasta in boiling water for 5 minutes. Drain it and add to the sauce in the saucepan. Mix well, cook for a few seconds, and serve with a bunch of fresh basil.

CHEF'S NOTEBOOK

ELENA ARZAC

SEARED BONITO WITH ONIONS AND MELON

PREPARATION TIME: 45 MINUTES
COOKING TIME: 20 MINUTES
TO SERVE: 4

INGREDIENTS
For the bonito
· 1 pound, 5 ounces (600 g) bonito tuna fillet with skin
· Salt and ginger
For the batter
· 1 tomato
· 2 ¼ ounces (60 g) bonito skin (taken from the fillet)
· 1 scant cup (200 ml) olive oil
· 2 ½ ounces (70 g) toasted almonds
· 1 tablespoon balsamic vinegar
· 2 ½ tablespoons (30 g) dry breadcrumbs
· 1 pinch of sugar
· Salt
For the onions with melon
· 2 small onions
· 1 small melon
· Olive oil
· Pinch of sugar
For the pickle dressing
· 6 ounces (70 g) pickles in vinegar
· 1 tablespoon minced parsley
· 4 tablespoons olive oil
· 2 tablespoons fresh breadcrumbs
· ⅓ cup (100 ml) water

METHOD
To make the batter, chop the tomato and grind in a food processor with a little olive oil. Skin the bonito fillet, reserving the skin. Fry the skin in half the olive oil, so that it is crisp. Drain it. Coarsely grind the almonds and combine all the batter ingredients with the rest of the olive oil, grind them and strain them through a sieve. Season with salt and sugar.
Slice the bonito fillet into 8 rectangles (2 per person) and season with salt and ginger. Dip them in the batter and fry for 4 to 5 minutes. They should still be juicy. Slice the small onions lengthwise. Heat a little olive oil in a skillet and sauté them until they are transparent.
Split the melon open and use a melon-baller to cut out little balls. Add them to the onions in the skillet with the sugar and mix well until lightly caramelized.
To make the pickle dressing, process all the ingredients in a blender. Arrange the bonito fillets in the center of the plates. Reheat the rest of the batter and add it to the dish with the onions and melon and serve with the pickle dressing. (Photo p. 13)

BROCHETTE OF FRUITS AND STRAWBERRY MILK

PREPARATION TIME: 20 MINUTES
COOKING TIME: 6 MINUTES
TO SERVE: 4

INGREDIENTS
For the spiced sugar
· ⅓ cup (100 g) sugar
· 2 teaspoons (10 g) dried basil
· 1 teaspoon chopped fresh mint
· 2 pinches black pepper
For the brochette
· 1 pear
· 1 kiwi fruit
· 1 apple
· 1 mango
For the strawberry milk
· 1 ¼ cups (300 ml) whole milk
· ⅓ cup (100 g) of strawberries, puréed in a blender
· 2 tablespoons (30 g) sugar
· 1 cup (250 g) ice cubes

METHOD
To make the spiced sugar, mix all the ingredients and reserve.
Peel the fruits and dice them into cubes of around 1 ½ inches (4 cm). Cover with the spiced sugar, mix thoroughly, and then thread them onto skewers. Broil them for 5 to 6 minutes, or until they are caramelized on all sides. Process all the strawberry milk ingredients in a blender and serve with the fruit skewers.
The recipe can be made with other fruits in season. (Photo p. 15)

ISABELLE AUGUY

ASPARAGUS AND FROGS' LEGS WITH OLIVE OIL EMULSION

PREPARATION TIME: 40 MINUTES
COOKING TIME: 50 MINUTES
TO SERVE: 4

INGREDIENTS
· 16 green asparagus
· 12 ounces (350 g) frogs' legs (fresh or frozen)
· 3 shallots
· 2 celery stalks
· 4 ounces (100 g) butter
· 1 bunch of chervil, tarragon, and parsley (4 sprigs each)
· 4 garlic cloves
· 1 sprig of thyme
· ⅔ cup (200 ml) dry white wine
· 1 ¼ cups (300 ml) chicken stock
· ½ cup (50 g) all-purpose flour
· 2 tablespoons oil
· ½ cup (100 ml) single cream
· 4 tablespoons (50 ml) olive oil (preferably from Verdale, see below)
· Salt and pepper

METHOD
Frogs' legs are sold in pairs with a little piece of bone corresponding to the spine. Slice them, then reserve this bone as well as the tips of the feet.
Chop the shallots and celery. Heat 3 teaspoons (20 g) butter in a saucepan over low heat. Add the chopped herbs, unpeeled garlic cloves, and the thyme. Cook on a low heat for 15 minutes without letting them color. Add the frog bones and feet, cover, and simmer for 5 minutes. Add the white wine and boil, uncovered, until almost all the liquid has evaporated. Add the chicken stock and bring to the boil. Skim the surface, reduce the heat, and simmer for 15 minutes. Remove from the heat and leave to rest for 10 minutes, then strain the liquid and leave it to cool.
While the broth is cooking, clean and trim the asparagus, leaving 3 in. (7 cm) of stalk. Cook for 4 to 5 minutes, depending on the thickness of the stems, in boiling water; they should still be crunchy. Check them for doneness with a knife point, which should resist slightly when inserted in the thickest part of the stem.
Pour the flour into a shallow bowl. Season the frogs' legs with salt and pepper and dredge them with flour. Shake to eliminate excess flour. Heat 1 ½ oz. (40 g) butter with the oil and fry the frogs' legs,

FACING PAGE: SOPHIE BISE'S FRUIT AND CREAM WITH MANGO SAUCE

169

turning them frequently so that they are nicely browned all over (3 to 4 minutes). Drain them on absorbent paper.

At the same time, complete the cooking of the stock. Add the cream, bring to the boil, then add the Verdale olive oil, beating to obtain an emulsion. Reheat the asparagus tips in the rest of the butter. Drain them and arrange them in serving dishes with the frogs' legs and emulsified broth. (Photo p. 17)

For frying the frogs' legs, I use clarified butter (melted butter from which the milk solids are removed). The trick of adding a little oil to the butter to stop it carbonizing during cooking is not 100 percent perfect but it usually works.

I add a little fresh butter before draining the frogs' legs.

The variety of Provençal olive known as aglandau is called "verdale" in Vaucluse. It produces a mild oil with a fragrance of almonds and a delicate fruitiness. Choose an AOC oil of good quality. For the clarified butter recipe, refer to the method explained on page 179 in Catherine Guerraz's sweetbreads recipe.

AUBRAC FARM BEEFSTEAK WITH MARCILLAC SAUCE

PREPARATION TIME: 30 MINUTES

COOKING TIME: 50 MINUTES

TO SERVE: 4

INGREDIENTS

For the meat
· 4 slices beefsteak, 7 ounces (200 g) each (from the tenderloin)
· 1 tablespoon oil
· 2 tablespoons (30 g) butter
· Coarse or kosher salt

For the Marcillac sauce
· 4 ounces (100 g) carrots
· 4 ounces (100 g) celery
· 4 ounces (100 g) onions
· 5 tablespoons (60 g) butter
· 2 tablespoons Cognac
· ½ cup (100 ml) red wine vinegar
· 1 ½ cups (350 ml) AOC Marcillac red wine
· 1 ½ cups (350 ml) veal or chicken stock
· 1 tablespoon mignonnette pepper
· Table salt and coarse salt

METHOD

First make the sauce. Dice the vegetables and sauté them in 3 teaspoons (20 g) butter. Add the Cognac and set it alight. Add the vinegar and cook over high heat until the liquid evaporates. Season with pepper, then add the red wine and the veal or chicken stock. Cook, uncovered, for around 30 minutes, or until only 1¼ cup (300 ml) liquid is left. Strain, season with salt, and keep hot on low heat.

To cook the steaks, heat the oil with 2 tablespoons (30 g) butter in a large skillet until pale brown. Quickly sauté the steaks over high heat for 1 minute on each side. Season on both sides with the coarse salt. Reduce the heat, and continue cooking until the steaks are cooked to your taste.

Arrange the steaks in a warmed serving dish, cover them with aluminum foil and leave to rest for 10 minutes.

Pour the reduced Marcillac sauce into the skillet in which the steaks were cooked. Bring to the boil, stirring, over high heat, then reduce the heat and add 3 tablespoons (40 g) butter, stirring constantly. Pour the sauce into a sauceboat and serve it with the steaks. (Photo p. 19)

"Aubrac Farm" cattle are raised on the Aubrac Mountains. The flesh is therefore firm and never fatty. But what a flavor it has! It is a meat as rare as it is delicious.

JUDITH BAUMANN

WINDBREAKER

PREPARATION TIME: 45 MINUTES

COOKING TIME: 1 HOUR

TO SERVE: 6

INGREDIENTS

For the tomato preserve
· 6 ripe beefsteak tomatoes, 2 inches (5 cm) in diameter
· 3 ½ tablespoons (50 ml) olive oil
· 6 pinches sugar
· 6 pinches ground cardamom
· 2 garlic cloves
· 3 sprigs thyme
· Salt and pepper

To finish
· Vinaigrette and balsamic vinegar

For the eggplant caviar
· 1 white eggplant weighing about 9 ounces (300 g)
· 3 ½ tablespoons (50 ml) olive oil
· 1 teaspoon chopped shallot
· 1 teaspoon butter
· Salt and pepper

For the eggplant cookies
· 1 small purple eggplant
· A splash of olive oil

For the athamantha butter
· 3 ½ ounces (100 g) athamantha (candy carrot) or a mixed bunch of parsley and chervil
· 4 tablespoons (60 g) softened butter
· Salt and pepper

To garnish
· 6 athamantha sprigs or a bunch of parsley
· 6 ribwort plantain leaves
· Espelette chili peppers

METHOD

For the preserved tomatoes, skin the tomatoes and sprinkle them with olive oil. Dust them with sugar and ground cardamom. Peel the garlic cloves and crush them. Add the thyme. Season and cook slowly in a preheated oven 210°F (100°C) oven for 1 hour, basting regularly with the juices that are produced.

To make the eggplant caviar, split the eggplant in half. Oil a sheet of aluminum foil and wrap the eggplant in it. Bake in a preheated 350°F (180°C) oven for 1 hour. Detach the flesh of the eggplant from the skin and grind it in a food processor. Add the rest of the olive oil.

Melt the butter in a skillet and cook the shallot over gentle heat. Incorporate the ground eggplant. Season with salt and pepper. Shape the eggplant into 12 patties. Refrigerate until required.

For the eggplant cookies, cut the eggplant into 12 slices about 1/8 inch thick. Brush them with oil, using a pastry brush. Place on a sheet of Silpat and cover with a second Silpat sheet. Bake in a preheated 250°F (130°C) oven for 15 minutes.

Remove the top Silpat sheet and increase the heat to 275°F (140°C) for 5 minutes. Leave to cool. Cover to keep out the air in a cool place, and store in a cool place until required.

To make the athamantha butter, blanch the athamantha or the parsley and chervil if using. Grind in a herb grinder. Add the softened butter and mix well. Season with salt and pepper. Form 12 small patties and refrigerate until required. Broil the preserved tomatoes under the broiler for 3 to 4 minutes. Sprinkle them with vinaigrette and balsamic vinegar.

On the left-hand side of a round plate, place 1 tomato. To its right, place 2 eggplant caviar patties. Arrange 2 eggplant cookies in the shape of a windbreaker. On the right of them, arrange 2 athamantha or herb patties. Complete the arrangement by topping the tomato with an umbel of athamantha and 1 ribwort plantain leaf. Sprinkle around them with Espelette or other small red chili peppers. (Photo p. 22)

SUMMER FRUIT MEDLEY

PREPARATION TIME: 1 HOUR

COOKING TIME: A FEW MINUTES

TO SERVE: 6

INGREDIENTS

For the elderflower soup
· ⅔ cup (150 ml) water
· 1 small handful of elderflowers
· 1 gelatin sheet, dissolved
· ⅔ cup (150 ml) Monbazillac wine
· 6 tablespoons (70 ml) elderflower syrup

For the melon sorbet
· 7 ounces (200 g) melon
· 1 ½ tablespoons (25 g) sugar
· 1 tablespoon (15 g) glucose syrup or 2 tablespoons (30 g) light corn syrup
· Juice of half a lemon
· ½ teaspoon Cognac

For the almond cookies
· 5 teaspoons (25 g) all-purpose flour
· 3 tablespoons (50 g) confectioner's sugar
· 5 teaspoons (25 g) ground almonds
· ¼ cup (50 g) egg white
· ¼ cup (50 g) melted butter

For the elderflower fritters
· 1 branch elderflowers
· 1 ¼ tablespoons (12 g) all-purpose flour
· 1 ¼ tablespoons (12 g) cornstarch
· ½ teaspoon (2 g) baking powder
· 1 teaspoon (5 g) egg yolk
· 2 tablespoons (30 ml) beer

To finish the dish:
· Peanut oil and confectioner's sugar

For the berries in syrup
· ⅓ cup (100 ml) port
· 2 teaspoons (10 g) sugar
· 2 tablespoons (30 g) black elderberries

Decoration
· 42 small melon balls
· 6 small mint sprigs

UTENSILS

· 1 ice-cream maker, 1 forcing bag, and 6 rum baba molds

METHOD

For the elderflower soup, infuse the elderflowers in ⅔ cup (150 ml) boiling water, and leave for 15 minutes. Strain them. Add the melted gelatin sheet, then the Monbazillac wine and elderberry syrup. Leave to cool, then chill until required.

Next, cut the melon flesh into pieces. Combine it with the sugar, glucose syrup, lemon juice, and cognac. Cover with plastic wrap and refrigerate for 4 hours. Pour it into an ice-cream maker and make the sorbet. Store in the freezer until required.

For the almond cookies, combine the flour and confectioner's sugar with the ground almonds. Beat the egg white into stiff peaks and gradually fold it into the flour mixture.

Incorporate the melted butter. Butter the rum baba molds and fill them using a forcing bag. Bake in a preheated 425°F (230 °C) oven for 8 minutes. Unmold them. To make the elderflower fritters, divide the elderflower branch into 6 twigs. Combine the flour, cornstarch, and baking powder with the egg yolk and beer. Leave to rest for 1 hour.

Make a syrup with the port and sugar. Cook the berries in this syrup for 5 minutes.

Heat the peanut oil to 300°F (170 °C). Dip the elderberry twigs in the batter and drain them. Deep-fry them in the oil until they are pale brown. Drain the fritters on absorbent paper, then sprinkle with confectioner's sugar.

Place an almond cookie in the center of a sundae glass. Place a scoop of melon sorbet on top of the cookie. Surround with a ring of elderberries. Pour the soup into the glass and sprinkle with the melon balls.

Complete by planting an elderberry twig in the top and garnish with a sprig of mint. (Photo p. 21)

NATHALIE BEAUVAIS

HAKE IN A BUCKWHEAT PANCAKE, WITH GUÉMENÉ SAUSAGE SAUCE

PREPARATION TIME: 25 MINUTES

COOKING TIME: 25 MINUTES
AT THE BEGINNING, THEN A FURTHER
8 MINUTES

TO SERVE: 6

INGREDIENTS

· 2 pounds, 12 ounces (1.2 kg) hake
· 2 tablespoons olive oil
· ⅓ cup (100 ml) white wine
· 1 ⅓ cups (300 g) tomatoes
· ⅓ cup (100 g) butter
· 6 buckwheat pancakes
· 5 ½ ounces (150 g) Guémené/Scorff sausage
· 1 cup (250 ml) heavy cream
· Juice of 1 lemon
· ½ bunch chives
· Salt and pepper

METHOD

For the fish fumet, ask the fishmonger to fillet the fish. Ask him to discard the skin and give you the bones and head. Clean the head and bones. Heat a little olive oil and sauté them briefly, then deglaze the pan with white wine. Simmer for 5 minutes, cover with water, then season with salt and continue to simmer for 20 minutes. Carefully strain the liquid and reserve it.

Skin the tomatoes and deseed them. To make the fish pancakes, spread softened butter over each pancake. In the center of each, place pieces of fish fillet, allowing around 3 ½ ounces (100 g) fish for each pancake. Season with salt and pepper and fold the pancakes over to form a rectangle. Refrigerate until required.

To cook the sausage broth, heat 1 scant cup (200 ml) of fish stock and add the tomatoes and sausage. Bring to the boil over high heat, add the cream and lemon juice, adjust the seasoning, and keep warm. Bake the pancakes in a preheated 475°F (250°C) for 8 minutes. Chop the chives finely and incorporate them into the sauce. Coat each plate with the sausage cooking liquid, and place a crisp pancake in the center of the plate. Serve immediately.

Buckwheat flour pancakes are a specialty of Brittany. There are two types of these pancakes, the *"galettes"* served in northern Brittany that are fairly thick pancakes, and the *"crêpes"* of southern Brittany that may be made from buckwheat flour or wheat flour. The batter is usually thinner in the south. Personally, I prefer buckwheat pancakes to be thin, as that makes them easier to digest.

BRAISED MONKFISH IN CURRY WITH STEAMED LEEKS AND TOASTED BUCKWHEAT

PREPARATION TIME: 40 MINUTES

COOKING TIME: 20 MINUTES

TO SERVE: 6

INGREDIENTS

· 4 pounds, 8 ounces (2 kg) monkfish
· 1 tablespoon curry powder
· 5 ½ ounces (150 g) butter
· 2 pounds, 12 ounces (1.2 kg) leeks
· 7 ounces (200 g) potatoes
· ⅓ cup (100 g) toasted buckwheat (kasha)
· ⅓ cup (100 g) heavy cream
· Juice of 1 lemon
· Salt and pepper

METHOD

Ask the fishmonger to skin the monkfish. Divide it into 6 slices. Lightly open out each slice along the bone in order to make the cooking more even. Arrange the fish slices in a gratin dish, season with salt and pepper and sprinkle with curry powder. Dot the fish with 5 tablespoons (100 g) butter cut into pieces. Refrigerate until required.

Clean the leeks, slice them thinly, and braise them in a covered pan in 2 ½ tablespoons (50 g) butter for 30 minutes. Keep them warm. Boil the potatoes in their skins in salted water. Drain them, peel them, and dice them.

Bring the toasted buckwheat to the boil in twice its volume of water, at a bare simmer. Season with a little salt. Reduce the heat, cover the pan, and simmer for 10 minutes. Keep warm.

Remove the gratin dish from the refrigerator and add the potatoes and 2 tablespoons of the braised leeks to the monkfish. Add enough water to come halfway up the monkfish. Bake in a preheated 475°F (250°C) oven for 20 minutes. To make the sauce and assemble the dish, arrange the monkfish slices on a serving platter, and keep warm. Pour the cooking liquid from the fish, leeks, and potatoes through a strainer into a saucepan. Add the heavy cream and lemon juice. Bring the sauce to the boil and blend it using a hand-held stick blender in the pan. Check the seasoning if necessary.

Coat the fish with this sauce and serve with the toasted buckwheat and the rest of the braised leeks.

TOASTED GINGERBREAD WITH ORANGE SORBET AND FRESH CITRUS

PREPARATION TIME: 20 MINUTES

COOKING TIME: A FEW SECONDS

TO SERVE: 6

INGREDIENTS

· 2 oranges
· 1 grapefruit
· 2 kiwi fruits
· 6 litchis
· 1 ¼ pounds (500 g) French gingerbread (*pain d'épices*)
· 4 teaspoons (20 g) butter
· 1 ⅓ cups (70 g) icing sugar
· 2 cups (500 g) orange sorbet

METHOD

Peel the oranges and grapefruit, discarding all the peel and white parts. Separate them into segments and reserve them with their juice. Peel the kiwi fruits and slice them. Peel the litchis and cut them open round the stone so as to form a flower.

Cut the gingerbread as thinly as possible and butter each slice on one side only. Arrange the slices on an ovenproof dish and sprinkle with icing sugar. Bake the slices for a few seconds in a preheated 475°F (250°C) oven until they are lightly toasted.

To assemble the dish, arrange the fruits in serving dishes as elegantly as possible and pour the reserved juices over each. Place a single slice of toasted gingerbread in the center and cover with a large scoop of orange sorbet. Cover the sorbet with a second slice of gingerbread. Serve immediately. (Photo p. 27)

SOPHIE BISE

STEAMED SOLE WITH GREEN PEA PURÉE FLAVORED WITH PEPPERMINT

PREPARATION TIME: 45 MINUTES

COOKING TIME: 5 MINUTES

TO SERVE: 4

INGREDIENTS

· 1 ¾ cups (400 g) shelled peas
· 1 ⅓ cups (150g) snowpeas
· 4 small leeks
· 8 green asparagus tips
· ⅔ cup (180 g) salted butter
· 4 carrots
· 4 baby artichokes
· 5 ½ ounces (150 g) peas in the pod
· 1 cup (250 ml) milk

· 8 fillets of sole
· Fresh mint leaves
· 1 bunch of basil
· 2 tablespoons olive oil

METHOD

To make the green pea purée, cook the garden peas in salted boiling water for 15 minutes. Drain and rinse them in ice water. Drain again and grind in a food processor, then push through a strainer.
Cook half the snowpeas with the small leeks and asparagus spears in a saucepan of salted boiling water. In a saucepan, heat 4 cups (1 liter) water and 3 tablespoons (40 g) salted butter and cook the carrots and artichokes. Reserve until required.
Bring 1 cup (250 ml) water to the boil and add the peas in their pods as well as the rest of the snowpeas. Add 2 cups (500 ml) milk and bring back to the boil; cook for 5 minutes. Grind in a food processor, then strain and keep warm. This mixture will be used as the sauce.
Wrap 2 fillets of sole head-to-tail with 3 tablespoons (40 g) salted butter in plastic wrap. Ensure the package is tightly closed and do the same with the other sole fillets. Steam for 5 minutes then leave to rest and remove the plastic wrap. Heat the pea purée with the rest of the salted butter. Add the chopped mint.
Arrange the mixture in the center of four plates. Place the sole fillets on top. Then top with the carrots and artichokes.
Garnish with a few mint leaves and a sprinkling of olive oil.
Surround with a trail of sauce and serve. (Photo p. 31)

SAUTÉED SLICE OF DUCK FOIE GRAS AND "DOLCE FORTE" APRICOT MARMALADE

PREPARATION TIME: 40 MINUTES
COOKING TIME: 2 MINUTES
TO SERVE: 4

INGREDIENTS

· 8 slices of duck foie gras, weighing around 1 ¾ ounces (50 g) each
· 2 tablespoons olive oil
For the sauce
· 2 cups (500 g) sugar
· Juice and grated rind of 1 lemon
· Juice and grated rind of 1 orange
· 1 scant cup (200 g) honey

· 4 teaspoons (20 g) ground coriander
· 10 cardamom seeds
· 2 birdseye chili peppers
· 1 vanilla bean (pod)
· 3 fresh lemon verbena leaves, torn into pieces
· 3 pounds, 5 ounces (1.5 kg) fresh apricots, pitted
· 4 teaspoons (20 g) sugar
For the polenta
· 2 cups (500 ml) milk
· 2 cups (500 ml) light cream
· 4 teaspoons (20 g) sugar
· 1 scant cup (200 g) yellow cornmeal
· 2 egg yolks
· 4 tablespoons oil

METHOD

First make a sugar syrup by dissolving the 2 cups (500 g) sugar in 1 quart (1 liter) water over medium heat. When the sugar has dissolved, increase the heat and boil for 10 minutes. Add the citrus juices, honey, spices, vanilla bean, lemon verbena, and grated citrus zest. Remove from the heat, cover, and leave to infuse for 15 minutes. Meanwhile, cook the apricots in half a cup (125 ml) water with 4 teaspoons (20 g) sugar. Strain the syrup through a conical sieve and combine with the cooked apricots. Reserve.
To make the polenta, first boil the milk with the cream and sugar. Add the cornmeal all at once and cook, stirring, for 20 minutes. Pour the polenta into a bowl, add the egg yolks and mix well. Pour this mixture into a greased jellyroll pan or similar low-sided flat pan. Leave to cool, then cut the polenta into 4 squares with a knife.
To serve, sauté the foie gras slices for 1 to 2 minutes on each side in a skillet with no extra grease. Sauté the polenta squares one after the other, each in 1 tablespoon olive oil for 2 minutes. Place each slice of polenta on a plate, top with the foie gras and surround with a trail of apricot sauce. (Photo p. 32)

DESSERTS IN A GLASS: JELLYCREAM IN A GLASS

PREPARATION TIME: 30 MINUTES
TO MAKE: 12 GLASSES

INGREDIENTS

· ½ cup (125 g) sugar
· 8 egg whites
· 2 unflavored gelatin leaves, soaked and squeezed

· 1 cup (250 g) heavy cream, whipped
· Soft fruits in season (raspberries, strawberries, etc.)
· Pistachio nuts, broken into pieces, to garnish

METHOD

Make a sugar syrup with the sugar and ¼ cup (60 ml) water. Dissolve the sugar in the water and cook it to a caramel or until a candy thermometer registers 250°F (120°C). Whisk the egg whites into stiff peaks with an electric beater, and gradually pour the sugar syrup into them, whisking constantly. Then add the gelatin leaves and beat until the mixture is smooth. Fold the whipped cream into the mixture and pour it into tall glasses to come three-quarters of the way up.
Garnish with fresh berries, such as raspberries. Top with a few broken pistachio nuts.

DESSERTS IN A GLASS: FRUIT AND CREAM WITH MANGO SAUCE

PREPARATION TIME: 30 MINUTES
COOKING TIME: 30 MINUTES
TO SERVE: 4–6

INGREDIENTS

· Summer fruits, such as peach, melon, apricot, berries, etc.
For the mango and jasmine sauce
· 1 mango
· 2 cups (500 ml) jasmine tea
For the crème brûlée
· 10 egg yolks
· ⅓ cup (100 g) sugar
· 2 cups (500 ml) cream (35 percent fat)
· 4 mint leaves, dipped in light corn syrup and then drained

METHOD

Dice the fruits into small pieces and put them in the bottom of 4 to 6 ramekins, reserving a few fruits for the garnish. To make the sauce, cut the mango into small pieces and cook it in the jasmine tea for 30 minutes. Grind in a food processor and strain through a fine sieve. Refrigerate until required.
To make the crème brûlée, beat the egg yolks with the sugar, add the light cream and cook in a double boiler or bain-marie, as for a custard, stirring constantly. The mixture should double in volume. When it coats the back of the spoon, it is ready. Cool, then refrigerate.

To assemble the dish, cover the fruits with the crème brûlée. Caramelize the surface by sprinkling with sugar and browning the sugar under a hot broiler for a few moments. Garnish with the reserved fruits and a candied mint leaf.
Serve with the mango sauce on the side.

CHANTAL CHAGNY

ROAST FROGS' LEGS WITH SALAD GREENS AND HERBS

PREPARATION TIME: 40 MINUTES
COOKING TIME: 15 MINUTES
TO SERVE: 4

INGREDIENTS

· 24 fresh frogs' legs
· 1 ¾ cups (400 ml) milk
· 2 tablespoons flour
· 2 tablespoons butter
· 4 tablespoons minced flat-leaved parsley mixed with 1 tablespoon minced garlic
· 2 cups (200 g) mixed salad greens
· 4 tablespoons hazelnut oil
· 1 tablespoon crunchy fresh almonds
· 4 small yellow tomatoes, marinated in 2 tablespoons olive oil and 2 sprigs of basil
· 8 lightly preserved tomatoes
· 4 tablespoons chopped chives

METHOD

Get the fishmonger to trim the tips of the feet and the spine of the frogs, so that only the pair of legs attached to each other remain. Soak them in the milk and roll in flour. Ensuring they are completely dry, heat the butter in a skillet and sauté them on one side for at least 10 minutes then turn them over and fry for another 5 minutes. When the butter foams, reduce the heat and sprinkle the parsley mixture into the skillet over the frogs legs. Transfer immediately to plates. Dress the salad greens with the hazelnut oil and arrange them round the frogs' legs. Sprinkle them with a few fresh, crunchy almonds.
Complete the garnish with the marinated yellow tomatoes and add a few slices of the lightly preserved tomatoes. Sprinkle with chopped chives.
(Photo p. 36)

BLACKCURRANT SORBET, BLACKCURRANT PURÉE, AND VANILLA ICE CREAM

PREPARATION TIME: 25 MINUTES
COOKING TIME: AROUND 15–20 MINUTES
TO SERVE: 4

INGREDIENTS

· 2 pounds, 4 ounces (1 kg) fresh or frozen blackcurrants
· 1 ¾ cups (400 ml) water
· 1 ⅔ cups (300 g) sugar
· 1 ¾ cups (400 g) vanilla ice cream

METHOD

To cook the blackcurrants, add them to the water and bring to the boil over high heat, adding the sugar as if making a preserve. When the mixture begins to foam, remove it from the heat. Grind the mixture in a vegetable mill, using the medium screen. Don't press the skin of the blackcurrants too hard, otherwise the tannin in them will get into the pulp. Discard the skins inside the mill after each quantity has been pressed. The blackcurrant purée should be liquid in consistency and fairly coarse in texture. Transfer two-thirds of it to an ice-cream maker and make it into a sorbet. When the sorbet has frozen, spread the reserved one-third of the blackcurrant pulp on plates. Place a scoop of vanilla ice cream on top and then a scoop of blackcurrant sorbet. Both should have more or less the same consistency. Serve immediately.

SALLY CLARKE

TARRAGON CHICKEN

PREPARATION TIME: 40 MINUTES
COOKING TIME: 90 MINUTES
TO SERVE: 6

INGREDIENTS

· 1 large free-range chicken, weighing 4 pounds 8 ounces to 6 pounds 8 ounces (2 to 3 kg)
· Sea salt and pepper
· 1 lemon, quartered
· 2 medium onions, coarsely chopped
· 2 medium carrots, coarsely chopped
· 4 celery sticks, chopped
· 1 fennel bulb, chopped
· 6 tablespoons (90 ml) olive oil
· 1 head of garlic, chopped
· 2 tablespoons chopped thyme
· 3 tablespoons chopped tarragon
· 1 bottle strong red wine
· 2 cups (500 ml) homemade chicken stock
· ⅓ cup (100 ml) heavy cream
· 6 fresh sprigs tarragon

METHOD

Preheat the oven to 370°F (180°C).
Remove any fat from the chicken and remove any trussing thread. Season inside with salt and pepper. Insert the lemon wedges. Put the vegetables, olive oil, and garlic into a heatproof dish and cook over high heat until they have colored, stirring from time to time. Place the chicken on top of them, breast upward, and sprinkle with a little olive oil. Season with salt and pepper and sprinkle with the chopped thyme and tarragon. Roast in the oven for 20 minutes. Remove the bird from the oven and turn it over, scraping the vegetables at the bottom of the dish. Return it to the oven, reduce the temperature to 300°F (160°C) and continue to cook for 20 minutes. Turn the chicken again so it is breast upward and cook until a skewer pushed into the thigh causes clear juices to flow out (around 20 to 30 minutes). Remove the chicken from the pan and reserve it in a warm place. Place the dish on medium heat and degrease the cooking juices. Pour the red wine into the dish, reduce it by half and add the broth. Simmer, scraping the vegetables until they are the right taste and consistency. Strain the juices into a small saucepan and add the cream and the rest of the tarragon. Taste and adjust the seasoning. Cut the chicken into serving pieces, serve it with the sauce, and garnish with sprigs of fresh tarragon.

CAKE FILLED WITH SABAYON CREAM, BLOOD ORANGES, AND PRUNE PURÉE

PREPARATION TIME: 30 MINUTES
COOKING TIME: 15 MINUTES
TO SERVE: 6

INGREDIENTS

1 sponge cake
For the sabayon
· 3 egg yolks
· ⅓ cup (110 g) sugar
· 6 tablespoons (75g) cake flour
· 1 scant cup (200 ml) marsala
· ¼ cup (50 ml) sweet white wine
· 1 ½ cups (370 ml) heavy cream
· 4 tablespoons prune purée
· 4 blood oranges
· 6 stewed prunes
· Mint leaves and icing sugar

METHOD

To make the cake filling, beat the egg yolks with the sugar. When the mixture is pale yellow, gradually incorporate the flour, beating constantly. Add the marsala and the wine, pour it all into a heavy-based saucepan, and cook on low heat at just below the boil. Leave to cool. Incorporate the cream into the filling just before using it on the cake. Split the sponge cake in half crosswise and spread the two layers with the prune purée. Delicately spread the sabayon over the bottom layer and place the top layer over it, with the cut side downward. Press gently. Refrigerate until ready to serve.
Meanwhile, peel the oranges, removing the white parts. Cut them into rounds and decorate the cake with the oranges and stewed prunes. Top with the mint leaves and sprinkle with sifted icing sugar. (Photo p. 40)

HÉLÈNE DARROZE

VENISON RAVIOLI WITH SWISS CHARD AND PARMESAN SHAVINGS

PREPARATION TIME: 30 MINUTES
COOKING TIME: 3 HOURS
TO SERVE: 12

INGREDIENTS

For the venison
· 1 pound, 5 ounces (600 g) lean venison, cubed
· 6 cups (1.5 l) tannic red wine
· 2 carrots
· 2 onions
· 1 celery stick
· ½ teaspoon (2 g) juniper berries
· ½ teaspoon (2 g) peppercorns
· 4 garlic cloves
· ⅓ cup (100 g) duck fat
· 3 tablespoons (40 g) all-purpose flour
· 1 bouquet garni
· 2 cups (500 ml) homemade chicken stock
· 2 cups (500 ml) homemade veal stock
· Chili pepper flakes
· Salt and pepper

For the swiss chard
· 1 bunch Swiss chard
· 3 ½ tablespoons (50 g) all-purpose flour
· Salt, pepper, pinch of chili pepper flakes

For the filling
· 3 ½ ounces (100 g) lean veal
· 3 ½ tablespoons (50 g) duck fat
· 2 cups (300 g) spinach
· 1 sheep's brain
· Vinegar
· ⅔ cup (150 g) mascarpone
· 3 ½ ounces (100 g) Basque sheep's milk cheese
· 2 sprigs flat-leaved parsley
· 5 chives
· Small fresh chili peppers
· Salt and pepper

METHOD

Twenty-four hours before stewing the venison, put the meat into a marinade consisting of the wine, plus the carrots, onions, celery, juniper berries, peppercorns, and a garlic clove. Refrigerate until required. Drain the meat well, reserving the marinade.
In a large sauté pan, sauté the pieces of venison in duck fat. When the meat is nicely browned, add the vegetables and spices from the marinade. Continue frying until lightly browned, then add the flour and wine, and the bouquet garni. Season with salt. Cook on medium heat, uncovered, for between 45 minutes and 1 hour, or until the wine has reduced by three-quarters. Then add the chicken broth and veal broth and cook, covered, for two and a half hours.
Clean the Swiss chard and cut the ribs into diamonds. Cut the green parts into long strips and reserve them for the filling.
Cook the white parts of the Swiss chard in 2 cups (500 ml) water with 2 tablespoons flour and some salt. Season the piece of veal and sauté it in duck fat until still pink inside. Grind it in a food processor. Wash the spinach and green parts of the Swiss chard and wilt them in a little duck fat. Chop them finely. Soak the brain in water to which a little vinegar has been added. Chop coarsely with a knife. Strain the venison stew, reserving the vegetables in one bowl and the meat in another. Pour the cooking liquid into a saucepan and cook over medium heat to reduce. Detach the meat from the bone and chop the meat with a knife. Combine the chopped veal, brain, spinach,

venison, mascarpone, and Basque sheep's milk cheese until you have a smooth mixture. Check the seasoning. This is the filling for the ravioli.

For the ravioli dough
INGREDIENTS
· 3 ½ cups (400 g) all-purpose flour
· 1 egg
· ⅓ cup (100 ml) olive oil
· Salt

METHOD
Combine all the ingredients for the ravioli dough. When the dough is smooth, leave it to rest, wrapped in plastic wrap, for at least 1 hour in a cool place. Roll it out several times in a pasta machine, making it thinner each time. The final dough should be very thin.
Put a teaspoon of filling on each square of the dough and make raviolis in the shape of a humbug. Transfer them to a plate dusted with flour and reserve.

For the garnish
INGREDIENTS
· Olive oil
· 1 tablespoon (15 g) butter
· 4 large shavings (20 g) Reggiano Parmesan
· ½ cup (120 g) Parmesan, grated
· 2 sprigs chervil

METHOD
Bring a large pot of salted water to the boil and add a little olive oil. Cook the ravioli, allowing six per person. The ravioli are cooked as soon as they rise to the surface.
Put four ladlefuls of the venison stew gravy into a large sauté pan. Add the butter and adjust the seasoning. Add the ravioli and Swiss chard ribs and coat with the gravy. Add a little grated Parmesan.
Divide the Swiss chard whites between the plates and arrange the ravioli on top. Coat with the venison gravy in which the ravioli were cooked. Then place the Parmesan shavings on top. Serve immediately. (Photo p. 46)

PATRICIA DESMEDT

LEMON-FLAVORED CRUNCHY CHEESECAKE WITH SEMI-SWEET CARAMEL SAUCE
PREPARATION TIME: 40 MINUTES
REFRIGERATION TIME: 1 HOUR
TO SERVE: 4

INGREDIENTS
· 2 egg yolks
· 2 ¾ tablespoons (75 g) superfine sugar
· 1 ¾ cups (400 ml) light cream
· 1 teaspoon vanilla sugar
· 1 cup (250 g) cream cheese (40 percent fat)
· Juice of 2 lemons
· 5 sheets unflavored gelatin, soaked in water then squeezed
· 8 ounces (250 g) spice cookies
· ⅓ cup (100 g) melted butter
· 4 tuiles or other types of cookie to garnish

For the caramel sauce
· 5 ½ ounces (150 g) sugar
· 1 tablespoon liquid glucose or light corn syrup
· 4 tablespoons (60 g) lightly salted butter
· 5 ½ ounces (150 ml) light cream

METHOD
To make the small cheesecake, combine the egg yolks and sugar. Beat the cream with the vanilla sugar. Incorporate the cream cheese and add the lemon juice and gelatin leaves. Stir just until smooth.
Pour the mixture into individual jelly molds and refrigerate for 1 hour. Break the spice cookies into small pieces and mix them with the melted butter. Press the mixture into individual buttered round molds.
To make the caramel, cook the sugar with the liquid glucose or light corn syrup and a little water until it turns caramel color.
Add the lightly salted butter and the cream, stirring gently. Leave to cool.
Arrange one of the spice cookie rounds in the center of each plate. Place the cheesecake on top and pour a little caramel sauce at the side. Finish with a cookie of your choice.

LOBSTERS WITH HOMEMADE POTATO CHIPS AND OSCIETRA CAVIAR
PREPARATION TIME: 45 MINUTES
COOKING TIME: 1 HOUR
TO SERVE: 4

INGREDIENTS
· 4 large floury potatoes
· 2 tablespoons olive oil
· ⅓ cup (100 ml) light cream
· 1 tablespoon celeriac purée
· 2 cooked lobsters, weighing around 1 pound, 5 ounces (600 g) each, shelled
· 3 tablespoons olive oil
· Salt and cayenne pepper
· 2 tablespoons lemon juice
· 24 x 2 inch (5 cm) slices steamed celery root
· 4 x 1 inch (2 cm) strips leek, steamed
· 2 teaspoons (10 g) salmon-trout roe
· 4 teaspoons oscietra caviar
· 4 strips lemon zest
· 8 strands spaghetti cooked and brushed with olive oil
· 8 chives
· 2 tablespoons olive oil
· Coarse salt

UTENSILS
· 1 mandolin slicer
· 1 x 2 ½ inch (6.5 cm) hoop

METHOD
Wash the floury potatoes, slice them thinly using a mandolin slicer and arrange 4 rounds on an oiled cookie sheet. Bake in a preheated 210°F (100°C) oven for 1 hour to make potato chips. Carefully remove them from the sheet using a spatula and drain them on kitchen paper.
Beat the light cream and season it with salt and pepper. Add the celeriac purée and refrigerate until required.
Dice the lobster into ½ inch (1 cm) cubes, add the olive oil (seasoned with salt, cayenne pepper, and lemon juice) and mix well in a bowl.
Place the rounds of celeriac in the center of the plate and place the 2 ½ inch (6.5 cm) hoop on top. Fill the hoop with the lobster, remove the hoop and surround with a strip of leek. Pour some of the celeriac purée around the lobster and garnish it with a little salmon-trout roe. Place a potato chip on the lobster. Add 1 teaspoon oscietra caviar, 1 small piece lemon zest, and the spaghetti. Garnish with the chopped chives, a sprinkling of olive oil, and some coarse salt, if the caviar is not too salty.

RABBIT AND CHICKEN BREAST WITH MORELS
PREPARATION TIME: 45 MINUTES
COOKING TIME: 12 MINUTES
TO SERVE: 4

INGREDIENTS
· 4 young rabbit backs
· 1 egg white
· 4 tablespoons (50 ml) light cream
· 1 corn-fed chicken breast, or two boneless breast halves
· 1 sheet phyllo dough
· 4 rabbits' kidneys
· 8 strips steamed leek
· 2 tablespoons (25 g) unsalted butter
· 4 thin strips steamed carrot
· 2 tablespoons aged ruby port
· ⅓ cup (100 ml) chicken stock
· 24 morels
· Salt and pepper

METHOD
Bone the rabbit, retaining the fillets, and cut them in half, or have your butcher do it. For the stuffing, grind the rest of the meat in a food processor, add the egg white and cream, and season with pepper and salt. Place a piece of rabbit fillet inside a 2 ½ inch (6.5 cm) hoop with a little stuffing and a piece of breast fillet, then add some stuffing, and finish with another piece of rabbit. Remove the hoop and place these small cakes in a buttered baking pan. Season with salt and pepper. Cook for around 12 minutes in a preheated 425°F (220°C) oven. Remove from the oven and leave to rest for 5 minutes under a sheet of aluminum foil. Garnish each rabbit cake with a slice of carrot, held in place with a strip of leek.
Cut the phyllo dough into 4 slices. Add some of the stuffing and a kidney on top and enclose in a strip of leek. Fry the little kidney packages. Drain them on absorbent paper. Deglaze the baking pan with the ruby port and chicken stock. Pour the mixture into a saucepan, reduce, and add half the butter. Clean the morels and sauté them in the rest of the butter; season with pepper and salt. Arrange the morels on plates, then place the rabbit and chicken cakes on top of the mushrooms. Arrange a few morels on the meat and pour the port-flavored sauce around it.
Put a little kidney package at the side of the plate. (Photo p. 50)

LYDIA EGLOFF

ROAST SQUAB WITH ANGELICA AND RED CABBAGE SAUERKRAUT
PREPARATION TIME: 45 MINUTES,
BUT THE SAUERKRAUT MUST BE MADE
A WEEK IN ADVANCE
COOKING TIME: 15 MINUTES
TO SERVE: 4

INGREDIENTS
For the sauerkraut
· 1 medium red cabbage

- 10 brown sugar lumps
- 2 cups (500 ml) aged vinegar
- 1 teaspoon ground juniper berries
- 2 cups (500 ml) Corbières wine
- 1 orange, sliced into rounds
- 4 fresh bay leaves
- Sea salt and Malabar pepper

For the roast squab
- 4 squab (around 3 weeks old)
- 4 ounces (125 g) candied angelica
- 3 ½ tablespoons (50 ml) hazelnut oil
- Sea salt and freshly ground black pepper (Malabar pepper if possible)

METHOD

To make the sauerkraut, discard two or three layers of the outer leaves as well as the core. Wash the cabbage leaves. Shred the cabbage using an electric shredder to a thickness of 1/8 inch (3 mm) and transfer it to an earthenware crock. Make a very light caramel with the sugar moistened with a little vinegar. As soon as it is a honey color, add the rest of the vinegar and the red wine and grind 8 turns of the peppermill over it. Reduce this caramel by half, add the rounds of orange, bay leaves, and a small handful of sea salt. Pour this mixture, while still boiling hot, over the red cabbage. Gently shake the crock to distribute the liquid evenly. Cover the crock with a saucer that is smaller than the mouth of the crock, and weigh down with a heavy weight, such as a can. Leave to cool and store in a cool place for 8 days.

Cut the angelica into pieces and slip pieces under the skin of the squab. Add a little hazelnut oil to an enameled flameproof cast iron casserole and sauté the birds all over on high heat. Season lightly with salt and pepper, cover, and cook in a preheated 300°F (150°C) oven for 15 minutes.

Strain the sauerkraut juice and pour it into a saucepan. Cook half of it on medium heat for 10 minutes to reduce it. Then add the red cabbage and braise, covered, on low heat for 10 minutes.

Remove the squab from the oven and check for doneness. The flesh should be pink and rosy. Cut them into serving pieces and keep them warm, ensuring that the angelica can be seen under the skin. Use the rest of the cabbage juice to glaze the casserole in which the squab were cooked and strain through a fine sieve. Reduce again if necessary.

Arrange a mound of the sauerkraut on a serving platter and place the pieces of squab around it. Surround with a trail of cooking liquid. Serve immediately.

SNAILS WITH HERB SAUCE AND BROCCOLI

PREPARATION TIME: 50–60 MINUTES

COOKING TIME: 7 MINUTES

TO SERVE: 4–6

INGREDIENTS
- 2 x 2 dozen fresh snails
- 2 bunches arugula
- 2 bunches basil
- 1 ¼ cups (300 ml) water
- 6 tablespoons (80 g) lightly salted butter
- 2 tablespoons olive oil
- 3 garlic cloves, blanched
- 4 tablespoons (60 g) all-purpose flour
- 4 tablespoons (60 g) medium farina (cream of wheat)
- 2 whole eggs
- 2 egg yolks
- ¼ cup (50 g) grated Parmesan cheese
- 1 tablespoon oil
- Salt and pepper

For the topping
- 14 ounces (400 g) flaky pastry dough
- 1 egg yolk
- 2 tablespoons milk
- 1 head broccoli
- 2 bunches arugula
- 2 tablespoons olive oil
- 3 tablespoons grated Parmesan
- 1 ⅓ cups (200 ml) whipped cream
- Salt and pepper

METHOD

Slice half the snails finely and chop one of the two bunches of arugula. For the pastry for the snails, wash and drain the arugula. Pull the leaves from the basil. Boil the water with salt, and add the basil and arugula and press them down into the liquid. Strain immediately while still hot and put in the bowl of a food processor with the butter, olive oil, and water, and blanched garlic cloves. Process until the liquid is very green and smooth like a thin sauce. Reserve 4 tablespoons for the finished dish in a small bowl. Pour the rest of the green liquid into a saucepan and cook for a few seconds on very low heat. Then add the flour and farina all at once. Cook stirring for a few moments. Beat the whole eggs with the yolks. Add the

chopped snails to the saucepan as well as the eggs, Parmesan, and chopped basil. Lightly oil a bowl so that the mixture does not stick to it and transfer the contents of the saucepan to the bowl.

Roll out the flaky pastry dough and cut out 4 strips about 10 inches (24 cm) long and 3 inches (8 cm) wide. Beat the egg yolk with the milk to make a pastry glaze and very light brush the dough with the glaze, ensuring it is not too wet. Put the snail mixture into a forcing bag with a wide, plain nozzle and pipe a cylinder of the paste along the strip across two-thirds of the width. Roll up and seal the rolls. Slice them into 16 slices so as to form little mouthfuls. Cook in a preheated 425°F (220°C) oven for 7 minutes. Separate the broccoli into florets and cook in boiling salted water for 3 minutes. Grind in a food processor and strain. Season to taste. Cook the remaining 2 dozen snails in the rest of the green sauce. Check the seasoning. Arrange the arugula on 4 plates and sprinkle with a few drops of olive oil. Top with the grated Parmesan cheese. Arrange the little pastry rolls on the plate with the snails cooked in green sauce. Put the whipped cream into sundae glasses and pour the broccoli juice over it. Serve immediately. (Photo p. 53)

NICOLE FAGEGALTIER

PINEAPPLE AND COCONUT CROUSTILLANT WITH COCONUT MOUSSE AND ORANGE ICE CREAM

PREPARATION TIME: 80 MINUTES

COOKING TIME: 10 MINUTES

TO SERVE: 4

INGREDIENTS
- 1 pineapple
- 1 vanilla bean
- 1 pinch pumpkin pie spice
- 4 teaspoons (20 g) butter
- 3 tablespoons sugar

For the pineapple sauce
- 4 teaspoons (20 g) sugar
- ½ cup (125 ml) pineapple juice

For the nut cookies
- ⅓ cup (100 g) sugar
- 3 tablespoons (40 g) butter
- 3 tablespoons (40 g) light corn syrup or sugar
- 2 tablespoons milk

- ⅓ cup (100 g) shortcrust dough, ground to a powder in a food processor

For the coconut mousse
- 1 sheet unflavored gelatin
- 3 cups (750 ml) milk
- 3 tablespoons (40 g) sugar
- 6 tablespoons (40 g) unsweetened shredded coconut
- ⅓ cup (100 g) whipped cream

For the orange ice cream
- 2 cups (500 ml) milk
- 1 teaspoon ground coriander
- 3 egg yolks
- 4 tablespoons (60 g) sugar
- 4 tablespoons (60 g) heavy cream
- 3 ½ tablespoons (50 g) light corn syrup or sugar
- 1 orange, rind blanched 3 times, then finely chopped into zest

METHOD

Peel the pineapple and cut 4 slices lengthwise without using the core. Then use a metal cookie-cutter to cut out 3 rounds with a diameter of 2 inches (4 cm) in each slice, making 12 rounds in all. Reserve the rest of the pineapple flesh. Make the pineapple sauce by putting the rest of the pineapple flesh in a food processor, adding a little water, the vanilla bean, and pumpkin pie spice. Process to a liquid, then strain.

Melt the butter in a skillet, sauté the 12 pineapple rounds. Sprinkle them with the sugar and allow to caramelize. When cooked, add half the filtered pineapple juice. Remove the skillet from the heat and place the pineapple rounds and liquid in separate bowls.

To make the pineapple sauce, make a caramel using the sugar. As soon as it starts to color, add the rest of the pineapple juice.

To make the cookies, in a saucepan, heat the sugar, butter, light corn syrup or sugar, and the milk. Bring to the boil, stirring, then remove from the heat and stir in the ground shortcrust dough. Spread the mixture on a sheet of Silpat, Flexipan, or similar nonstick release baking paper. Bake in a preheated 325°F (160°C) oven for 10 minutes. Cut out 4 strips measuring around 3 x 2 inches (8 cm x 5 cm) and use a greased metal tube or the handle of a wooden spoon to make 4 cylinders just under 2 inches (4 cm) in diameter and around 3 inches (8 cm) long.

To make the coconut mousse, soak the gelatin in cold water. Boil the milk with the sugar and add the coconut. Off the heat, squeeze the sheet of gelatin and add it to the pan. Stir, then leave to cool and when cold, add the whipped cream. Refrigerate until required. To make the orange ice cream, boil the milk with the ground coriander and remove from the heat. Leave to infuse while you beat the egg yolks with the sugar. Pour the heavy cream over this mixture and stir well. Pour back into the pan and return to the heat. Cook this custard, stirring constantly until it coats the back of the spoon. Add the light corn syrup or sugar and orange rind. Pour the mixture into an ice-cream maker, process, and put it aside.

To assemble the dish, draw lines of caramel on each serving plate, then stand a cylindrical cookie vertically on the caramel. Place a round of pineapple inside the cylinder, topped with a layer of coconut mousse. Do this twice more then top with a scoop of ice cream.

Serve with the warmed pineapple juice.

NOUGATINE MILLE-FEUILLE FILLED WITH COFFEE MASCARPONE, WITH TAFFY ICE CREAM

PREPARATION TIME: 45 MINUTES
COOKING TIME: 10 MINUTES
TO SERVE: 4

INGREDIENTS
For the chocolate nougatine
· ⅓ cup (100 g) sugar
· 2 tablespoons milk
· 3 tablespoons (40 g) butter
· 3 tablespoons (40 g) glucose
· 1 teaspoon (5 g) unsweetened cocoa powder
· 3 tablespoons (70 g) chopped almonds
For the coffee sauce
· 2 tablespoons (30 g) sugar
· 1 tablespoon very strong espresso coffee
For the coffee cookie dough
· 2 eggs
· 3 tablespoons (80 g) sugar
· 5 ½ tablespoons (75 g) all-purpose flour
· 2 tablespoons strong coffee
For the mascarpone mousse
· ⅔ cup (150 g) mascarpone
· 2 tablespoons (30 g) sugar
· 1 ⅓ cup (150 g) whipped cream

For the taffy ice cream
· 1 cup (250 ml) milk
· 2 ½ ounces (70 g) taffy
· 3 egg yolks
· 3 tablespoons sugar
· 4 tablespoons (60 g) light cream
· 3 ½ tablespoons (50 g) light corn syrup or sugar

METHOD
To make the chocolate nougatine, boil the sugar with the milk, butter, glucose, and unsweetened cocoa. Then add the chopped almonds. Pour this mixture on a sheet of Silpat release paper or aluminum foil. Bake in a preheated 325°F (160°C) oven for 10 minutes. Cut into rectangles measuring around 1 x 5 inches (3 cm x 13 cm).
To make the coffee sauce, heat the sugar in a dry skillet. As soon as it starts to turn color, add the coffee. Cook on low heat to reduce the liquid.
To make the coffee cookies, separate the egg whites from the yolks and beat the egg yolks and sugar together until the mixture is pale and fluffy. Add the flour and beat until smooth. Whip the egg whites until they are stiff and incorporate them. Spread the mixture on a nonstick cookie sheet to a depth of ½ inch (1 cm) and bake in a preheated 325°F (160°C) oven for 10 minutes. Cut into rectangles measuring around 1 x 5 inches (3 cm x 13 cm).
To make the mascarpone mousse, add the sugar to the mascarpone cheese, then fold in the whipped cream.
To make the ice cream, boil the milk with the taffy and stir until dissolved. Beat the egg yolks with the sugar until pale and fluffy and pour the light cream over them. Return to the heat and cook, stirring, as if for a custard. Add the corn syrup or sugar and transfer to an ice-cream maker.
To serve, soak the cookies in the strong coffee. Put the mousse into a forcing bag. Pipe a layer of mascarpone mousse over the cookies, and sprinkle with the coffee sauce. Arrange a piece of the nougatine on top followed by another layer of cream and coffee sauce. Continue layering, finishing with a piece of nougatine.
Serve with the taffy ice cream in a circle of nougatine cookie, and add a trail of coffee sauce.
(Photo p. 57)

AVEYRON VEAL AND SÉGALA, ALMOND CREAM AND PRESERVED FENNEL WITH COMBAVA*

PREPARATION TIME: 40 MINUTES
COOKING TIME: 1 HOUR
TO SERVE: 4

INGREDIENTS
· 1 pound, 12 ounces (800 g) boned rib of veal, with the bone
· 1 carrot, sliced
· 1 onion, sliced
· 1 leek, sliced
· 1 bouquet garni
· 1 x 14-ounce (400-g) fennel bulb
· 4 tablespoons olive oil
· 4 teaspoons (20 g) butter
· Combava (*a mixture of sel Guérande—French sea salt—and combava, a tiny lemon grown on the island of Réunion)
· Pepper
For the almond-flavored creamed potatoes
· 3 tablespoons (40 g) potatoes
· ½ cup (120 ml) milk
· 1 ¾ cups (400 ml) light cream
· 4 teaspoons (20 g) ground almonds

METHOD
To make a gravy with the rib of veal, put it into a large pot with the sliced carrot, onion, leek, and the bouquet garni. Add water to cover, season with salt and pepper, and simmer for 1 hour on low heat. Strain the liquid and reduce it to a syrupy consistency (there should be around 5 tablespoons left).
Split the fennel bulb into 4 pieces lengthwise. In a sauté pan, heat 4 tablespoons olive oil with the fennel, combava and pepper, then add water to cover. Cover and cook just below the boil, checking the fennel for doneness by inserting a small knife into it. Cut the boned rib of veal into 4 equal portions. Heat the rest of the oil and the butter in a sauté pan. Season the meat with salt and pepper and place it in the pan. Cook until browned, and finish cooking in a preheated 425°F (220°C) oven for 10 minutes. Remove the meat and let it rest. To make the creamed potatoes, dice them and cook in a saucepan in the milk and cream. When cooked, around 15 minutes, add the ground almonds. Process in a food processor and then strain. Before serving, arrange the cooked fennel on the serving plates, pour

1 tablespoon of the creamed potatoes onto the plate. Slice the veal thickly and place slices next to the fennel. Pour the gravy over them and sprinkle a little combava over the veal. (Photo p. 58)

ANNIE FEOLDE

SPAGHETTI ALLA CHITARRA WITH DRIED TOMATOES AND CREAM OF GARDEN PEAS

PREPARATION TIME: 30 MINUTES
COOKING TIME: 3 HOURS, 40 MINUTES
(INCLUDING 3 HOURS FOR THE TOMATOES THE DAY BEFORE)
TO SERVE: 4

INGREDIENTS
· 12 very thin slices Canadian bacon or salt pork
· 1 ⅓ cup (320 g) freshly made spaghetti *alla chitarra*, bought from an Italian deli (or see below)
· Extra-virgin olive oil
· 1 bunch small-leaved basil
· Salt and pepper
For the dried tomatoes
· 12 very ripe plum tomatoes
· 1 teaspoon fresh thyme leaves
· Olive oil
· Coarse salt
For the cream of garden peas
· 1 shallot
· 1 slice Canadian bacon or salt pork
· 8 ounces (200 g) shelled fresh garden peas
· 1 ¼ cups (300 ml) chicken stock
· Extra-virgin olive oil
· Salt and pepper

METHOD
The day before, dip the tomatoes in boiling water for 30 seconds, rinse them in cold water, and peel them. Cut them into quarters, discard the seeds, and drain them for 30 minutes in sieve.
Arrange the quartered tomatoes on an ovenproof dish, season them with coarse salt and thyme, and sprinkle them with olive oil. Bake them for 3 hours in the oven at 200°F (90°C).
To make the cream of garden peas, chop the shallot, and cut the bacon or pork into very small pieces. Sauté the shallot and meat in a little olive oil, add the peas, mix well, and immediately add the stock. Simmer for 20 minutes. Purée them in a blender then pour the liquid through a fine conical

sieve to eliminate all the skins. You should have around ⅔ cup (150 ml) of cream of garden peas. Season with salt and pepper and reserve.

Preheat the oven to 350°F (180°C). Arrange the 12 slices of Canadian bacon or salt pork on a cookie sheet between two sheets of nonstick baking paper. Place an even weight on top of them (such as a fairly heavy round cookie sheet that will flatten them during cooking). Bake for 10 minutes. Slice the dried tomatoes into pieces.

Immerse the spaghetti into 3 quarts (3 l) salted boiling water. As soon as the spaghetti rises to the surfaces, remove and drain; it will be al dente. Combine the spaghetti and tomatoes in a skillet, add a little olive oil and mix for 1 minute over low heat.

Reheat the cream of garden peas and distribute it between the plates. Then top with the spaghetti and slices of bacon or pork. Decorate with basil leaves, season with pepper, and serve immediately. (Photo p. 64)

We make our own *alla chitarra* pasta. The *chitarra* (guitar) is a kitchen tool that is used in southern Italy. It has metal strings for slicing spaghetti. If you have one of these utensils, or a manual pasta-maker, here are the proportions to use:
2 cups (250 g) flour, 4 egg yolks, 1 tablespoon oil, 1 tablespoon water. Mix the pasta and knead it. Cover it with a damp cloth and leave to rest for at least 30 minutes in the refrigerator.

Roll out the dough with a rolling pin to a thickness of 1/8 inch (2 mm), then slice it into rectangles the same size as the *chitarra* and press it onto the strings of the instrument with a rolling pin. Immediately sprinkle the spaghetti with flour and keep wrapped in a damp cloth in a cool place.

CHRISTINE FERBER

PRALINE NUT SHORTCRUST PASTRY

PREPARATION TIME: 20 MINUTES, PLUS
1 HOUR MINIMUM FOR RESTING
TO MAKE 20 OUNCES (600 G) OF
DOUGH (TWO LAYERS)

INGREDIENTS
· 2 cups (250 g) all-purpose flour
· ⅔ cup (150 g) softened butter
· 1 cup (100 g) powdered (confectioner's) sugar
· 2 tablespoons (25 g) crushed praline or praline powder (from a gourmet store, gourmet section of the supermarket, or make your own)
· 4 tablespoons (50 g) ground hazelnuts
· 1 dash of salt
· 1 egg, beaten

METHOD
Sift the flour over the work surface and make a well in the center. Put the softened butter into the well, together with the sugar and crushed praline. Sprinkle the salt and ground hazelnuts around the edge. Mix the ingredients in the center until you have a thick, creamy batter.

Gradually move the flour into the center of the well, rubbing it between your fingers and thumb until the mixture has a sandy texture. Make a well in the center of this new mixture and pour the beaten egg into it. Knead the dough lightly without working it too much, then roll it into a ball, and wrap it in plastic wrap. Leave it to rest for at least 1 hour in the refrigerator before using it or, better still, make it the night before. It is easiest to make this quantity of dough. You can freeze whatever you don't need for use another time. The flour can be flavored with a dash or two of cinnamon, or the ground seeds of two cardamom pods.

The dough is ideal for baking blind (without a filling), because it does not shrink, which means you won't need to cover the inside base with nonstick baking paper, dried beans, or grains of rice. Make sure it fits tightly to the walls and angles of the pan if it is square or rectangular.

CARDAMOM-FLAVORED ALMOND CREAM

PREPARATION TIME: 10 MINUTES
TO MAKE AROUND 1 1/4 CUPS (300 G)
ALMOND CREAM

INGREDIENTS
· 3 ounces (75 g) softened butter
· 2 ounces (60 g) confectioner's sugar
· 2 small eggs
· 2 tablespoons (30 g) all-purpose flour
· 3 ounces (75 g) ground almonds
· Ground seeds from 2 cardamom pods

METHOD
Beat the butter and sugar together with an electric beater. Add the eggs, flour, ground almonds, and cardamom, beating well, until the cream becomes pale and smooth. This cream can also be flavored with a little grated zest from untreated oranges or lemons, a few drops of orange-flower water, cinnamon, or ground anise. If this almond cream is spread over a pie shell when cooking fruit pies, the almond cream will become impregnated by the juice released by fruits during baking and will keep the pastry firm and crunchy.

SOUR CHERRIES WITH PEPPER

PREPARATION TIME: 45 MINUTES
COOKING TIME: 10 MINUTES
TO MAKE 5 MASON-TYPE JARS OF
7-OUNCE (200-G) CAPACITY.

INGREDIENTS
· 1 ¾ pounds ounces (800 g) sour cherries
· ½ cup (125 ml) white vinegar
· ½ cup (100 ml) water
· ½ cup (100 g) preserving sugar
· ⅓ cup (125 g) flower honey
· 40 black peppercorns

METHOD
To make the sweet-and-sour sauce, pour the vinegar into a small stainless-steel saucepan. Add the water, sugar, and honey. Bring to the boil, skim well, and reserve. Wash the sour cherries, then dry them in a kitchen towel. Carefully remove the stems.
Prick each cherry with a needle to allow the juice to penetrate. Arrange the cherries in layers in the preserving jars (about 36 to a jar with 8 peppercorns).
Bring the sweet-and-sour juice to just below the boil and, when the liquid is simmering, pour it over the cherries. They must be completely covered.
Seal the jars and turn them upside down until the next day. Keep them in the refrigerator for 2 to 3 weeks before opening. The cherries are served as an appetizer with salami or pepperoni sausage or pork rillettes, or to accompany a raclette.

ROSE-HIP PURÉE

The berries of the wild rose or dog rose, known as "rose hips," are delicious in a jam, as long as the little hairs on the inside are completely removed.
They should only be picked when they are dark red, after the first frost has softened them. There are two ways of making them into a purée:

FIRST METHOD
Quickly rinse the hips under cold running water. Wearing thin rubber or plastic gloves, remove the stems with a sharp knife, remove the cap (the little black patch), then slice them in half lengthwise, removing all the seeds and hairs. Rinse the cleaned berries again, put them in a heavy-based saucepan, and cover them with water. Bring to the boil, then simmer them for about 30 minutes, stirring occasionally. Leave them to cool, then mill the cooking liquid and berries in a vegetable mill with a fine screen, so that the skins are left behind.

SECOND METHOD
Clean the hips as above, put them whole into a saucepan, and cover with water. Bring to the boil and cook for 30 minutes, or until the fruits burst open. Leave them to cool. Grind the fruits several times in a vegetable mill, using a finer screen each time. This will ensure that the seeds, hairs, and skins are left behind.
Finally, push the pulp through a silk screen to eliminate the last hairs.

ROSE-HIP PRESERVE WITH VANILLA

PREPARATION TIME: 2 HOURS
COOKING TIME: 35 MINUTES
(INCLUDING 30 MINUTES TO MAKE THE
ROSE-HIP PURÉE)
TO MAKE 5 OR 6 7-OUNCE (200-G) JARS

INGREDIENTS
· 2 ¼ pounds (1 kg) rosehip purée (see above), using around 5 ½– 6 ½ pounds (2 ½–3 ½ kg) raw fruits
· 1 vanilla bean (pod), split lengthwise
· 4 cups (800 g) preserving sugar

METHOD
Boil the jars and lids and drain them on a clean kitchen towel. Make the rose-hip purée, using

either of the methods indicated, then pour it into a preserving pan with the split vanilla pod and the sugar.

Bring to the boil, stirring constantly. Continue at a rolling boil for 5 minutes, stirring constantly. To check to see if the preserve is cooked, drop a teaspoonful on a very cold saucer and tip it up slightly. If the liquid does not run but "coats" the saucer, remove the pan from the heat. If not, continue cooking until the right consistency is reached.

Remove the vanilla bean and chop it into pieces. Pour the preserve into the preserving jars, adding a piece of vanilla to each. Seal the jars and turn them over. The next day, store the preserve in a cool place, away from the light.

This preserve is incomparably smooth. I'm reminded of one of my favorite desserts, which consisted of a little fritter filled with rose-hip preserve. Try it with an Alsace Muscat made from so-called "noble" (late-harvested) grapes.

ROSE GRAY AND RUTH ROGERS

BUFFALO MOZZARELLA, BEAN AND PECORINO CHEESE SALAD

PREPARATION TIME: 15 MINUTES
TO SERVE: 6

INGREDIENTS
· 5 pounds 8 ounces (2.5 kg) fresh young beans in the pod
· ⅓ cup (100 ml) extra-virgin olive oil
· Juice of 1 lemon
· Maldon sea salt and freshly ground black pepper
· 1 bunch arugula leaves
· 1 bunch fresh mint leaves
· ⅔ cup (150 g) fresh Pecorino cheese, thinly sliced
· 6 balls buffalo mozzarella

METHOD
Shell the beans and put them into a bowl. Add the oil and lemon juice. Mix well and season with salt and pepper.
Mix the rocket and mint leaves in another bowl. Add the beans with their seasoning and toss lightly. Sprinkle the slices of Pecorino cheese on top. Then sprinkle with

olive oil. Drain the mozzarella and slice it, arranging it on top just before serving. (Photo p. 72)

WILD HERB MEDLEY

PREPARATION TIME: 25 MINUTES
COOKING TIME: 15 MINUTES
TO SERVE: 4

INGREDIENTS
· 8 ounces (250 g) endive or escarole
· 7 ounces (200 g) arugula
· 7 ounces (200 g) Swiss chard (silverbeet)
· 7 ounces (200 g) turnip or radish greens
· 4 tablespoons extra-virgin olive oil
· 4 garlic cloves
· 2 small dried chili peppers
· 2 lemons
· Maldon salt*
· Freshly ground black pepper
· Lemon wedges to serve

METHOD
Wash all the greenery. If radish greens are used instead of turnip greens, rinse them in several waters, because they are often full of soil and sand.
Cook each type of greenery separately in salted boiling water with coarse salt. The arugula should take around 3 minutes, the turnip or radish tops, 4 minutes, the endive or escarole, 8 minutes, and the Swiss chard 10 minutes. Drain well, squeezing to remove excess moisture, then chop the largest leaves coarsely.
Peel and finely chop the garlic cloves, and crumble the chili peppers. Heat a large, heavy-based saucepan and add the oil, garlic, and chili pepper. Sauté until the garlic turns color, then mix in the greens and cook for a few seconds, stirring.
Season with Maldon salt and pepper. Serve with lemon wedges.

*Maldon salt. These flakes of English sea salt are pleasantly crunchy in the mouth. The salt is sold at gourmet stores. If not available, it can be replaced by other types of sea salt.

ROAST TURBOT WITH CAPERS

PREPARATION TIME: 20 MINUTES
COOKING TIME: 20–25 MINUTES
TO SERVE: 6

INGREDIENTS
· 6 slices of turbot, including backbone, weighing 8–9 ounces (225–300 g) each
· Juice of 3 lemons
· 1 lemon sliced
· 6 tablespoons chopped tender celery leaves
· 6 tablespoons minced flat-leaved parsley
· 12 tablespoons capers, drained from their vinegar
· 2 tablespoons olive oil
· Maldon salt (or other sea salt)
· Freshly ground black pepper

METHOD
Preheat the oven to 450°F (230°C). Brush the turbot slices with olive oil, and season with salt and pepper. Arrange them in an ovenproof dish and roast for 15 to 20 minutes, depending on the thickness.
Remove them from the oven and arrange them on warmed serving dishes. Pour the lemon juice into the ovenproof dish, add the chopped celery leaves, half the chopped parsley, and the capers. Heat for 1 minute on high heat, stirring well. Pour the mixture over the turbot slices, and sprinkle with the rest of the parsley. Serve with the lemon slices. (Photo p. 71)

CATHERINE GUERRAZ

SWEETBREAD BROCHETTES WITH LEMONGRASS AND CARAMELIZED SALSIFY

PREPARATION TIME: 40 MINUTES
COOKING TIME: 30 MINUTES, PLUS 3 HOURS SOAKING THE SWEETBREADS
TO SERVE: 4

INGREDIENTS
For the sweetbreads
· 1 ¾ pounds (800 g) calves' sweetbreads
· ⅓ cup (75 g) clarified butter (see below)
· 4 lemongrass stalks
· 1 cup (100 g) all-purpose flour
· Salt and pepper
For the sauce
· 1 cup (250 ml) chicken stock
· 2 lemongrass bulbs
· 1 quart (1 l) crème fraîche or heavy cream
· ½ cup (100 g) butter
· Salt and pepper
For the garnish
· 1 ¾ pounds (800 g) salsify (scorzonera or oyster plant)

· Juice of ½ a lemon
· 2 tablespoons (30 g) butter
· 7 ounces (200 g) sugar
· Salt and pepper

METHOD
Soak the sweetbreads in running water for 3 hours.
Put them in a heavy-based saucepan of cold water and bring to the boil. Remove them from the heat, drain them, and rinse under running water.
Clean the sweetbreads, discarding the cartilage, fat, and nerves. Cut them into pieces and reserve in the refrigerator.
To make the sauce, finely chop the lemongrass bulbs, add them to the chicken stock, and boil vigorously, uncovered, to reduce the liquid for 2 minutes. Add the cream and butter and cook on a lower heat to reduce the liquid. Strain, blend, and season with salt and pepper.
To make the garnish, peel the salsify. Add the lemon juice to the water and leave the salsify in the water. Make caramel with the sugar and butter. Add 1 cup (230 ml) water, season with salt and pepper, and cook the salisify in this until it is soft. Cut it into equal pieces and reserve.
Finish cooking the sweetbreads by seasoning them, then dredging them in the flour.
Heat the clarified butter in a skillet on a high heat and sauté the sweetbreads until they are golden and crunchy. Thread them onto the lemongrass stalks.
Reheat the lemongrass sauce and beat it with an electric hand-blender until it foams.
Serve the sweetbreads with the sauce and salsify.

Clarified butter is butter from which the milk solids are removed, making it possible to use it for cooking and frying at high temperatures without burned particles forming. Make it in advance and store it in the refrigerator. Use it in the same quantities as any recommended cooking fat.
Method: melt one or two sticks of butter on a low heat in a saucepan and wait for the white milk solids to separate out; they will sink to the bottom. Recover the liquid on the top. Store in a cold place.

CHOCOLATE FONDANT WITH BUTTERED CARAMEL

PREPARATION TIME: 25 MINUTES
COOKING TIME: 15 MINUTES
TO SERVE: 4

INGREDIENTS

For the fondant
· 2 ¼ ounces (60 g) chocolate truffle bar
· 2 whole eggs
· 2 tablespoons (50 g) sugar
· ¼ cup (30 g) all-purpose flour
· ⅓ cup (70 g) butter, melted and cooled, plus 4 tablespoons (20 g) butter for buttering the molds

For the caramel
· ½ cup (125 g) superfine sugar
· 1 ½ ounces (40 g) salted butter
· ½ cup (100 ml) light cream

METHOD

To make the fondant, break the chocolate into pieces and melt in a double boiler or bain-marie with the butter. Butter and flour four individual soufflé molds.
Beat the eggs and sugar vigorously until you have a creamy mixture that falls in ribbons from a spoon. Incorporate the flour into the melted chocolate and eggs. When the mixture is smooth and well blended, pour it into the molds. Refrigerate for 30 minutes. Preheat the oven to 400°F (200°C).
Slide the molds into the oven and bake them for 9 minutes.
To make the caramel, cook the sugar until it caramelizes, then add a little lemon juice to stop the caramelizing, remove from the heat, and add the salted butter and cream. Return the pan to the heat and bring it to the boil, then remove from the heat and serve it with the chocolate fondants. (Photo p. 76)

FATÉMA HAL

COUSCOUS WITH ROSES

PREPARATION TIME: 30 MINUTES
TO SERVE: 4

INGREDIENTS

· 1 cup (250 g) fine couscous
· 2 tablespoons (25 g) butter
· 5 teaspoons (50 g) sugar
· 1 tablespoon rose water
· 3 teaspoons crushed rose petals and a fourth rose or rosebuds for decoration (obtainable at gourmet stores and some supermarkets)
· 1 teaspoon salt

METHOD

Fill the bottom part of a couscoussier (couscous pot) with water and bring to the boil.
Pour the fine couscous into a big bowl and gradually sprinkle it with water, mixing with the flat of the hands, pulling it up from the bottom to make circles in the air.
Fill the top part of the couscoussier with the couscous and place it over the lower part of the pot. Take a piece of dampened cheesecloth and wrap it round the join between the two halves of the pot so the steam cannot escape.
As soon as steam passes through the couscous grains, remove the top of the pot and empty the contents in a large bowl. Sprinkle again with water, moistening well, and separating the grains by hand or, if they are too hot, with a fork.
When the grains are well separated return them to the top part of the couscous pot. Leave for a few minutes for the steam to pass through the grains, then remove the top half of the couscous pot and repeat the operation with the water. Return the pot to the couscousier.
Repeat the operation once more, this time adding 1 teaspoon salt. Sprinkle with water gradually, aerate the couscous well, and replace it on the top of the couscous pot. As soon as steam passes through the grains again, remove them, put them in a large dish, add the butter, and continue to mix, separating the grains.
Pour the cooked couscous into a bowl and stir it again. Incorporate the sugar, taste and add more if necessary.
Sprinkle with the rosewater. Add the crushed rose petals, mix well, and shape into a mound. Arrange the rest of the roses to form a pretty star on top of the mound.

CHICKEN TAJINE WITH PRUNES AND SESAME SEEDS

PREPARATION TIME: 30 MINUTES
COOKING TIME: 1 HOUR
TO SERVE: 4

INGREDIENTS

· 1 free-range chicken, cut into 8 pieces
· 5 tablespoons oil
· 1 cinnamon stick
· 3 teaspoons saffron or a dozen threads
· 2 onions, sliced
· ½ teaspoon black pepper
· 1 teaspoon salt
· 1 ¾ cups (350 g) pitted prunes
· ⅓ cup (100 g) superfine sugar
· 1 teaspoon ground cinnamon
· ⅓ cup (100 g) butter
· 4 tablespoons sesame seeds

METHOD

Heat the oil in a heavy-based pan and add the cinnamon stick, saffron, sliced onions and the chicken. Sprinkle with pepper. Season with salt, cover with water, and cook on low heat for 45 minutes.
When the chicken is cooked, remove it from the pan and keep it warm. Discard the cinnamon stick. Put the prunes into the pot with the sugar, ground cinnamon and the butter. Add a half a cup (125 ml) of water, mix well, and simmer until you have a creamy sauce.
Return the chicken to the pot and simmer for another 15 minutes. Serve on a large platter, arranging the chicken in the sauce and sprinkling the prunes with sesame seeds. (Photo p. 79)

MURUZIYA

PREPARATION TIME: 25 MINUTES
COOKING TIME: 70 MINUTES
TO SERVE: 6

INGREDIENTS

· ½ teaspoon each of salt and pepper
· 1 pinch of saffron filaments
· 2 teaspoons ras el hanout (spice mixture found in gourmet stores)
· 2 cups (500 ml) water
· 2 pounds 4 ounces (1 kg) lamb, cut into pieces
· 2 tablespoons peanut oil
· 2 onions, grated
· 1 tablespoon *semneh* or clarified butter
· 5 ½ ounces (150g) blanched almonds
· 1 ⅓ cups (300 g) raisins
· ⅓ cup (100 g) honey

METHOD

In a bowl, combine the salt, pepper, saffron, ras el hanout, and ½ cup (125 ml) water. Marinate the meat in half this mixture. Arrange the pieces in a cast-iron pot with the oil and the rest of the water, the grated onions, the *semneh* or clarified butter, and the blanched almonds. Simmer on low heat for 45 minutes.

Meanwhile, soak the raisins in warm water for 15 minutes. Drain them and add them to the meat with the other half of the spices. Simmer for another 20 minutes, then add the honey and keep on a low heat until the almonds and raisins are caramelized.
Serve hot, surrounding the meat with the almonds and raisins.

BASTILLA OF SQUAB

PREPARATION TIME: 45 MINUTES
COOKING TIME: 70 MINUTES
TO SERVE: 6

INGREDIENTS

For the dough
· 30 phyllo dough sheets
· 5 ½ ounces (150 g) melted butter
· 2 egg yolks

For the squab stuffing
· 3 tablespoons oil
· 4 large onions, chopped
· 2 bunches fresh coriander (cilantro), chopped
· 1 teaspoon salt
· 1 tablespoon sugar
· ½ teaspoon pepper
· ¼ teaspoon nutmeg
· ¼ teaspoon ginger
· ¼ teaspoon saffron pistils
· 1 teaspoon cinnamon
· 6 tender squab
· 10 eggs
· 4 bunches flat-leaved parsley
· 1 cup (250 ml) water
(The spices, salt, and sugar can be replaced by a heaping teaspoon of *ras el hanout*.)

For the almond paste
· 2 cups (400 g) almonds
· 2 tablespoons oil for frying the almonds
· ⅓ cup (100 g) sugar
· ½ teaspoon cinnamon
· 1 tablespoon orange-flower water

For the garnish
· ⅔ cup (100 g) icing sugar
· 1 teaspoon cinnamon

METHOD

First make the stuffing. Pour the oil into a large bowl. Add the chopped onions, coriander, salt, sugar, and spices or ras el hanout. Mix well and spread over the whole squab. Cook the squab on high heat. Add 1 cup (250 ml) water. Bring to the boil then reduce the heat, cover and simmer for 45 minutes. Remove the squab and simmer the mixture for another 20 minutes.
Bone the squab, keeping the wings whole. Break the eggs one at a

time into the sauce in the pot, and beat them in over low heat. Remove from the heat.
Blanch the almonds, dry them, and fry them until golden, but do not let them burn. Grind them and transfer them to a bowl. Add the sugar, cinnamon, and orange-flower water. Butter a large round mold and arrange 3 or 4 buttered phyllo dough sheets on top of each other, so that the weight of the filling does not tear the bottom of the bastilla.
Form a ring of buttered phyllo sheets all around it to cover the bottom. The sheets should overlap and gradually reach the edge of the mold, overlapping the edge generously. Do not forget to brush each sheet with melted butter, using a pastry brush. Arrange a layer of the almond paste in the bottom of the mold, then a layer of squab stuffing with squab, alternating the layers until they are used up. Close up the bastilla like a pie, sealing the top and sides together, brushing the seal with egg yolk.
Bake for about 20 minutes in an oven preheated to 375–400°F (180–210°C).
Place the pie on a ceramic serving platter. Sprinkle it with sifted icing sugar all over and decorate with ground cinnamon.
(Photo p. 80)

ANGELA HARTNETT

CITRUS CRUNCH
PREPARATION TIME: 45 MINUTES
COOKING TIME: 20 MINUTES
TO SERVE: 4

INGREDIENTS
For the citrus marmalade
· 1 large grapefruit and 1 large orange
· 2 tablespoons sugar and 2 pinches of pectin (or the same amount of special preserving sugar)
For the orange tuile cookies
· 1 cup (125 g) confectioner's sugar
· ½ cup (50 g) all-purpose flour
· Juice and grated rind of ½ an orange
· ⅔ cup (60 g) softened butter
For the lemon cream
· Juice and grated rinds of 2 untreated lemons
· ⅔ cup (135 g) sugar
· 3 eggs
· ¾ cup (185 g) butter

For the orange caramel
· 1 cup (125 g) confectioner's sugar
· ⅔ cup (150 ml) orange juice
To serve
· 7 ounces (200 ml) lemon sorbet (one scoop per person)
· 2 tablespoons candied citrus peel, thinly sliced

METHOD
To make the citrus marmalade, peel the fruits over a bowl, removing all the white parts. Divide them in half, remove the white membranes in the center, then slice them crosswise.
Pour the juice in the bowl into a saucepan. Bring to the boil with the sugar and pectin (or special preserving sugar). Add the sliced fruits and cook them for 3 to 4 minutes, stirring gently. Remove from the heat and leave to cool.
To make the tuile cookies, preheat the oven to 350°F (180°C). Combine the sugar and flour, and add the juice and rind of the half orange. Incorporate the butter, then mix just until smooth. Cover a cookie sheet with nonstick baking paper and drop small balls of the dough onto it, spacing them out since they will spread into flat cookies. Bake them for 5 to 6 minutes or until golden.
When you take them out of the oven, put a sheet of paper over them to eliminate any air bubbles, then quickly transfer them to a rolling pin, and curl them round it so that they take on the classic tuile shape.
To make the lemon cream, beat the sugar, eggs, and rind until the mixture has a light, foaming consistency. Add the lemon juice and cook in a double boiler or bain-marie, beating constantly with a whisk. Remove from the double boiler or bain-marie, wait for the cream to cool slightly, then gradually incorporate the butter, continuing to beat.
To make the orange caramel, put the sugar into a dry skillet until it solidifies and starts to color, then add the orange juice to liquefy it.
Arrange the citrus slices in the marmalade on dessert plates with the lemon cream and tuile cookies. Serve with the caramel sauce and lemon sorbet, and sprinkle with the candied peel.
(Photo p. 83)

PROFITEROLES WITH CHOCOLATE SAUCE
PREPARATION TIME: 40 MINUTES
COOKING TIME: 35 MINUTES
TO SERVE: 6

INGREDIENTS
To make 20 balls of choux paste
· 1 scant cup (200 ml) water (or half milk, half water)
· ⅓ cup (100 g) butter
· 1 cup (130 g) flour
· 4 eggs, beaten
· 1 pinch salt
· 1 teaspoon sugar
· 1 spray can whipped cream
For the chocolate sauce
· 2 cups (500 ml) milk
· 7 teaspoons (35 g) sugar
· 2 teaspoons (10 g) unsweetened cocoa powder
· 2 tablespoons (25 g) cornstarch
· 1 tablespoon (15 g) confectioner's sugar
· 4 squares (125 g) dark semi-sweet baking chocolate
· 1 pinch salt

METHOD
To make the choux paste, pour the water into a saucepan, add the butter, salt, and sugar. Bring to a fast boil. Remove from the heat and add the flour all at once. Return the saucepan to the heat and beat the mixture until it is smooth and leaves the sides of the pan. Remove from the heat and beat in the beaten eggs.
Preheat the oven to 400°F (200°C). Transfer the paste to a forcing bag (or use two teaspoons) and drop walnut-sized balls of the paste on a nonstick or buttered cookie sheet. Bake for 10 minutes, then increase the heat to 425°F (220°C) and continue cooking for 15 minutes or until the paste is golden and crunchy. Remove from the oven and leave to cool.
Make a little hole in each profiterole and fill it with the whipped cream, giving two or three squirts from the can. Put in a cool place while you make the sauce.
To make the chocolate sauce, boil the milk with 4 teaspoons (20 g) of the sugar and the cocoa powder. Mix the cornstarch with a little cold water, then mix it into the chocolate milk. Bring to the boil, then remove from the heat. Add the salt, the rest of the sugar, and the chocolate broken into small pieces. Mix to a smooth consistency.

Serve the profiteroles with the warm or chilled chocolate sauce.
(Photo p. 84)

MARIE-CHRISTINE KLOPP

EEL TAGINE FROM THE SOMME WITH BAY LEAF, CHARLOTTE POTATOES, COCO DE PAIMPOL BEANS, AND PICKLED LEMONS
PREPARATION TIME: 30 MINUTES
COOKING TIME: 20 MINUTES
TO SERVE: 4

INGREDIENTS
· 4 preserved lemons
· 1 ⅓ cups (300 g) coco de Paimpol beans or other coco beans
· 2 ½ tablespoons (50 g) finest unsalted butter
· 3 shallots, sliced
· 1 head of garlic, cloves peeled
· 3 bay leaves
· 4 tomatoes, skinned and diced
· 3 pounds, 5 ounces (1.5 kg) eels
· 1 ¼ pounds (500 g) of medium-sized Charlotte potatoes
· 3 tablespoons oil
· 1 ¼ cups (300 ml) Pinot Blanc d'Alsace white wine
· 1 tablespoon olive oil
· Salt and pepper

METHOD
To preserve the lemons, after washing them, wrap them in 2 thicknesses of aluminum foil, put them in an earthenware dish, and place in an oven preheated to 200°F (100°C). Leave overnight. Or use ready-made untreated pickled lemons.
Shell the coco beans and cook them in boiling water for 10 minutes. Drain them. Melt the butter and add the beans and sliced shallots, and cook them with the garlic, one bay leaf, and the diced tomatoes. Moisten with 1 cup (250 ml) warm water and simmer for 30 minutes on low heat.
Ask the fishmonger to clean the eels. Peel the Charlotte potatoes and slice them into rounds about ½ inch (1 cm) thick. Wash the other 2 bay leaves, skin the eels, and cut them into short lengths. Sprinkle the potato slices with oil, salt, and pepper, and put them in a tagine or other stewpot. Sprinkle the eels with oil, salt, and pepper and add them to the pot. Add the

partially cooked beans. Quarter the preserved lemons and discard the pips but retain the pulp. Add the white wine, the olive oil, and cook for 20 minutes on the stove top. Cooking this dish in a tagine retains all the pleasantly soft texture of the eel and the flavors of the vegetables like no other cooking utensil.

TANDOORI BABY BACK RIBS, POTATOES, AND BABY PURPLE ARTICHOKES

PREPARATION TIME: 35–40 MINUTES

COOKING TIME: 20 MINUTES

TO SERVE: 6

INGREDIENTS

· 1 rack 13 baby back ribs
· 3–4 tablespoons garam masala or tandoori spices
· 1 cup (250 ml) clarified butter
· 1 garlic clove, minced
· 8 gray shallots, minced
· 1 cup (250 ml) fragrant vegetable stock
· 2 pounds, 4 ounces (1 kg) fresh waxy potatoes, such as Charlotte
· 8 baby purple artichokes
· 2 tablespoons lemon juice
· 2 tablespoons olive oil
· 1 large red onion, sliced
· ⅔ cup (150 ml) dry white wine
· Salt and pepper

METHOD

Bone and trim the baby back ribs or get the butcher to do so. Season with salt and pepper and sprinkle with garam masala or tandoori spices. Arrange in a heated roasting pan and brush with some of the clarified butter. On the stovetop, brown it on both sides, then add the minced garlic and shallots, transfer to a preheated 350°F (180°C) oven and roast for 15 to 20 minutes, basting several times during cooking.
Remove the ribs from the oven and keep them warm in aluminum foil. Deglaze the pan with the fragrant vegetable stock, strain it, and reserve the liquid.
Peel and trim the Charlotte potatoes, wash and dry them carefully, so they do not stick. Then heat 3 tablespoons clarified butter in a skillet and sauté them. When lightly browned, add them to the ribs.
Trim the baby purple artichokes, leaving 1 third of the stems. Cut them in half and remove the choke. Sprinkle them with the lemon

juice, and add them to a tagine with the olive oil, red onion, the white wine, and the strained stock. Cook on the stovetop for 8 minutes. To finish the dish, place the Charlotte potatoes at the top of the plate, and arrange the artichokes on the plate, sprinkling with the cooking juices.
Trim the ribs and place them on each plate with the cooking juices poured round them. (Photo p. 87)

MILK CHOCOLATE TRIANGLES WITH GIN MOUSSE AND GRANNY SMITH APPLES

PREPARATION TIME: 35–40 MINUTES

COOKING TIME: 30 MINUTES

TO SERVE: 6

INGREDIENTS

For the milk chocolate triangles
· 7 ounces (200 g) milk baking chocolate

For the gin mousse
· 3 egg yolks
· 3 tablespoons (40 g) superfine sugar
· 4 teaspoons (20 g) cornstarch
· 4 teaspoons (20 g) all-purpose flour
· 1 ¼ cups (300 ml) milk
· ⅓ cup (100 ml) of la Houlle juniper gin or Dutch gin
· 1 leaf unflavored gelatin, softened in water and squeezed
· 1 scant cup (200 ml) whipped cream

For the almond cream
· 6 tablespooons (80 g) softened butter
· 3 tablespooons (80 g) superfine sugar
· 1 egg at room temperature
· 6 tablespooons (80 g) ground almonds
· 2 Granny Smith apples, peeled, cored, and thinly sliced

METHOD

To make the milk chocolate triangles, melt the milk chocolate in a microwave oven on medium power and spread it on a sheet of silicone release paper. Cover with another sheet of silicone release paper and refrigerate. When it has set, use a sharp knife to cut it into triangles. Keep refrigerated until required. For the gin mousse, first make a confectioner's custard. Beat the egg yolks and sugar until foaming and gradually add the flour and cornstarch, beating constantly until smooth. Boil the milk and pour it

over the mixture. Pour back into the pan and cook, stirring, until the mixture coats the back of a spoon. Pour into a bowl, add the gin and leave to cool. Then incorporate the gelatin and stir until dissolved. Leave to cool, then refrigerate. When cold, fold in the whipped cream. Cover with plastic wrap and return to the refrigerator. To make the almond cream, combine the butter and sugar, then beat in the egg and ground almonds. Pour into a nonstick shallow pan and bake at 350°F (170°C) until it is set but pale (25 to 30 minutes).
Cool to room temperature then refrigerate. Cut into triangles. Arrange the triangles of almond cream in the dish, put the gin mousse into a forcing bag and pipe it on the triangles, interspersing with the thin triangles of milk chocolate, and complete with thin slices of Granny Smith apples surrounding the dessert. (Photo p. 88)

LÉA LINSTER

SCALLOPS COOKED IN THE SHELL WITH WILD MUSHROOMS

PREPARATION TIME: 40 MINUTES

COOKING TIME: 14–15 MINUTES

TO SERVE: 4

INGREDIENTS

· 4 small cep (porcini) mushrooms
· ⅓ cup (100 g) horn-of-plenty mushrooms
· 1 shallot
· 4 teaspoons (20 g) butter
· 8–12 scallops, cleaned
· 4 scallop shells (both halves)
· 3 ½ ounces (100 g) flaky pastry dough
· 1 egg yolk
· Fine sea salt

For the sauce
· 1 shallot
· 2 ½ tablespoons (50 g) butter
· 1 knifepoint chopped garlic
· Wild mushroom peelings
· 1 scant cup (200 ml) homemade chicken stock
· 3 ¼ cups (800 ml) whole milk
· 6 tablespoons (80 ml) light cream
· 4 teaspoons (20 ml) sherry
· Fine sea salt and freshly ground black pepper

To serve
· Coarse sea salt

METHOD

Clean the ceps with a damp cloth but do not wash them. Peel them and slice thickly. Wash the horn-of-plenty mushrooms, dry them, and slice them in half or quarters, depending on the size. Reserve the peelings for the sauce.
Peel the shallot and slice it thinly. Heat the butter in a skillet and, when hot, add the mushrooms and shallot and season lightly with salt. Cook until the shallot is transparent, and then leave to cool.
Wash the scallops under cold, running water and dry them on kitchen paper. Refrigerate until required. Brush the shells thoroughly inside and out and leave them to dry.
Roll out the flaky pastry dough to a thickness of around ⅛ inch (3 mm) and cut out 4 rings about the size of the shells and 1 inch (3 cm) in diameter. Beat the egg yolk lightly with 1 tablespoon water. Preheat the oven to 400°F (200°C). Season the scallops with salt and put 2 or 3 of them in each concave shell. Surround with the mushrooms and close with the flat shell. Brush the dough rounds with egg yolk on one side. Seal the gap between the shell halves with the coated side of the dough. Press the dough around the join of the shells to seal them together, then brush with the egg yolk mixture. Bake the sealed shells for 14 to 15 minutes, or until the pastry is golden-brown.
To make the sauce, while the scallops are cooking, peel and slice the shallot. Melt the 4 teaspoons (20 g) of the butter in a small pan and add the scallops, garlic, and mushroom peelings. Cook for a few minutes, then add the chicken stock. Reduce the liquid by half, then strain it through a fine sieve. Add the milk and cream. Grind in a food processor, gradually adding the rest of the butter cut into small pieces. Season the sauce with salt and pepper and add the sherry.
To assemble the dish, check the seasoning of the sauce and blend it again, so that it is foaming. Sprinkle a large handful of coarse salt in the center of 4 shallow bowls. Arrange the cooked scallop shells on top of the salt. Serve the shells closed, accompanied by the sauce. (Photo p. 92)

JOCELYNE LOTZ-CHOQUART

BURGUNDY SNAILS WITH SPINACH, PINK RADISH CREAM WITH HORSERADISH

PREPARATION TIME: 30 MINUTES
COOKING TIME: 20 MINUTES
TO SERVE: 4

INGREDIENTS
· 24 canned Burgundy snails
· 1 lemon
· 4 cups (250 g) spinach
· 7 ounces (200 g) radishes (half to be grated, half for the sauce)
· 1 scant cup (200 ml) heavy cream
· 2 tablespoon grated preserved horseradish
· 2 tablespoons hazelnut oil
· Salt and freshly ground pepper
· Guérande sea salt

METHOD
Peel 4 thin zests from the lemon. Bring them to the boil in a saucepan of water, then rinse them and repeat the operation twice to remove any bitterness. Slice them into thin strips lengthwise.
Break the spinach stems and pull them so as to remove as much of the ribs as possible. Wash the leaves then steam them in their own liquid for 2 minutes. Remove from the heat and reserve.
To prepare the radishes, wash them and put half of them in a juicer or blender to obtain their juice. Slice the rest very thinly.
Rinse the snails under the cold faucet, wipe them, then wrap each of them in a spinach leaf.
In a heavy saucepan combine the cream, lemon juice, processed radish juice, horseradish, and sliced radish. Simmer on low heat for 10 minutes (the sliced radishes should still be slightly crunchy). Season with salt. Steam the snails for 5 minutes. Remove them and sprinkle them with the hazelnut oil. Pour the radish cream into individual serving dishes. Arrange the snails on top with the lemon zest, a few grains of sea salt, and freshly ground black pepper. Serve immediately. (Photo p. 96)

BRESSE CHICKEN BREAST IN "VIN JAUNE" WITH MORELS

PREPARATION TIME: 35 MINUTES
COOKING TIME: 40 MINUTES
TO SERVE: 6

INGREDIENTS
· 4 chicken breasts, skinned and boned
· 1 ½ ounces (40 g) dried morels
· 8 pearl onions
· 4 ounces (100 g) butter
· 1 ⅔ cups (400 ml) chicken stock
· 1 ½ cups (300 ml) heavy cream
· 2 cloves
· 2 bay leaves
· 2 tablespoons soy sauce
· 1 scant cup (200 ml) Vin Jaune (sweet dessert wine)
· 1 vanilla bean (pod), split in half
· Salt and pepper

METHOD
Soak the morels in water for around 30 minutes to reconstitute them. Rinse them, drain them, and slice them in half.
Peel the pearl onions, cook them for 3 minutes in salted boiling water, drain and rinse them in cold water. Put them in a saucepan with a little cold water and 4 teaspoons (20 g) butter. In a sauté pan, combine the halved morels, chicken stock, heavy cream, cloves, bay leaves, soy sauce, half the Vin Jaune and the split vanilla bean. Mix well and season with salt and pepper. Add the chicken breasts and cook on low heat, with the liquid simmering but not boiling for 10 to 15 minutes, depending on the thickness of the meat. The breasts should still be slightly pink. Remove them from the pan and reserve them covered in aluminum foil.
Discard the vanilla bean, cloves, and bay leaves.
Reduce the sauce containing the morels until it is syrupy. Then add the rest of the Vin Jaune and butter, stirring constantly. Put the breasts into this sauce in order to heat them without boiling. Reheat the pearl onions for 2 minutes. Arrange the chicken breasts on heated plates with the pearl onions and morels, and coat with the Vin Jaune sauce. (Photo p. 96)

The Bresse AOC produces the finest chickens in France, with a flavor and texture that are exceptional. They deserve to be combined with other exceptional flavors, such as that of the yellow, sweet dessert wine of Jura and the wild mushrooms known as morels. However, this festive dish can also be prepared with other premium chicken fillets.

GISÈLE LOVICHI

SARTÈNE-STYLE TRIPE

PREPARATION TIME: 1 HOUR
COOKING TIME: 5–6 HOURS
TO SERVE: 10

INGREDIENTS
· 5 kg veal or beef blanket tripe, bleached and cut into strips measuring 10 cm x 2 cm (4 inches x 1 inch)
· ⅔ cup (150ml) oil
· 2 ¼ pounds (1 kg) onions, sliced
· 1 head garlic
· 4 or 5 bay leaves
· 2 bunches of parsley
· 6 cloves
· 2 cups (500 ml) white wine (optional)
· 5 tablespoons tomato paste
· 1 pig's foot or a knuckle of veal
· Salt and cracked pepper

METHOD
Heat the oil and fry the tripe in a large pot. Add the onions, garlic, bay leaves, parsley, cloves, salt and pepper. Add white wine to taste and simmer for about 15 minutes to reduce the liquid. Add the tomato paste and water to cover the contents.
Cook for 1 hour at a rolling boil, then reduce the heat and add the pig's foot or knuckle of veal. Simmer the meat for 4 to 5 hours. Stir frequently. Serve very hot.

PEARS POACHED IN WINE AND SPICES

PREPARATION TIME: 30 MINUTES
COOKING TIME: 25 MINUTES
TO SERVE: 6

INGREDIENTS
· 8 large pears, peeled and cored, stems retained
· 1 quart (1 liter) strong red wine
· 1 scant cup (200 g) sugar
· 4 cinnamon sticks
· 1 vanilla bean
· 5–6 cloves
· 6 slices orange, cut crosswise
· 6 slices lemon, cut crosswise

METHOD
Put the pears into a saucepan Add the red wine, sugar, spices, and orange and lemon slices. Cover with aluminum foil just over the pears and stew slowly.
Check the pears for doneness by piercing them with a knife point and remove them when they are cooked. Reduce the wine until it is syrupy enough to coat the pears. Serve the pears with vanilla ice cream and decorate it with the orange and lemon slices. Coat them with the sauce. (Photo p. 99)

JOHANNA MAIER

WHITEFISH CARPACCIO WITH BASIL AND SPRING GREEN SALAD

PREPARATION TIME: 30 MINUTES
TO SERVE: 4

INGREDIENTS
· 4 fera or whitefish fillets
· ⅔ cup (150 ml) extra-virgin olive oil
· Juice of 1 lemon
· 12 small vine tomatoes, peeled and diced
· 10 basil leaves, torn into pieces
· Salt and freshly ground black pepper
For the salad
· A large handful of mixed salad leaves (arugula, romaine lettuce, Boston lettuce, etc.)
· 6 tablespoons (80 ml) olive oil
· Juice of 1 lemon
· 4 tablespoons (50 ml) balsamic vinegar
· A pinch of salt and pepper

METHOD
Fillet the fish or have a fishmonger do it. Place the fillets between 2 thicknesses of plastic wrap and carefully flatten them with a steak-hammer. Roll up the fillets and freeze them for 30 minutes to 1 hour to firm them up. Then slice them very thinly.
Pour a few drops of oil onto four flat plates and season with salt and pepper. Arrange the slices of fish on them—the fish should still be slightly frozen.
Mix the rest of the oil with the lemon juice and diced tomato, and season with salt and pepper. Sprinkle the raw fish with this dressing and leave to marinate at room temperature for at least 30 minutes. Sprinkle with the basil and garnish with salad leaves that have been previously seasoned with olive oil, salt and pepper, lemon juice and balsamic vinegar.

BREADED LAMB CUTLETS

PREPARATION TIME: 30 MINUTES
COOKING TIME: 10 MINUTES
TO SERVE: 4–6

INGREDIENTS
- (800 g) chine and leg of lamb
- Salt and freshly ground pepper
- 2 eggs
- 2 tablespoons lightly sweetened whipped cream
- 6 tablespoons (80 g) all-purpose flour
- 1 ½ cups (200 g) soft white breadcrumbs mixed with 1 tablespoon finely chopped thyme and 1 tablespoon chopped rosemary
- 1 cup (250 ml) corn oil
- 2 pounds, 4 ounces (1 kg) waxy potatoes
- 4 flat-leaved parsley sprigs, minced
- Salt and ground cumin
- 5 cups (1.25 l) beef stock
- ¾ cup (180 ml) white wine vinegar
- Salt and freshly ground black pepper
- 1 teaspoon German mustard
- 50 g parsley and basilic
- 2 tablespoons oil

METHOD
Trim the meat and separate it into cutlets. Season them with salt and pepper.
Combine the eggs with the sweetened whipped cream.
Dredge the cutlets in flour, then dip them in the egg and cream mixture.
Then roll them in the breadcrumb and herb mixture. Heat two-thirds of the oil until a cube of bread will brown in 60 seconds.
Fry the cutlets in the hot oil for 8 to 10 minutes until the coating is golden.
Scrub the potatoes and cook them in their skins in boiling water with the parsley, salt, and cumin. Peel them while still hot and dice them.
In a bowl combine the beef stock, white wine vinegar, salt, pepper and mustard, add the rest of the corn oil, and beat with a whisk.
Add the potatoes and leave them to marinate for 15 minutes.
Grind the herbs in a blender with a little oil and sprinkle on the warm potatoes just before serving.
Serve the cutlets with the potato and herb salad. (Photo p. 106)

ELDERBERRIES WITH CHAMPAGNE AND STRAWBERRIES
PREPARATION TIME: 50 MINUTES, PLUS COOKING TIME
TO SERVE: 4

For the champage mixture
INGREDIENTS
- 3 unflavored gelatin leaves, previously soaked and squeezed
- 1 ¾ cups (400 ml) champagne
- 2 vanilla beans (pods)
- Juice of 2 lemons
- 20 strawberries, diced
- Sugar to taste

METHOD
Combine the squeezed gelatin leaves with the champagne.
Add the vanilla beans and lemon juice, and sprinkle with the sugar.
Add the diced strawberries and pour the mixture into sundae glasses.
Chill in the refrigerator.

For the strawberry jelly
INGREDIENTS
- ⅓ cup (100 g) strawberry paste
- Sugar and lemon juice to taste
- 1 gelatin leaf

METHOD
Combine all the ingredients into a creamy mixture.

For the elderberry purée
INGREDIENTS
- 1 scant cup (200 ml) yogurt
- 1 scant cup (200 ml) elderberry syrup
- Juice of 1 lemon
- Superfine sugar to taste
- 3 gelatin leaves, previously soaked and squeezed
- 1 ⅔ cups (300 g) whipped cream

METHOD
Combine the yogurt with the elderberry syrup, lemon juice, and superfine sugar. Incorporate the gelatin and stir until a thin cream is obtained.
Add the whipped cream, folding it in without beating.
Refrigerate the mixture and, as soon as the jelly has set, add half the elderberry purée. Top with the strawberry jelly and fresh strawberries.

For the hazelnut shortcrust
INGREDIENTS
- 1 ⅓ cups (150 g) cake flour
- ⅓ cup (100 g) butter, diced
- 3 ½ tablespoons (50 g) superfine sugar
- 1 small egg
- 6 tablespoons (40 g) ground hazelnuts
- 1 sprig of mint

METHOD
Make a well in the center of the flour. Add the butter, sugar, and the egg. Mix with the fingertips, adding the ground hazelnuts. Shape into a ball, wrap in plastic wrap, and refrigerate for 2 hours. Roll out the dough until it is 5 mm (¼ inch thick).
Cut it into slices and bake in a preheated 325°F (160°C) oven until it is golden.
Arrange the cooked pastry in molds and fill with the remaining elderberry purée. (Photo p. 103)

FLORA MIKULA

BROILED JOHN DORY AND ARTICHOKES WITH PICKLED LEMONS
PREPARATION TIME: 35 MINUTES
COOKING TIME: 35 MINUTES
TO SERVE: 4

INGREDIENTS
- 4 John Dory fillets, each weighing around 5 ounces (150 g)
- 4 raw globe artichoke bottoms, choke discarded
- 1 carrot
- 2 garlic cloves
- 2 shallots
- 7 tablespoons olive oil
- ½ teaspoon coriander seeds
- 1 cup (250 ml) dry white wine
- 3 sprigs thyme
- 1 bay leaf
- Salt and pepper
- 1 pickled lemon (available from Middle Eastern grocery stores)
- 8 gnocchi (fresh)

METHOD
Preheat the oven to 425°F (210°C). Cut the artichoke bottoms into quarters and dice the carrot. Peel and mince the garlic and shallots.
Heat 6 tablespoons of the olive oil in a sauté pan and sauté the shallots, garlic, and carrot. Add the artichokes, coriander seeds, white wine, thyme, and bay leaf. Season with salt and pepper, then simmer for 20 minutes (the artichokes should remain firm to the bite). Rinse the pickled lemon under cold water and cut it into quarters. Add it to the pan with the gnocchi, which will swell in the hot liquid. Transfer to serving plates and keep warm.
Brush the John Dory fillets with the rest of the olive oil and season with salt and pepper. Bake in the preheated oven for 7 to 8 minutes. Arrange the fish fillets on the artichokes and gnocchi and serve at once.
The fish can be sprinkled with pistou before serving (see the recipe for Goat Cheese Pastries, below). Grouper can be used if John Dory is not available.

GOAT CHEESE PASTRIES WITH ICED TOMATO SOUP AND PISTOU
PREPARATION TIME: 50 MINUTES
COOKING TIME: 2 HOURS, 15 MINUTES, INCLUDING 2 HOURS THE DAY BEFORE FOR THE SOUP
TO SERVE: 4

INGREDIENTS
For the iced soup
- 2 ¼ pounds (1 kg) tomatoes
- ½ red bell pepper
- ½ onion
- 2 garlic cloves
- 1 tablespoon sugar
- Olive oil
- Tabasco sauce, salt, and pepper
- ½ bunch of basil

For the pistou
- 1 bunch of basil
- 2 garlic cloves, peeled
- 1 tablespoon grated Parmesan
- 1 teaspoon pine nuts
- ⅔–¾ cup (150–200 ml) olive oil

For the pastries
- 2 small eggplants
- 4 sheets phyllo dough
- ½ red bell pepper
- ½ green bell pepper
- 1 tablespoon black olives, chopped
- 1 tablespoon green olives, chopped
- 1 fresh goat cheese
- 1 cup (250 ml) olive oil (for deep frying)
- Salt, pepper

METHOD
Make the soup the day before. Cut up the vegetables—tomatoes, bell pepper, onion, and garlic. Arrange them on a large cookie sheet. Sprinkle them with the sugar and a little olive oil and the basil. Bake in a preheated oven at 300°F (150°C) for 2 hours.
Pour the vegetables into a food processor and process them. Strain them through a sieve, pressing down hard to eliminate all the vegetable skins. Refrigerate the liquid until required.
To make the pistou, trim the basil,

chop the leaves, and put them in a food processor with the garlic, Parmesan, and pine nuts. Process the mixture while pouring the oil into the mixture through the funnel, continuing until the consistency is creamy. Refrigerate until required.

The next day, season the soup with salt and 3 drops of Tabasco sauce. Refrigerate until required.

Make the filling for the pastries. Slice the eggplant lengthwise into 8 slices around ¼ inch (5 mm) thick. Heat the olive oil in a skillet and fry the eggplant for 3 minutes on each side. Drain well on absorbent paper and season with salt and pepper.

Cut the red and green bell peppers into ¼ inch (5 mm) dice. Add the chopped olives and fresh goat cheese, and season with salt and pepper. Mix well.

Slice the sheets of phyllo dough in half. Place a slice of cooked eggplant and a little goat cheese filling on each. Roll them up, folding the ends inward like a burrito.

Heat the olive oil. Add the pastries and deep-fry for 2 or 3 minutes or until golden. Drain them and sprinkle with pistou. Serve hot with the iced soup decorated with basil leaves. (Photo p. 109)

The pistou can be stored in a sealed jar for several weeks in the refrigerator. It can be used to flavor salads, soups, and pasta.

OLYMPE

CRUNCHY BLOOD SAUSAGE PACKAGES WITH MIXED SALAD LEAVES

PREPARATION TIME: 25 MINUTES

COOKING TIME: 1–2 MINUTES

TO SERVE 4

INGREDIENTS

· 4 handfuls (around 8 cups) mixed salad leaves, with a lot of wild arugula
· 20 slices blood sausage, ½ inch (1.5 cm) thick
· 5 phyllo dough sheets cut into 4
· 1 scant cup (200 ml) peanut oil or grape seed oil for deep-frying
· 1 tablespoon fresh coriander (cilantro), washed and chopped

For the dressing
· 3 tablespoons olive oil
· 1 tablespoon vinegar

· 2 teaspoons strong mustard
· Salt and pepper

METHOD

Wash and drain the salad greens. Wrap each slice of blood sausage in a ¼ phyllo dough sheet. Heat oil to a depth of ½ inch in a large skillet.

Deep-fry the blood sausage for about 1 minute on each side, then drain them on kitchen paper. Mix the dressing ingredients. Transfer the salad leaves to a bowl and toss them in the salad dressing. Arrange the blood sausage packages on a serving platter and sprinkle with coriander. Serve hot. (Photo p. 116)

PASTILLA WITH ALMOND MILK

PREPARATION TIME: 25 MINUTES

COOKING TIME: 15–20 MINUTES

TO SERVE 4

INGREDIENTS

· 5 teaspoons (50 g) blanched, slivered almonds
· 2 cups (500 ml) unpasteurized milk
· ½ cup (125 g) superfine sugar
· 1 scant tablespoon cornstarch
· 1 small teaspoon almond extract
· 5 teaspoons (50 g) pine nuts
· 5 teaspoons (50 g) chopped pistachios
· 5 teaspoons (50 g) chopped hazelnuts
· 6 tablespoons peanut oil
· 12 phyllo dough sheets cut into quarters, making 48 pieces
· 3–4 tablespoons icing sugar

METHOD

In a dry nonstick skillet, toast the slivered almonds. Watch them carefully as they toast very quickly. Bring the milk to the boil in a saucepan. Add the superfine sugar and cornstarch. Beat well to prevent the formation of lumps. Leave to thicken over high heat for 2 to 3 minutes.

When the milk becomes creamy, remove it from the fire. Pour it into a large bowl and add the almond extract. Beat well, leave to cool, and then refrigerate. Mix the rest of the nuts in a bowl and reserve.

Pour the peanut oil into a skillet. Place 3 sheets of phyllo dough on top of each other, add them to the skillet, and fry them in this manner for 30 seconds on each side. Drain on kitchen paper and repeat the operation until you have 16 packages of fried phyllo dough. Put 2 phyllo packages in each plate and sprinkle with the mixed nuts, then with the icing sugar. Top with 2 more phyllo packages, and sprinkle with the rest of the mixed nuts. Sprinkle again with icing sugar and add the chilled almond milk mixture.

Serve immediately. (Photo p. 113)

You can make the pastilla in advance and assemble it at the last minute.

AGATA PARISELLA

AGATA'S MILLE-FEUILLE

PREPARATION TIME: 1 HOUR, 45 MINUTES

COOKING TIME: 25 MINUTES

TO SERVE: 6–8

INGREDIENTS

For the puff pastry dough
· 4 cups (500 g) all-purpose flour
· 2 cups (500 g) vegetable margarine or butter
· 1 pinch of salt

For the pastry cream
· 5 egg yolks
· ⅔ cup (150 g) superfine sugar
· ⅔ cup (60 g) sifted all-purpose flour
· 1 quart (1 l) milk
· 1 vanilla bean (pod)
· 1 quart (1 l) ice-cold heavy cream

For the garnish
· 3 ½ ounces (100 g) extra-fondant dark chocolate
· 3 tablespoons (50 g) slivered almonds
· About 1 cup (125 g) confectioner's sugar, sifted

METHOD

For the flaky pastry dough, on a work surface, mix 3 ¼ cups (375 g) flour with a pinch of salt and just enough water to make the mixture pliable. Knead the dough until it is has a smooth consistency. Wrap it in a piece of damp cheesecloth and refrigerate for at least 30 minutes, or until required. Mix the rest of the flour with the butter to make a paste. Wrap it in a piece of damp cheesecloth and refrigerate until required. Roll out the dough into a rectangle and place the butter and flour mixture in the center. Fold one third of the rectangle toward the center then fold the uncovered third over the top of the other two thirds. Roll the dough out again

with the rolling pin. Wrap the dough in damp cheesecloth and refrigerate it for 15 minutes. Repeat this operation six times, with 15 minute intervals, always wrapping and refrigerating the dough in between times.

The dough will then be ready to roll out to a thickness of ½ inch (1 cm). Bake the dough in a preheated 375°F (180°C) oven for 15 to 20 minutes. Once it has been baked, sprinkle the dough liberally with confectioner's sugar and bake in a preheated 400°F (200°C) oven for 5 minutes to caramelize the sugar. Watch carefully, as the dough can color very quickly. Leave to cool, then cut the pastry into rectangles.

To make the pastry cream, in a copper or heavy-based pan, combine the egg yolks, sugar, and flour. Beat the mixture with a hand whisk but do not whisk it. In another saucepan, add the vanilla bean to the milk and bring to the boil. Pour this over the yolks, return to the pan and cook, stirring constantly, for 5 to 6 minutes.

Leave to cool completely, then whip the ice-cold heavy cream and add it to the cooled egg yolk and milk mixture.

For the pastry topping, melt the chocolate in a double boiler or bain-marie and make 10 little chocolate leaves by placing teaspoons of the chocolate on a sheet of silicone release or nonstick baking paper. Leave to cool. Toast the almonds in a preheated 375°F (180°C) oven or in a dry nonstick skillet until they are golden, around 5 minutes. To assemble the cake, place a large tablespoon of the pastry cream in the center of a dessert plate, add a few pieces of pastry and the slivered almonds. Sprinkle with confectioner's sugar and decorate with the chocolate leaves. (Photo p. 121)

SPAGHETTI ALL'AMATRICIANA

PREPARATION TIME: 35 MINUTES

COOKING TIME: 6 MINUTES

TO SERVE: 6

INGREDIENTS

· 3 tablespoons olive oil
· 1 small chili pepper, chopped
· 5 ½ ounces (150 g) salt pork belly or pancetta, sliced into short strips

- 1 onion, sliced
- ½ cup (125 ml) white wine
- 2 cups (500 g) tomatoes, skinned and crushed
- 1 pound, 5 ounces (600 g) spaghetti
- 1 scant cup (200 g) grated Pecorino Romano cheese
- 2 pinches of salt
- 3 ½ ounces (100 g) bacon slices, broiled and broken into pieces

METHOD

Heat the oil in a sauté pan. Add the chopped pepper, the salt pork or pancetta, and the sliced onion. Sauté for 4 or 5 minutes, stirring constantly until the mixture is crunchy. Add the white wine and continue cooking until it evaporates. Add the crushed tomatoes and cook for 5 to 6 minutes.

Meanwhile, cook the spaghetti in salted boiling water until it is half-cooked, around five minutes. Drain and add to the pan. Complete the cooking, then sprinkle with half the grated cheese and mix well. Serve hot topped with the broiled bacon, and sprinkle with the rest of the grated cheese.
(Photo p. 120)

SPAGHETTI A CACIO E PEPE

PREPARATION TIME: 25 MINUTES
COOKING TIME: 15 MINUTES
TO SERVE: 4

INGREDIENTS

- 1 teaspoon white peppercorns
- 1 teaspoon black peppercorns
- 14 ounces (400 g) spaghetti
- 2 tablespoons olive oil
- 1 scant cup (200 g) grated Pecorino cheese

METHOD

Grind the two types of peppercorn in a mortar.

Heat a large pot of salted water, bring to the boil and add the spaghetti. Cook it until it is al dente.

Heat the oil in a sauté pan. Drain the spaghetti and add it to the hot oil. Mix well.

Sprinkle with the grated Pecorino and serve very hot. Serve the crushed peppercorns separately.
(Photo p. 118)

ANNE-SOPHIE PIC

SEA BASS STEAMED WITH WAKAME, OYSTERS, AND SWEET-AND-SOUR CUCUMBER

PREPARATION TIME: 45 MINUTES
COOKING TIME: 25 TO 30 MINUTES
TO SERVE: 4

INGREDIENTS

For the sweet-and-sour cucumber
- 7 ounces (200 g) cucumber
- 1 small piece ginger root
- 1 garlic clove
- 4 limes
- 2 tablespoons (50 ml) white wine vinegar
- 2 tablespoons (50 ml) white wine
- 1 ½ tablespoons (40 g) honey
- 1 pinch mixed spice
- Salt and pepper

For the butter sauce
- 3 small cucumbers
- 4 oysters (see below)
- ⅔ cup (150 g) chilled butter
- 1 lime
- 2 tablespoons (20 ml) vodka

For the sea bass
- 1 pound (480 g) fillet of sea-bass
- A handful of wakame seaweed (see below)
- Salt and pepper

METHOD

To make the cucumber chutney, chop the cucumber, ginger, and garlic. Squeeze the limes to get ⅓ cup (100 ml) juice. Add the white wine vinegar, white wine, honey, mixed spice, ginger, and garlic. Bring to the boil, and boil on high heat until reduced by half. Add the cucumber and cook until the liquid evaporates (around 15 minutes). Season with salt and pepper.

To make the butter sauce, put the three cucumbers through a juicer to obtain their juice. Open the oysters and save their liquid. Mix it with the cucumber juice. Pour this liquid into a saucepan and bring to the boil. Reduce for 5 minutes. Cut the butter into small pieces and add it, piece by piece, while beating with a beater, until the liquid is of creamy consistency. Add a sprinkling of lime juice and the vodka. Adjust the seasoning. Season the sea bass with salt and pepper and steam in a steamer with the wakame for 3 minutes at 210°F (100°C).

Pour the oysters and the vodka liquid into a saucepan over low heat, just to warm them through.

On each warmed plate, place 1 tablespoon sweet-and-sour cucumber, 1 oyster, and 1 slice of sea-bass fillet. Decorate with lime zest and serve with the cucumber butter. (Photo p. 123)

Wakamé is a crunchy seaweed that is rich in iodine. It grows in long, green, translucent strips. It can bought fresh from fishmongers and in Japanese food stores. It is also sold in dehydrated form, in which case it just needs rehydrating in water.

I like to use special Gillardeau oysters (the no. 3 size). These oysters are raised on oyster beds in Normandy. They are farmed for 4 years, giving them an exceptional quality. Their flesh is crunchy, mild, and pleasantly firm.

POACHED GRANNY SMITH APPLE CRUMBLE AND CHAMPAGNE SORBET

PREPARATION TIME: 40 MINUTES,
PLUS 4 HOURS' REFRIGERATION TIME
COOKING TIME: 35 MINUTES
TO SERVE: 4

INGREDIENTS

For the crumble
- 3 ½ tablespoons (50 g) softened butter
- 3 ½ tablespoons (50 g) sugar
- 2 egg yolks
- 4 tablespoons (60 g) all-purpose flour

For the champagne jellycream
- ⅔ cup whipping cream
- 4 tablespoons sugar
- 1 scant cup champagne
- 2 leaves unflavored gelatin or 1 teaspoon powdered gelatin

For the poached apples
- Juice of 1 lemon
- 4 Granny Smith apples
- 1 tablespoon (15 g) sugar and ½ teaspoon (3 g) powdered pectin (or 4 teaspoons [20 g] preserving sugar)

METHOD

To make the crumble, preheat the oven to 300°F (150°C). Combine the butter and sugar, mixing well, then beat in the egg yolks, and then the flour. Roll out this dough on a sheet of nonstick baking paper laid on a cookie sheet. Bake it in the oven for 20 to 30 minutes, or until golden. Chop it up coarsely and leave to cool.

To make the champagne jellycream, whip the cream until it has almost stiffened. Combine the sugar and the champagne. Soften the gelatin leaves in cold water, then drain them and squeeze them dry, or prepare the powdered gelatin according to the manufacturer's instructions. Warm half the champagne mixture, and stir the softened gelatin into it, then add the rest of the champagne mixture and fold this into the whipped cream. Refrigerate for at least 4 hours.

Squeeze a little of the lemon juice into a large bowl of water. Peel the apples and core them. Cut them into balls with a melon-baller, reserving the excess. Put them into water with a little lemon juice to prevent oxidation. Reserve them.

For the apple jelly, put all the trimmings from the apples into a juicer with the rest of the lemon juice. Mix this juice with the sugar and pectin (or preserving sugar) and bring to the boil. Remove from the heat immediately. Drain the apple balls. Pour the boiling liquid over the apple balls and leave to cool. Refrigerate for at least 4 hours.

Arrange the apple balls on serving plates with the apple jelly and the crumble. Accompany with the champagne jellycream.

Serve as it is, or add a champagne sorbet and apple chips (see recipe below). (Photo p. 126)

APPLE CHIPS

PREPARATION TIME: 10 MINUTES, PLUS
24 HOURS' MACERATION
COOKING TIME: 3 HOURS
TO MAKE: AROUND 20 CHIPS

INGREDIENTS

- 2 Granny Smith apples
- ⅓ cup (100 g) sugar
- Juice of ½ a lemon

METHOD

Slice the apples into thin slices and put them in a bowl. Boil 2 cups water with the sugar and lemon juice.

Remove from the heat and pour this over the apples. Refrigerate for 24 hours.

Then drain the apples and arrange them on nonstick baking paper covering a cookie sheet. Bake for about 3 hours on the lowest oven setting, or until the apple rounds are as crunchy as potato chips. Use the chips to decorate the

Poached Granny Smith Apple Crumble recipe or to accompany fruit compotes and ice creams.

CHAMPAGNE SORBET

PREPARATION TIME: 10 MINUTES
COOKING TIME: 2 MINUTES
TO MAKE: ABOUT 1 1/2–1 3/4 CUPS
(350–400 ML) SORBET

INGREDIENTS
· 1 scant cup (200 ml) champagne
· 6 tablespoons (85 g) sugar
· 2 tablespoons (30 g) liquid glucose or honey, or 4 tablespoons light corn syrup
· Juice and grated rind of half an orange

METHOD
Pour ⅓ cup (100 ml) water into a saucepan with the sugar and glucose, honey, or corn syrup. Add the orange rind and juice. Bring to the boil, remove from the heat, add the champagne, and mix well. Strain through a fine sieve to remove the zest. Leave to cool and process in an ice-cream maker. Store in the freezer if the sorbet is not to be eaten immediately.

VALERIA PICCINI

VARNELLI LIQUEUR AND TOBACCO ICE CREAM WITH COFFEE MOUSSE AND RHUBARB SAUCE

PREPARATION TIME: 1 HOUR
COOKING TIME: 15 MINUTES
TO SERVE 4

INGREDIENTS
· 2 cups (500 ml) custard
· ⅔ cup (150 g) heavy cream
· 6 tablespoons (85 ml) Varnelli aniseed liqueur
· Pinch of Kentucky tobacco
· 3 ½ ounces (100 g) baking chocolate (70% cocoa mass)
· 1 egg
· ⅔ cup (150 g) sugar
· 3 tablespoons (40 g) ricotta
· ½ cup (120 ml) espresso coffee (preferably Giovanni Erbisti 1947)
· 5 tablespoons (70 ml) coffee liqueur
· 1 unflavored gelatin leaf
· 10 ½ ounces (300 g) fresh rhurbarb
· 2 tablespoons (30 ml) rhubarb liqueur

METHOD
To make the ice cream, combine the custard with the heavy cream, aniseed liqueur, and tobacco. Blend in an ice-cream maker and freeze until required.
To make cigar-shaped cookies, make cones from aluminum foil measuring around 2 inches (6 cm) high. Melt the chocolate in a bain-marie or double boiler, and pour chocolate into the cones to line them. Refrigerate until required. Beat the egg yolk with 3 tablespoons of the sugar, and add the ricotta and tobacco cream. Beat the egg whites and fold them in. Fill the chocolate cones with the mixture and freeze until required.
To make the mousse, combine the coffee and the coffee liqueur. Add the softened gelatin then whisk with an electric beater. Pour the mousse thus obtained into sundae glasses and chill until required.
To make the rhubarb sauce, peel the rhubarb and cook it with the rest of the sugar and ½ cup (125 ml) water. Strain. Add the rhubarb liqueur to the rhubarb.
To assemble the dish, use a large plate 14–16 inches (35–40 cm) in diameter. Place a sundae glass of coffee mousse on it and surround with the rhubarb sauce. Peel away the aluminum foil from the chocolate cigars and add them. Lastly, add scoops of ice cream.

PECORINO AND BROAD BEAN TORTELLI WITH CHICKEN STOCK AND ARTICHOKES

PREPARATION TIME: 20 MINUTES
COOKING TIME: 30 MINUTES
TO SERVE 4

INGREDIENTS
· 3 whole eggs
· 1 ⅓ cup (150 g) all-purpose flour
· 1 ¾ ounces (50g) farina (cream of wheat)
· 4 tablespoons extra-virgin olive oil
· 3 artichoke bottoms
· 1 cup (250 ml) chicken stock
· 2 tablespoons (30g) minced white onion
· 10 ½ ounces (300g) fresh sheep's milk ricotta cheese
· 3 ounces (85g) Tuscan pecorino cheese
· 1 ⅓ cup (150 g) fresh broad beans, shelled
· 4 ounces (120 g) foie gras
· Salt and pepper

METHOD
Beat 2 of the eggs with the flour and farina. Sprinkle with 1 tablespoon of the oil and season with salt and pepper. Leave the dough to rest for about 30 minutes. Meanwhile, heat 1 tablespoon of the oil in a saucepan and sauté the beans. Season with salt, then add the ricotta and pecorino cheeses. Beat the remaining egg and add it to the mixture. This will be the filling for the tortelli. Refrigerate it until required.
To make the sauce, thinly slice the artichoke bottoms. Heat the rest of the oil in a skillet and sauté the artichokes with the onion. Add the chicken stock and cook for 10 minutes. Then transfer the contents of the skillet to a food processor and process until smooth. Strain through a conical sieve.
Slice the foie gras into small pieces around ¼ inch (5 mm) thick. Roll out the dough as thinly as possible and cut into 1-inch (2.5 cm) squares. Place a teaspoon stuffing in the center of each tortelli with a piece of foie gras on top. Pinch the dough around the filling. Bring a large pan of salted water to the boil and add the tortelli. Cook for 5 minutes.
Pour a trail of sauce in each dish. Drain the tortelli well and arrange them on each plate on top of the sauce. (Photo p. 130)

CORNELIA POLETTO

WHITE ASPARAGUS RISOTTO WITH MINT AND SHRIMP

PREPARATION TIME: 20 MINUTES
TO SERVE: 4

INGREDIENTS
· 1 pound, 2 ounces (500 g) white asparagus
· Pinch of sugar
· Juice of ½ a lemon
· ⅓ cup (100 g) butter
· 1 shallot, peeled and minced
· 1 garlic clove, peeled and minced
· About 1 scant cup (200 g) Carnaroli or other risotto rice
· 3 tablespoons (50 ml) dry white wine
· 8 medium-sized shrimp
· Sea salt and freshly ground black pepper
· About ⅔ cup (150 g) grated Parmesan cheese
· 1 bunch of mint, leaves finely chopped

METHOD
Peel and trim the asparagus and make 1 ¾ cups (400 ml) broth with the peelings, trimmings, a pinch of sugar, and the lemon. Heat half the butter in a saucepan and cook the minced shallot and garlic on low heat.
Cut the asparagus stems into short lengths. Cook the spears separately. Add the pieces of asparagus and the rice to the saucepan and fry them, stirring frequently. Then add the wine. Add the asparagus broth gradually, cooking each time until the rice has absorbed the liquid. Once all the liquid has been absorbed, continue cooking the rice until it is al dente.
Season the shrimp with salt and pepper and sauté them on high heat on both sides. Add them to the risotto, bind with the rest of the butter, and incorporate the Parmesan. Finally, add the chopped mint leaves.

CREAM CHEESE DUMPLINGS WITH VANILLA

COOKING TIME: 15 MINUTES
PREPARATION TIME: 20 MINUTES
TO SERVE: 4

INGREDIENTS
· 1 ½ cups (300 g) cream cheese
· 2 tablespoons (30 g) butter
· 2 eggs, separated
· 1 vanilla bean (pod)
· Juice and grated rind of 1 lemon
· 1 tablespoon sugar
· 1 cup (120 g) soft white breadcrumbs
· Dry breadcrumbs, sugar, cinnamon

METHOD
Combine the cream cheese with the butter and egg yolks. Split the vanilla bean lengthwise and scrape out the vanilla seeds and add them to the mixture with the lemon rind.
Beat the egg whites into stiff peaks with the sugar and fold into the egg yolk mixture, alternating with the soft white breadcrumbs.

Shape the mixture into dumplings and poach them in lightly salted water for about 15 minutes. Drain them and roll them in a mixture of dry breadcrumbs, sugar, and cinnamon. Serve them sprinkled with icing sugar.

CREAM CHEESE MOUSSE

PREPARATION TIME: 20 MINUTES
REFRIGERATION TIME: 4 HOURS
TO SERVE: 4

INGREDIENTS

· ½ cup (125 g) cream cheese
· Juice and grated rind of ½ a lemon
· Juice and grated rind of ½ an orange
· 1 vanilla bean (pod)
· ⅓ cup (80 g) sugar
· 3 unflavored gelatin leaves, soaked in water and squeezed
· 2 tablespoons (30 ml) Grand Marnier liqueur
· 3 egg whites
· Salt
· 2 cups (250 g) whipped cream

METHOD

Combine the cream cheese with the citrus rind. Split the vanilla bean and add the vanilla seeds to the mixture with half the sugar.
Soak the unflavored gelatin leaves in cold water, drain them, and squeeze them. Dissolve the gelatin in the Grand Marnier, adding the citrus juice. When dissolved, add the cream cheese mixture and mix well.
Whisk the egg whites into stiff peaks with the rest of the sugar and a pinch of salt. Fold them into the cream cheese, alternating with the whipped cream.
Refrigerate for at least 4 hours, or until set.

CREAM CHEESE ICE CREAM

PREPARATION TIME: 10 MINUTES
TO SERVE: 4

INGREDIENTS

· Juice of 1 lemon
· Juice of 1 orange
· 6 tablespoons (75 g) sugar
· 1 cup (250 g) cream cheese

METHOD

Combine the citrus juice, sugar, and cream cheese. Freeze the mixture in an ice-cream maker.

MARIE-FRANCE PONSARD

HOT SOUFFLÉ WITH LORRAINE MIRABELLE PLUM LIQEUR

PREPARATION TIME: 35 MINUTES
COOKING TIME: 6–7 MINUTES
TO SERVE: 4

INGREDIENTS

· 1 scant cup (200 g) ready-made confectioner's custard
· ½ cup (120 ml) Mirabelle plum liqueur
· 4 tablespoons (60 g) butter and 2 tablespoons sugar for the ramekins
· 8 egg whites
· 2 rounded tablespoons (60 g) superfine sugar
· ⅓ cup (100 g) Mirabelle plums in syrup
· 2 tablespoons Mirabelle liqueur plus extra for the finish

METHOD

Pour the confectioner's custard into a large bowl, incorporate a little of the Mirabelle liqueur and mix well. Butter the ramekins and sprinkle them with sugar. Beat the egg whites with an electric beater. When they start to stiffen, add the sugar all at once. Continue beating for 5 minutes, or until the whites are stiff and glistening.
Fold in the custard cream with a wooden spoon. Put a few of the Mirabelle plums in syrup in the center of each ramekin and cover with the custard and meringue mixture. Bake in a preheated 475°F (240 °C) oven for 6 to 7 minutes.
Remove from the oven and serve immediately. As each soufflé is placed in front of a guest, pierce it with the point of a knife and pour a little more liqueur into the center.
Serve with sponge cake or white cake.

CARME RUSCALLEDA

SEA BREAM, ARTICHOKES, AND TOMATO SAUCE WITH CAPERS

PREPARATION TIME: 45 MINUTES
COOKING TIME: 2 HOURS, 10 MINUTES
TO SERVE: 4

INGREDIENTS

· Fillets from a sea bream weighing 2 pounds, 12 ounces (1.2 kg)
· Olive oil
· Salt and pepper
For the vegetables and garnish
· 4 pounds, 8 ounces (2 kg) tomatoes
· Salt and pepper
· Olive oil
· 1 small chili pepper
· 2 tablespoons (50 g) capers in vinegar
· 1 ¼ pounds (500 g) pumpkin
· 1 large artichoke bottom
· Juice of ½ a lemon
For the stock
· Bones, head, and trimmings from the fish
· 1 carrot
· 1 onion
· 1 leek
· 1 tomato
· 2 garlic cloves
· 3 sprigs of parsley
· 1 bay leaf
· 1 scant cup (200 ml) dry sherry
· Salt and pepper

METHOD

Prepare the tomatoes for the garnish by boiling them for 30 seconds, rinsing and skinning them. Divide them in half and reserve one half for oven-drying. Put the rest aside.
Cut the tomatoes to be oven-dried into quarters, season them with salt and pepper, and arrange them on a cookie sheet. Sprinkle them with a little olive oil. Bake them for 2 hours at 250°F (120°C).
Prepare the stock by putting into a heavy-based pan the bones, trimmings, and head of the bream, the vegetables cut into small pieces, the parsley, bay leaf, sherry and ⅓ cup (100 ml) water. Cook for 30 minutes. Strain, season to taste, and leave to simmer on a very low heat.
Remove the seeds from the reserved half of the tomatoes, chop them coarsely, then sauté them in 2 tablespoons oil with the chili pepper. Cook for 20 minutes, add half the drained capers, and season with salt and pepper. Keep in a warm place.
Peel the pumpkin then cut it into regular, rectangular pieces and steam it for 4 minutes or cook it in salted, boiling water. Reserve it.
Remove the dried tomatoes from the oven. Increase the heat to 375°F (190°C).

Slice the artichoke bottom very thinly and sprinkle it with lemon juice to prevent oxidation.
Sauté the sea bream fillets and pumpkin rectangles on a griddle or in a nonstick pan with a little oil. Season with salt and pepper and bake for about 5 minutes.
Deep-fry the artichokes in about ⅓ cup (100 ml) olive oil. Drain on kitchen paper and season with salt. Arrange the pumpkin, artichoke, and bream on warmed plates. Serve with the dried tomatoes and the fried tomatoes, the stock, and the rest of the capers.

REINE SAMMUT

CRUNCHY BROUSSE CHEESE CANNOLI WITH PICKLED LEMON AND HONEY ICE CREAM

PREPARATION TIME: 40 MINUTES
COOKING TIME: 5 MINUTES
TO MAKE: 4 CANNOLI

INGREDIENTS

· 4 tablespoons (50 g) sugar
· 4 tablespoons (50 g) ground almonds
· 3 tablespoons (40 g) butter. melted
· 1 lemon, rind grated
· ⅓ cup (100 ml) orange juice
· 2 tablespoons (15 g) all-purpose flour
· ⅓ cup (100 g) candied fruits such as pears and apricots
· 1 ¾ cups (400 g) sheep's-milk cheese such as brousse
· 4 tablespoons (50 g) superfine sugar
· 4 cups (500 g) strawberries
· ⅓ cup (100 g) granulated sugar
For the honey ice cream
· 5 egg yolks
· 4 tablespoons (50 g) sugar
· 2 cups (500 ml) whole milk
· ⅓ cup (100 g) mixed flower honey
· ⅓ cup (100 g) light cream

UTENSILS

· 1 1-inch (2.5-cm) diameter rolling pin, 5 inches (12 cm) long
· 1 electric ice-cream maker

METHOD

Preheat the oven to 400°F (200°C).
Whisk the sugar, ground almonds, melted butter, grated lemon rind, and orange juice, then add the flour.

Cover a cookie sheet with nonstick baking paper and spread 1 tablespoon of the mixture over it. Spread it out into a disk, using the back of a spoon. Bake for 5 minutes.

Remove the cookie sheet from the oven and use a metal spatula to gently detach the disk while it is still hot. Roll it around a rolling pin. Repeat the operation 4 times. Dice the candied fruits.

Combine the brousse cheese, superfine sugar, and candied fruits using a whisk, and refrigerate until required.

To make the honey ice cream, in a bowl beat the egg yolks and sugar until the mixture is pale and foaming. In a saucepan, bring the milk and honey to the boil and pour it over the egg yolk mixture, whisking constantly. Pour it all back into the saucepan and cook on low heat, stirring constantly with a wooden spoon, until the mixture coats the back of the spoon. Strain the custard through a fine sieve then leave it to cool. Refrigerate until chilled.

Pour the chilled custard into a bowl and whisk it until it is firm. Whip the light cream with the honey mixture and beat it into the custard. Transfer to an ice-cream maker and process for around 15 minutes. Wash the strawberries and place them with the sugar in the bowl of a food processor. Grind them together, then strain through a fine sieve. Use a forcing bag to fill the cheese cannoli with the mixture. Arrange 1 cannoli on each plate with a scoop of the vanilla ice cream, surrounded by a trail of strawberry sauce.

This dessert is of Sicilian origin, as is Grandma Guy.

The sheep's-milk cheese must be fresh and creamy. Try and use the finest candied fruits.

CRUNCHY, SPICY CHICKEN WINGS WITH GARLIC JELLY

PREPARATION TIME: 30 MINUTES
COOKING TIME: 12–15 MINUTES
TO SERVE: 4

INGREDIENTS
· 2 eggs
· Salt and pepper
· Pinch of mixed spice
· 20 chicken wings
· 1 cup breading mixture for deep-frying

· 3 tablespoons peanut oil
· 24 garlic cloves
· 2 cups (500 ml) homemade chicken stock
· 5 sheets unflavored gelatin, soaked and squeezed
· 3 tablespoons olive oil
· 1 tablespoon balsamic vinegar
· 2 ½ cups (400 g) mixed salad leaves

METHOD
Beat the eggs as for an omelet with salt, pepper, and the mixed spice. Dip the chicken wings in this mixture, then in the bread coating. Put a little of the peanut oil in a skillet and cook the chicken wings on low heat.

Peel the garlic cloves and remove any green shoots inside. Cook them for 8 to 10 minutes in the chicken stock. Then transfer the garlic cloves to 4 ramekins, and incorporate the softened gelatin into the chicken stock. Pour the stock over the ramekins and refrigerate until required.

Make a dressing with the olive oil and vinegar and season with salt and pepper.

Unmold a garlic-flavored aspic mold onto each plate. Toss the salad leaves in the dressing, then add a few leaves and 5 crunchy chicken wings to each plate. (Photo p. 146)

HOT CHOCOLATE SOUFFLÉ

PREPARATION TIME: 25 MINUTES
COOKING TIME: 10 MINUTES
TO SERVE: 6

INGREDIENTS
· ½ cup (110 g) butter
· ⅓ cup (100 g) dark semi-sweet chocolate (64 percent cocoa)
· 4 egg yolks
· 2 tablespoons (30 g) superfine sugar
· 3 ½ tablespoons (50 g) all-purpose flour
· 1 tablespoon (15 g) butter for the ramekins

METHOD
In a double boiler or bain-marie melt the butter and the chocolate. Beat the egg yolks with the sugar until the mixture is pale and fluffy. Mix this with the melted chocolate. Sift the flour and add it to the mixture. Pour into individual buttered molds or ramekins. Place these soufflés in

the freezer and keep them at -4°F (-20°C) for around 1 hour; then bake them in a preheated oven at 375°F (180 °C) for 10 minutes. Serve immediately.

NADIA SANTINI

TORTELLI OF SOFT GOAT CHEESE AND WHITE TRUFFLE

PREPARATION TIME: 35 MINUTES
COOKING TIME: 2 MINUTES
TO SERVE: 4

INGREDIENTS
For the tortelli dough
· 2 cups (250 g) wheat flour
· 3 egg yolks
· 1 whole egg
· 1 pinch of salt
For the filling
· ⅓ cup (100 g) grated Parmesan
· 4 teaspoons (20 g) creamy goat cheese
To serve
· 2 to 3 tablespoons grated Parmesan
· 3 tablespoons (40 g) melted butter
· 1 white truffle

METHOD
To make the dough, combine the flour, eggs, and salt. Pour a little flour onto the work surface, then roll out the dough on it as thinly as possible. This will be easier if the work surface is wooden, because the warmth of the wood makes it easier to roll out the dough very thinly.

Cut the dough into squares. Mix the grated Parmesan and creamy goat cheese. Using two teaspoons, place a little of this two-cheese filling on each square of dough. Fold over one corner diagonally to make a triangle, then press the edges together to seal them. Then bring the corners of the triangle together to produce a rounded shape.

Bring a large quantity of salted water to the boil in a saucepan. Throw the tortelli into it and cook them for around 2 minutes. Drain them and arrange them on a serving dish. Sprinkle them with very hot melted butter and then with Parmesan. Always sprinkle with the butter before the Parmesan so that it makes the cheese melt.

Grate the white truffle over the dish and serve immediately.

MIXED FRUITS IN BERRY TEA

PREPARATION TIME: 25 MINUTES
COOKING TIME: 15–20 MINUTES
TO SERVE: 4

INGREDIENTS
· 2 cups (500 ml) aromatic white wine
· ⅓ cup (100 g) sugar
· 2 cups (500 ml) berry tea
· 1 pear
· 1 apple
· 4 plums
· 4 prunes
· 1 peach
· 2 apricots
· 1 bunch of grapes

METHOD
In a large saucepan, combine the wine, sugar, and berry tea. Mix well and bring to the boil. Meanwhile, wash, peel, pit or deseed the fruits, and slice them into pieces. Put the fruits into the saucepan, turn off the heat, and cover the pot. Leave to infuse for around 30 minutes. Serve warm with fruit sorbet. (Photo p. 149) You can use fruits of your choice, depending on the region and the season. Give your imagination free rein for the best results.

ANNA SGROI

OCTOPUS CARPACCIO WITH ASPARAGUS AND OYSTER MUSHROOMS

PREPARATION TIME: 25 MINUTES
COOKING TIME: 1 HOUR
TO SERVE: 4

INGREDIENTS
For the baby octopus
· 1 baby octopus
· 1 onion stuck with a clove
· 2 cups (50 cl) white wine vinegar
· Salt and peppercorns
For the vegetables
· 8 green asparagus
· ⅓ cup (100g) petit pois (garden peas)
· 1 cup (250 g) oyster mushrooms
· 1 quarter of leek white parts
· 5 tablespoons olive oil
· Salt and pepper
· 1 head escarole
· Juice of half a lemon
· 1 tablespoon minced parsley

METHOD
Put the baby octopus into a saucepan with the onion, vinegar,

salt and a few peppercorns. Cook on a low heat for about 45 minutes, or until a knifepoint can easily be inserted. Drain and leave to cool. Slice the octopus thinly.
Cook the asparagus and peas in salted boiling water, for 3 minutes and drain them. Wash the oyster mushrooms but do not soak them. Slice them and do the same with the white part of the leek.
Heat 2 tablespoons of the oil in a wok or skillet and sauté the leek and oyster mushrooms. Slice the asparagus and season with salt and pepper. Mix the vegetables with the octopus, and add the separated leaves of the escarole. Sprinkle with the lemon juice, minced parsley, and the rest of the olive oil. Mix well before serving. (Photo p. 157)

SCALLOP SALAD WITH RED WINE SAUCE

PREPARATION TIME: 45 MINUTES
COOKING TIME: 50 MINUTES
TO SERVE: 4

INGREDIENTS
For the scallops
· 8 pearl onions
· ⅔ cup (150 ml) dry white wine
· 6 baby artichokes
· Juice and grated rind of 1 lemon
· Olive oil
· 1 head of lettuce
· 1 leek, white part only
· 8 large scallops
· Salt and pepper
For the sauce
· 1 ¼ pounds (500 g) shallots
· 1 tablespoon olive oil
· 2 cups (500 ml) strong red wine
· 1 bay leaf
· Salt and pepper

METHOD
To make the sauce, slice the shallots and sauté them in the olive oil for 5 minutes. Add the wine and bay leaf. Cook for 30 minutes on low heat until the liquid is reduced by three-quarters.
Meanwhile, cook the pearl onions for 10 minutes in the white wine and drain them.
Clean the artichokes, discard the tough outer leaves, remove the choke and sprinkle them with the lemon juice. Then sauté them in 2 tablespoons olive oil.
Separate the lettuce leaves, reserving the heart. Blanch them for 1 minute, then drain them.
Slice the white part of the leek and cook on low heat for 3 minutes in a little olive oil. Thinly slice the lettuce heart.
Cut the scallops in half crosswise and season with salt and pepper.
Combine the lettuce heart and leek with the scallops and add the grated lemon rind. Wrap in the blanched lettuce leaves to make little packages. Preheat the oven to 375°F (190°C). Brush an ovenproof dish with oil and place the scallop packages in the center with the artichokes and pearl onions around them. Bake for 8 minutes.
Strain the shallot sauce, reheat it, and season with salt and pepper. Arrange the scallops and vegetables on warmed plates and coat them with the sauce. (Photo p. 155)

SWEET VANILLA CREAM

PREPARATION TIME: 15 MINUTES
COOKING TIME: 10 MINUTES
TO SERVE: 4

INGREDIENTS
· 3 ½ ounces (100 g) milk
· 3 ½ ounces (100 g) crème fraiche
· 2 ¾ ounces (80 g) sugar
· ⅓ ounce (10 g) cornstarch
· 2 egg yolks
· Seeds from half a vanilla bean (pod)

METHOD
Mix together all the ingredients. Cook over a low heat in a saucepan, stirring continuously until a creamy consistency is obtained. Leave to cool.

LUISA VALAZZA

RED PARTRIDGE RISOTTO

PREPARATION TIME: 35 MINUTES
COOKING TIME: 10 MINUTES
TO SERVE: 4

INGREDIENTS
· 2 large red partridges
· Salt and pepper
· 2 sprigs rosemary
· Slices of fat bacon for larding
· 3 tablespoons olive oil
· 1 cup (250 ml) dry white wine
· 1 carrot, sliced
· 1 onion, sliced
· 1 celery stick, sliced
· 1 scant cup (200 g) Carnaroli or other short-grain rice
· 1 quart (1 l) chicken broth
· 2 tablespoons (30 g) butter, diced
· 1 ¾ ounces (50 g) Parmesan cheese, sliced

METHOD
Season the partridges inside with salt and pepper, insert a sprig of rosemary in each and cover them with the bacon slices, trussing the slices in place, or have the butcher do it for you. Heat the olive oil in a deep pan and sauté the partridges on high heat, turning them frequently. Deglaze them with the white wine, scraping to dislodge the juices in the bottom of the pan. then add the sliced carrot, onion, and celery. Cook in a preheated 400°F (200°C) oven for 10 minutes. Remove from the oven, cover loosely with foil and leave them to rest. Recover the cooking juices.
Put the rice into a large pot, gradually adding the chicken broth, then incorporate the diced butter and sliced Parmesan. Add 2 tablespoons of the partridge cooking liquid. Mix well.
Arrange the rice on the serving dishes, add half a partridge per person, and coat with the rest of the cooking juices. (Photo p. 167)

GRATIN OF NEW POTATOES WITH PARMESAN AND WHITE TRUFFLES

PREPARATION TIME: 20 MINUTES
COOKING TIME: 30 MINUTES
TO SERVE: 4

INGREDIENTS
· 4 medium potatoes, unpeeled
· ⅓–⅔ cup (100–150 ml) milk
· 5 egg yolks
· 1 tablespoon of Parmesan
· Salt and pepper
· 1 white truffle, weighing around 3 ounces (80 g)

METHOD
Cook the potatoes in boiling water in their skins for 30 minutes. Drain them, peel them, and scoop out a hollow in each one that is large enough to hold an egg yolk. Keep them warm.
Mash the scooped-out potato with a little milk. Beat in 1 egg yolk and 1 tablespoon Parmesan cheese, salt, and pepper. The purée obtained should be fairly soft.
Season the scooped-out potatoes with salt, place an egg yolk inside each of them, cover with the creamed potatoes, and brown in a preheated 400°F (200°C) oven for 5 minutes. Remove the potatoes from the oven, grate the truffle over them, and serve immediately.

FIG FRITTERS AND FIG SORBET WITH BLUEBERRY SAUCE

PREPARATION TIME: 25 MINUTES
COOKING TIME: 1–2 MINUTES
TO SERVE: 4

INGREDIENTS
· 1 cup (250 g) sugar syrup
· 12 fairly large, very ripe Mission figs
· 2 eggs
· 1 tablespoon all-purpose flour
· 3 tablespoons milk
· 1 cup (250 g) blueberries
· 2 tablespoons sugar
· Oil for deep-frying
· 3 to 4 tablespoons icing sugar

METHOD
Pour the sugar syrup over 4 of the figs. Pour the mixture into an ice-cream maker and leave to set.
In a bowl, combine the eggs, flour, and milk to make the batter.
Cook the blueberries with the sugar for 5 minutes and strain through a sieve to make the sauce. Split the remaining figs in half, dip them in the batter and fry them for 1 or 2 minutes in boiling oil. Spread 2 tablespoons of the blueberry sauce on the plates. Arrange 1 scoop of fig sorbet in the center, and surround with the fig fritters. Sprinkle with icing sugar and serve. (Photo p. 165)

RESTAURANT ADDRESSES

ELENA ARZAK
Arzak
273 Avenida del Alcalde
Jose Elosegui
20015 Donostia/San Sebastian
Spain
Tel: 943 27 84 65
Fax: 943 27 27 53
restaurante@arzak.es
www.arzak.es

ISABELLE AUGUY
Grand Hôtel Auguy
2 allée de l'Amicale
12210 Laguiole
France
Tel: 05 65 44 31 11
Fax: 05 65 51 50 81
grand-hotel.auguy@
wanadoo.fr
www.hotel-auguy.fr

JUDITH BAUMANN
Pinte des Mossettes
La Valsainte
1654 Cerniat
Switzerland
Tel: 26 927 20 97
Fax: 26 927 20 97
Books: *Saveurs sauvages de la
Gruyère*, Éditions de l'Aire,
1994; *Un monde de saveurs*,
Favre, 2003.

NATHALIE BEAUVAIS
Le Jardin Gourmand
46 rue Jules Simon
56100 Lorient
France
Tel: 02 97 64 17 24
Fax: 02 97 64 15 75
Books: *La Bretagne
gourmande*, Acanthe, 2004.
Contributions: *Femmes Chefs*,
Actes Sud, 2004; *Saveur et
Terroir*, Hachette, 1996.

SOPHIE BISE
• L'Auberge du Père Bise
Route du Port
74290 Talloires
France
Tel: 04 50 60 72 01
Fax: 04 50 60 73 05
reception@perebise.com
www.perebise.com

• Chez Ma Cousine
2036 Route Annecy
74210 Doussard
France
Tel: 04 50 32 38 83
Fax: 04 50 32 91 66
info@chezmacousine.fr
www.chezmacousine.fr

CHANTAL CHAGNY
Restaurant Le Cep
Place de l'Église
69820 Fleurie
France
Tel: 04 74 04 10 77
Fax: 04 74 04 10 28

SALLY CLARKE
Clarke's
124 Kensington Church
Street
London W8 4BH
Great Britain
Tel: 020 7221 9225
Fax: 020 7229 4564
restaurant@sallyclarke.com
www.sallyclarke.com
Books: *Sally Clarke's Book:
Recipes from a Restaurant,
Shop and Bakery*, Macmillan,
2003.

HÉLÈNE DARROZE
Hélène Darroze
4 rue d'Assas
75006 Paris
France
Tel: 01 42 22 00 11
Fax: 01 42 22 25 40
darroze@relaischateaux.com

PATRICIA DESMEDT
't oud Konijntje
53 Bostraat
8790 Waregem
Belgium
Tel: 056 60 19 37
Fax: 056 60 92 12
Books: *Culinaire confidenties:
De Keuken van't oud Konijntje
stichting Kunstboek*, Allmedia,
2002.
Contributions: *De Chef is een
vrouw*, Lannoo, 2004; *The
Culinary Chronicle*, Opt Art,
2003.

LYDIA EGLOFF
La Bonne Auberge
15 rue Nationale
57350 Stiring-Wendel
France
Tel: 03 87 87 52 78
Fax: 03 87 87 18 19

NICOLE FAGEGALTIER
Hôtel Restaurant du Vieux
Pont
12390 Belcastel
France
Tel: 05 65 64 52 29
Fax: 05 65 64 44 32
hotel-du-vieux-
pont@wanadoo.fr
www.hotelbelcastel.com

ANNIE FEOLDE
Enoteca Pinchiorri
87 Via Ghibellina
50122 Florence
Italy
Tel: 055 24 27 77
Fax: 055 24 49 83
ristorante@enotecapinchiorri.
com
www.enotecapinchiorri.com

CHRISTINE FERBER
Maison Ferber
18 rue des Trois-Épis

68230 Niedermorschwhir
France
Tel: 03 89 27 05 69
Fax: 03 89 27 48 03
Books: *La Cuisine des fées*,
Éditions du Chêne, 1999;
Ma cuisine des fruits,
Marabout, 2003; *Mes aigres-
doux: terrines et pâtés*, Payot,
1999; *Mes confitures: The
Jams and Jellies of Christine
Ferber*, Michigan State
University Press, 2002;
*Mes tartes: The Sweet and
Savory Tarts of Christine
Ferber*, Michigan State
University Press, 2003.

**ROSE GRAY &
RUTH ROGERS**
The River Cafe
Thames Wharf
Rainville Road
London W6 9HA
Great Britain
Tel: 020 7386 4200
Fax: 020 7386 4201
info@rivercafe.co.uk
www.rivercafe.co.uk
Books: *The Cafe Cookbook*,
Clarkson Potter, 1996;
London River Cafe Cookbook,
Random House, 2003; *River
Cafe Italian Kitchen*, Ebury
Press, 2000; *River Cafe Two
Easy*, Ebury Press, 2005;
Rogers and Gray Italian Cookbook,
Random House, 1996.

CATHERINE GUERRAZ
Chez Catherine
3 rue Berryer
75008 Paris
France
Tel: 01 40 76 01 40
Fax: 01 40 76 03 96

FATÉMA HAL
La Mansouria
11 rue Faidherbe
75011 Paris
France
Tel: 01 43 71 00 16
Fax: 01 40 24 21 97
contact@fatemahal.com
www.fatemahal.com
Books: *La Cuisine du Maroc*,
Pacifique, 2001; *The Food of
Morocco: Authentic Recipes
from the North African Coast*,
Pacifique, 2002; *Le Grand
livre de la cuisine marocaine*,
Hachette, 2005; *Le Livre du
couscous*, Stock, 2000; *Les
Saveurs et les gestes: Cuisines et
traditions du Maroc*, Stock,
1995.

ANGELA HARTNETT
The Connaught
Carlos Place
Mayfair
London W1K 2AL

Great Britain
Tel: 020 7499 7070
Fax: 020 7495 3262
info@the-connaught.co.uk
www.the-connaught.co.uk

**MARIE-CHRISTINE
KLOPP**
La Flamiche
20 place de l'Hôtel de Ville
80700 Roye
France
Tel: 03 22 87 00 56
Fax: 03 22 78 46 77
restaurant.flamiche@
worldonline.fr
www.flamiche.fr
Books: *L'Anguille*, Épure, 2004.

LÉA LINSTER
Le Restaurant
17 route de Luxembourg
5752 Frisange
Luxembourg
Tel: 23 66 84 11
Fax: 23 67 64 47
info@lealinster.lu
www.lealinster.lu
Books: *Einfach und genial*,
Mozaik, 2002.

**JOCELYNE LOTZ-
CHOQUART**
Mungo Park
11 rue Jean Petit
25000 Besançon
France
Tel: 03 81 81 28 01
Fax: 03 81 83 36 97
contact@mungo-park.com
www.mungo-park.com

GISÈLE LOVICHI
Auberge Santa Barbara
Route de Propriano Alzone
20100 Sartène
France
Tel: 04 95 77 09 06
Fax: 04 95 77 09 09

JOHANNA MAIER
Hubertus
1 am Dorfplatz
5532 Filzmoos
Austria
Tel: 064 53 82 04
Fax: 064 53 82 046
info@hotelhubertus.at
www.hotelhubertus.at
Books: *Johanna Maier*, Rolf
Heyne, 2003; *Lass dir das
Leben schmecken*, Ecowin, 2004.

FLORA MIKULA
Flora
36 Avenue George V
75008 Paris
France
Tel: 01 40 70 10 49
Fax: 01 47 20 52 87
Books: *Ma Provence dans
votre assiette*, Aubanel, 2003.

OLYMPE (alias for
DOMINIQUE VERSINI)
Casa Olympe
48 rue St-Georges
75009 Paris
France
Tel: 01 42 85 26 01

AGATA PARISELLA
Agata e Romeo
45 Via Carlo Alberto
00185 Rome
Italy
Tel: 064 466 115
Fax: 064 465 842
ristorante@agataeromeo.it
www.agataeromeo.it
Books: *Palermo: Oli e aceti
d'Italia*, Gremese, 1998; *La
Pittura in cucina*, Sellerio di
Giogianni, 2000.

ANNE-SOPHIE PIC
• Pic
285 avenue Victor Hugo
26000 Valence
France
Tel: 04 75 44 15 32
Fax: 04 75 40 96 03
pic@relaischateaux.com
www.pic-valence.com

• Auberge du Pin
285bis avenue Victor Hugo
26000 Valence
France
Tel: 04 75 44 53 86
Fax: 04 75 40 96 03
Books : *L'Artichaut*, Épure,
2002; *Au nom du père*,
Éditions Glénat, 2004.

VALERIA PICCINI
Da Caino
3 via Canonica
58050 Montemerano
Italy
Tel: 0564 602 817
Fax: 0564 602 807
info@dacaino.it
www.dacaino.it
Books: *Caino: La Cucina di
Valeria Piccini*, Giunti, 2005.

CORNELIA POLETTO
Poletto
145 Eppendorfer Landstrasse
21251 Hamburg
Germany
Tel: 040 4 80 21 59
Fax: 040 41 40 69 93
www.poletto.de

**MARIE-FRANCE
PONSARD**
Le Bistroquet
97 Route Nationale
54940 Belleville
France
Tel: 03 83 24 90 12
Fax: 03 83 24 04 01
le-bistroquet@wanadoo.fr

CARME RUSCALLEDA
Restaurant Sant Pau
10 Nou
08395 Sant Pol de Mar
Spain
Tel: 93 760 06 62
Fax: 93 760 09 50
santpau@ruscalleda.com
www.ruscalleda.com
Books: *Any amb Carma
Ruscalleda*, Salsa, 2004;
Cuinar per ser feliç, Columna,
2001; *Deu anys de cuina al
Sant Pau*, Restaurant Sant
Pau, 1998.

REINE SAMMUT
Auberge La Fenière
Route de Cadenet
84160 Lourmarin
France
Tel: 04 90 68 11 79
Fax: 04 90 68 18 60
contact@reinesammut.com
www.reinesammut.com
Books: *La Cuisine de Reine,
heures et saveurs
méditerranéenne*s, Hachette,
1997; *Méditerranée*,
Hachette, 2001.

NADIA SANTINI
Ristorante dal Pescatore
17 Runate
Canneto sull'Oglio
46013 Mantua
Italy
Tel: 0376 72 30 01
Fax: 0376 703 04
santini@dalpescatore.com
www.dalpescatore.com
Books: *La Cucina di Nadia e
Antonio Santini*, Giunti
Gruppo, 2001 (also available
in French and Japanese).

ANNA SGROI
Sgroi
40 Lange Reihe
20099 Hamburg
Germany
Tel: 040 28 00 39 30
Fax: 040 28 00 39 31

SUZEL (alias for
ODETTE JUNG)
La Ferme de Suzel
15 rue des Vergers
67350 Ringendorf
France
Tel: 03 88 03 30 80

LUISA VALAZZA
Al Sorriso
18 Via Roma
28018 Soriso
Italy
Tel: 0322 983 228
Fax: 0322 983 328
info@ alsorriso.com
www.alsorriso.com

RECIPE INDEX

The editor wishes to thank all the chefs who made
this book possible by giving both their valuable
time and recipes.

Translated from the French by:
Louise Guiney (preface and introductory texts)
Joseph West (introductory texts for Sally Clarke,
    Rose Gray & Ruth Rogers, Cornelia Poletto, and
    Anna Sgroi)
Josephine Bacon (recipes and captions)
Copyediting: Penny Isaac
Typesetting: Claude-Olivier Four
Proofreading: Chrisoula Petridis

Color Separation: Repro Scan

Distributed in North America by Rizzoli
International Publications, Inc.

Simultaneously published in French as *Elles sont
chefs: les grandes dames de la cuisine contemporaine et
leurs meilleures recettes*
© Éditions Flammarion, 2005
English-language edition
© Éditions Flammarion, 2005

05 06 07 4 3 2 1

FC0487-05-IX
ISBN: 2-0803-0487-9
EAN: 9782080304872
Dépôt légal: 09/2005

Printed in Italy by Canale